CULTS, RELIGION, AND VIOLE

Cults, Religion, and Violence explores the question of when and against new religious cults erupts and whether and how su   ..t conflicts can be foreseen, managed, and averted. The authors, leading international experts on religious movements and violent behavior, focus on the four major episodes of cult violence during the last decade: the tragic conflagration that engulfed the Branch Davidians in Waco, Texas; the deadly sarin gas attack by the Aum Shinrikyô in Tokyo; the murder-suicides by the Solar Temple in Switzerland and Canada; and the collective suicide by the members of Heaven's Gate. They explore the dynamics leading to these dramatic episodes in North America, Europe, and Asia and offer insights into the general relationship between violence and religious cults in contemporary society. The editors, in the prologue to the book, examine the most recent incident of religiously motivated violence – the hijacking of three American airplanes and attacks on the Pentagon and World Trade Center by operatives of the Al Qaeda network on September 11, 2001. They explain some of the background and history of the Islamic fundamentalist movement that spawned Al Qaeda and place the September 11th incident within the context of the findings from this study.

Violent episodes involving cults are relatively rare historically. But their potential to affect and disrupt civic life looms large, and efforts to manage these incidents involve controversial issues of religious freedom, politics, state intervention, and pubic security. The interpretive challenge of this book is to provide a social scientific explanation for these rare events. The authors conclude that they usually involve some combination of internal and external dynamics through which a new religious movement and society become polarized. This extreme distancing leads one or both parties to conclude that a moment of moral reckoning is at hand. What follows is a dramatic incident in which a final solution to the conflict is sought either by destruction of enemies or by a collective exodus from the world.

David G. Bromley is Professor of Sociology and an Affiliate Professor in the Department of Religious Studies at Virginia Commonwealth University. He has written or edited more than a dozen books on religious movements, is former president of the Association for the Sociology of Religion, and is the founding editor of the annual series *Religion and the Social Order.*

J. Gordon Melton is the founder and director of the Institute for the Study of American Religion in Santa Barbara, California, and Research Specialist in the Department of Religious Studies at the University of California, Santa Barbara. He has authored more than twenty-five books and is past president of the Communal Studies Association.

CULTS, RELIGION, AND VIOLENCE

Edited by

DAVID G. BROMLEY

Virginia Commonwealth University

J. GORDON MELTON

Institute for the Study of American Religion

CAMBRIDGE
UNIVERSITY PRESS

45.99

201.76
Cults

PUBLISHED BY THE PRESS SYNDICATE OF THE UNIVERSITY OF CAMBRIDGE
The Pitt Building, Trumpington Street, Cambridge, United Kingdom

CAMBRIDGE UNIVERSITY PRESS
The Edinburgh Building, Cambridge CB2 2RU, UK
40 West 20th Street, New York, NY 10011-4211, USA
477 Williamstown Road, Port Melbourne, VIC 3207, Australia
Ruiz de Alarcón 13, 28014 Madrid, Spain
Dock House, The Waterfront, Cape Town 8001, South Africa

http://www.cambridge.org

First published 2002

Printed in the United Kingdom at the University Press, Cambridge

Typeface Garamond 3 11/13 pt.   *System* LATEX 2$_\varepsilon$ [TB]

A catalog record for this book is available from the British Library.

Library of Congress Cataloging in Publication Data
Cults, religion, and violence / edited by David G. Bromley, J. Gordon Melton.
p. cm.
Includes bibliographical references and index.
ISBN 0-521-66064-5 – ISBN 0-521-66898-0 (pbk.)
1. Violence – Religious aspects.   2. Cults.   I. Bromley, David G.   II. Melton, J. Gordon.
BL65.V55 C85   2002
306.6′99 – dc21   2001037861

ISBN 0 521 66064 5 hardback
ISBN 0 521 66898 0 paperback

CONTENTS

Contents

ACKNOWLEDGMENTS

This project has been more than five years in the making. It originated in informal conversations among a network of scholars who were actively analyzing and developing theoretical interpretations for the recent series of incidents of violence involving new religious movements. The project began to take shape with the recruitment of papers for several sessions on "Violence in the New Religions" at the 1996 annual meeting of the Society for the Scientific Study of Religion. In these sessions, papers were presented on a variety of theoretical issues and specific cases of violent episodes. The sessions were sponsored jointly by the Institute for the Study of American Religion (ISAR) in Santa Barbara, California, and the Center for Studies on New Religions (CESNUR) in Turin, Italy. The support of these organizations in initiating this project is gratefully acknowledged.

The editors wish to acknowledge the editorial assistance of Jena D. Morrison in preparing this manuscript.

"Mass Suicide and the Branch Davidians" by John R. Hall is a revised and emended version of John R. Hall, "Public Narratives and the Apocalyptic Sect." In *Armageddon in Waco*, edited by Stuart A. Wright. Chicago: University of Chicago Press, 1995: 205–235. © 1995 by The University of Chicago. All rights reserved. Reprinted with permission.

CONTRIBUTORS

Robert W. Balch received his Ph.D. in sociology from the University of Oregon in 1972. Currently he is Professor of Sociology at the University of Montana in Missoula. In addition to Heaven's Gate, he has conducted participant-observer studies of the Love Family, the Baha'is Under the Provisions of the Covenant, the Church Universal and Triumphant, Aryan Nations, and Elohim City.

Eileen Barker, OBE, FBA, is Professor of Sociology with Special Reference to the Study of Religion at the London School of Economics (LSE). Her main research interest over the past 25 years has been "cults," "sects," and new religious movements, but since 1989 she has spent much of her time investigating changes in the religious situation in postcommunist countries. She has more than 180 publications, which include the award-winning *The Making of a Moonie: Brainwashing or Choice?* and *New Religious Movements: A Practical Introduction*, which has been published in seven languages and is currently being translated into four more. In the late 1980s, with the support of the British government and mainstream churches, she founded INFORM, a charity based at the LSE that provides information about the new religions that is as accurate, objective and up-to-date as possible. She has also acted as an advisor to a number of governments, official bodies, and law-enforcement agencies around the world. She has served as President of the Society for the Scientific Study of Religion. In 1998 she was elected as a Fellow of the British Academy, and she was appointed an Officer of the Order of the British Empire in the Queen's 1999–2000 New Year's Honours list.

David G. Bromley is Professor of Sociology and an Affiliate Professor in the Department of Religious Studies at Virginia Commonwealth University. His research interests include sociology of religion, social movements, deviance, and political sociology. He has written or edited more than a dozen books on religious movements. Among his recent books are *The Politics of Religious Apostasy* (Praeger, 1998); *Anticult Movements in Cross-Cultural Perspective*, edited with Anson Shupe (Garland Publishers, 1994); *Handbook on Cults and Sects in America*, 2 vols. edited with Jeffrey K. Hadden (Association for the Sociology of Religion, Society for the Scientific Study of Religion, and JAI Press, 1993); and *The Satanism Scare*, (edited with James Richardson and Joel Best) (Aldine de Gruyter, 1991). He is former president of the Association for the Sociology of Religion; founding editor of the annual series *Religion and the Social Order*, sponsored by the Association for the Sociology of Religion; and former editor of the *Journal for the Scientific Study of Religion*, published by the Society for the Scientific Study of Religion.

Lorne L. Dawson is an Associate Professor of Sociology and Chair of the Department of Religious Studies at the University of Waterloo in Canada. He has published many articles dealing with new religious movements, has edited the book *Cults in Context* (Transaction Books, 1998), and is the author of *Comprehending Cults* (Oxford University Press, 1998). Many of his recent publications focus on aspects of religion and the Internet and theoretical analyses of the cultural significance of new religious movements under the social conditions of late modernity.

John R. Hall is Professor of Sociology and Director of the Center for History, Society, and Culture at the University of California-Davis. He is the author of books and articles on social theory, epistemology, the sociology of religion, and the sociology of culture. His most recent book is *Apocalypse Observed: Religious Movements and Violence in North America, Europe, and Japan*, coauthored by Philip D. Schuyler and Sylvaine Trinh (Routledge, 2000). He also has written *Culture: Sociological Perspectives*, coauthored by Mary Jo Neitz (Prentice-Hall, 1993), and *Cultures of Inquiry: From Epistemology to Discourse in the Methodological Practices of Sociohistorical Research* (Cambridge University Press, 1999).

Massimo Introvigne is Managing Director of the Center for Studies on New Religions (CESNUR) in Torino, Italy, and is the author or editor of 30 books in Italian, Spanish, English, German, and French and of more than 100 chapters and articles in scholarly journals about the history and sociology of new religious movements.

Jean-François Mayer is a Swiss historian who received his doctoral degree from the University of Lyon, France, in 1984. He worked for several years as an analyst in international affairs for the Swiss federal government. Since 1998 he has been a lecturer in religious studies at the University of Fribourg, Switzerland. He is the author of several books and numerous articles on contemporary religion, some of them translated into several languages. In 1994 he participated as an expert to the Swiss police investigation of the Order of the Solar Temple.

J. Gordon Melton is the Director of the Institute for the Study of American Religion in Santa Barbara, California, and Research Specialist in the Department of Religious Studies at the University of California, Santa Barbara. He founded the Institute for the Study of American Religion in 1969 as a research facility focusing on the study of America's many religious groups and organizations, especially the many small and unconventional religions. He has authored more than 25 books, including *The Cult Experience* (1982), the *Biographical Dictionary of Cult and Sect Leaders* (1986), *The Encyclopedic Handbook of Cults in America* (1986), the *New Age Encyclopedia* (1990), and the *Encyclopedia of African American Religion* (1993). His *Encyclopedia of American Religions*, now in its sixth edition, has become a standard reference book on North American religious bodies. He is senior editor of four series of books on American religions and is past president of the Communal Studies Association.

Ian Reader is currently Professor of Religious Studies at Lancaster University, England. Previously he has held academic positions in Japan, Scotland, Hawaii, and Denmark. He teaches and researches primarily religion in modern Japan and is the author of several books in this area, including *Religious Violence in Contemporary Japan: The Case of Aum Shinrikyô* (Curzon Press and University of Hawaii Press, 2000), and he has coauthored with George J. Tanabe, Jr., *Practically Religious: Worldly Benefits and the Common Religion of Japan* (University of Hawaii Press 1998). He is currently writing a book about pilgrimage in Japan.

Thomas Robbins received his Ph.D. in sociology from the University of North Carolina in 1973. He is the author of *Cults, Converts, and Charisma* (Sage, 1988) and of numerous articles, essays, and reviews in social science and religious studies journals. He is coeditor of six collections of original papers including *In Gods We Trust* (Transaction, 1981, 2d ed., 1990),

Millennium, Messiahs, and Mayhem (Routledge, 1997), and *Misunderstanding Cults* (University of Toronto Press, 2001).

David Taylor received his Ph.D. in sociology from Queen's University in Belfast, Northern Ireland, in 1983. Besides investigating Heaven's Gate with Robert Balch, he has studied the Unification Church and Ian Paisley's church and political party in Northern Ireland. Currently he is Training and Development Director for the City of Portland, Oregon, and Adjunct Professor of Sociology at Marylhurst University in Portland.

Stuart A. Wright is Professor of Sociology and Associate Dean of Graduate Studies at Lamar University. He received his Ph.D. from the University of Connecticut in 1983. He was National Institutes of Mental Health Research Fellow and Lecturer at Yale University in 1984–1985 before arriving at Lamar. He is the author of the monograph *Leaving Cults: The Dynamics of Defection* (Society for the Scientific Study of Religion, 1987) and editor of *Armageddon in Waco* (University of Chicago Press, 1995). Dr. Wright worked with the congressional subcommittees in 1995 investigating the government's role in the Waco siege and standoff. He also testified in the hearings as an expert. Later, he was hired as a consultant in the Oklahoma City bombing trial of Timothy McVeigh by defense attorneys. He is currently completing a book manuscript on the Oklahoma City bombing based on his experience in the case.

PROLOGUE

September 11, Religion, and Violence

This book was already in production when another major incident with similarities to those analyzed in this book occurred on September 11, 2001. Agents of an obscure organization named Al Qaeda directed aircraft into the Pentagon (a symbol of America's military power) and the World Trade Center in New York City (a symbol of America's economic power). While the analysis of the events is just beginning and it is far too early to draw any definitive conclusions, as we move beyond the shock, grief, and anger that the terrorist action produced, the events of September 11 emerge as a dramatic new incident by which the themes and conclusions developed during the five years of work that went into this study of violence involving new religious movements can be extended.

Among the conclusions reached by this study was the very pessimistic prediction that, while they will be rare, in light of the number of groups and people involved in new religious movements, future episodes of violence involving these movements would occur and that "they will occur in a much more complex and politicized environment." One could hardly imagine a more politicized environment than that surrounding Al Qaeda and its Amir, Osama bin Laden. For more than a decade, Al Qaeda and the related groups of the World Islamic Front have been involved in an ongoing set of violent incidents that would include among other events: the 1993 bombing of the World Trade Center and the trial and conviction of Sheik Omar Abdul-Rahman for his role in the Trade Center bombing; the bombing of the U.S. embassies in Kenya and Tanzania in August 1998, followed by the United States' retaliatory missile strikes against Al Qaeda in August 1998 and the conviction of four people for the embassy bombings in May 2001; and the bombing of the *USS Cole* at Aden, Yemen, in October 2000 and the subsequent arrest of eight suspects.

This political history underscores a second theme developed through-out this book that fits violent incidents into a prior history of escalating conflict and hostility. Such a history certainly stands behind Al Qaeda and the thousands of deaths that occurred on September 11. Law enforcement agencies and terrorism experts have subjected bin Laden and Al Qaeda to hours of intense analysis with the hope of understanding the members and tracking them for international law breaking. What has been most lacking in the study of Al Qaeda has been the religious dimension that is so inte-gral to its operation. Al Qaeda has been defined as a terrorist organization and has thus been treated much as other violent criminal groups. However, without additional perspective on its essential religious nature, much is lost in grasping its agenda, the tenacity of its operatives (even to the point of suicide), its support throughout the Muslim world, and the problems that will be encountered in the attempt to prevent future incidents. In the weeks following the Pentagon and Trade Center attacks, the American government carefully separated Al Qaeda and its action from mainstream Islam in the public consciousness. At the same time, the overwhelming majority of Muslims also attempted to distance themselves from Al Qaeda, just as almost all Christians wanted to distance themselves from the Peoples Temple and Buddhists from Aum Shinrikyô.

However, in separating Al Qaeda from mainstream Islam, it has been tempting to go further and see Al Qaeda in purely secular terms, to see it as a terrorist rather than a religious group, when it is best viewed as a new religious group that has integrated terrorism into its very fabric. Also, while understanding the manner in which Al Qaeda differs radically from mainstream Islam, it would be misleading to separate it and the related Islamic sects completely from the wider Islamic milieu out of which it developed and within which it continues to exist. It is important not to impugn the Muslim/Arab community, which bore no responsibility for the events of September 11, while at the same time confronting the religious life that informs and dictates Al Qaeda's actions.

The Twentieth-Century Islamist Revival

To fill out our picture of Al Qaeda, we must reach back into the recent past and the crisis occasioned for many Muslims by the fall of the Ottoman Empire and the Caliph who ruled it. The decline of the Ottomans coincided with the increase of Western influence in the Middle East. The Caliphate, in one form or another, had been a part of Islamic life since the death of the Prophet Muhammad in 632 A.D. It began with the selection of the first Caliph to assume leadership of the fledgling community and the growing assumption that religious and secular leadership in the Muslim world should be intimately connected. Through the years, many Caliphs did not live up to the ideal set by the first two Caliphs, but returning to the ideal was always possible until the rise of modern national states that replaced the old Empire and the final destruction of even the fiction of a Caliphate in the 1920s.

Already in the nineteenth century, reactions to the failing Caliphate and the tampering of Western powers in Ottoman lands appeared, the most prominent being the Wahhabi movement, which fought a war with the Empire as the Saud family attempted to establish hegemony in the Arabian peninsula. Integral to the Wahhabi agenda was the establishment of a Muslim society that merged religious and governmental authority. This agenda was dictated by a rather literal reading of the Muslim scripture, the Qu'ran, and the collection of accepted sayings and stories of Muhammad and his companions, the Hadith. Osama bin Laden (b. 1957) was raised in a devout Wahhabi family and opted not to go to the West for college in order to attend the King Abdu Aziz University in Saudi Arabia.

The modern Islamist revival, however, really began in Egypt in the 1920s. Just six years after the fall off the Caliphate, Al-Imam Hassan Al-Banna (1906–1949) founded Al-Ikhwan Al-Moslemoon, the Muslim Brotherhood, that began as a movement among Egyptian youth with an emphasis on ridding people of non-Muslim elements in their religious life (especially folk magic) and on living by the Qu'ran and Hadith. The movement spread rapidly. Changes in neighboring Palestine in the 1930s appear to be the catalyst that diverted the Brotherhood from its reformist program to a new agenda that focused on the political situation. This new emphasis was a natural outgrowth of Al-Banna's conviction that Islam speaks to all spheres of life from personal conduct to the running of government and business. He also taught his followers that action should flow from belief; for while good intentions are important, they must generate righteous deeds.

The Brotherhood became increasingly involved in the conflict between the Palestinians (Muslims) and the new Jewish settlements in Palestine, a conflict that escalated further following the proclamation of the nation of Israel. In 1948, members of the Brotherhood joined the forces that unsuccessfully attempted to block Israel's stabilization as a national entity, and at the same time, in Egypt, it attempted to change the government by assassinating various officials, including one prime minister. A keynote of the Brotherhood had become a return to an Orthodox Islamic state in which a true Islamic ruler (not the "puppet" then ruling Egypt) would sit on the throne and Islamic law would shape the community's life. The violence in Egypt came back on the Brotherhood in 1949 when Al-Banna was himself assassinated.

Gamel Nasser, who came to power in 1954, attempted to suppress the movement, and its major impulse passed to other groups, possibly the most important being the Jamaat-e-Islam, founded in 1941 by Indian Muslim Sayyid Abul A'la Mawdudi (1903–1979). The Jamaat emerged in the context of the Indian independence movement and Mawdudi's critique of Indian nationalism, which he saw as a threat to Muslim community identity. To resist the modern forces in India (and later Pakistan), he came to see the need of a complete reconstruction of Islamic thought.

Just prior to the founding of the Jamaat, Mawdudi published his small book, *A Short History of the Revivalist Movement in Islam* (1972), which summarized the direction of the needed reconstruction. Islam, according to Mawdudi, was aiming at the eventual establishment of the kingdom of God on earth and the enforcement of the system of life Allah gave to humanity (Islamic law). The present need was to revolutionize the intellectual and mental perspective of the population, to regiment the behavior of those peoples who had already accepted Islam in an Islamic pattern, and to organize the various segments of social life on an Islamic basis. The pattern to guide the reconstruction was the period of the "rightly guided caliphs," those men who had ruled the Islamic community in the mid-seventh century. In every age there is the need for leaders who will make extraordinary strides in reviving Islam and bringing it back to its true course of kingdom building, from which it has shown a marked tendency to deviate. The Jamaat built a comprehensive program to accomplish the step-by-step reconstruction of first cultural and social life and then the government.

In Egypt, Siyyid Qutb (1906–1966), who emerged as the new ideological leader of the Brotherhood, integrated Al-Banna's perspective of Islam as a complete way of life with the new program offered by Mawdudi for the Islamization of society. The plan demanded nothing less than a total reformation of Egyptian government and society from the top down. However, in 1954 Nasser immediately moved to crush the Brotherhood. Qutb was arrested and spent the next decade in jail, where he penned his major work. Finally published in 1966, *Milestones* summarized plans for reforming the government that Qutb now gave the Brotherhood. After reading the book,

Nasser immediately moved against the Brotherhood. Qutb was among those arrested and executed.

By the 1960s, in the writings of Al-Banna, Mawdudi, and Qutb, the intellectual/theological foundation had been laid for a whole set of revivalist Muslim movements that were dedicated to the reformation of the Muslim world with the goal of establishing rulers patterned on the original righteous Caliphs who would merge religious and political authority and restructure the legal system with Islamic law. At the same time, they emphasized an additional threat – the decadent influence of the West manifest in the spread of Western immorality among Muslims and the injection of Western political influence into Middle East affairs. Qutb had been particularly upset by the behavior he had seen during his stay in the United States (1948–1950).

With the thought world provided by Al-Banna, Mawdudi, and Qutb (among others), a spectrum of revivalist religious movements appeared, all of which shared their general theological framework. They emerged country by country, each developing a program dictated by individual national situations. Among the more famous groups are Hizballah (the Party of God, aka Islamic Jihad, Lebanon); Hamas (the Islamic Resistance Movement, Lebanon), an outgrowth of the Palestinian branch of the Muslim Brotherhood; the Islamic Salvation Front (Algeria); the National Islamic Front (Sudan); and Al-Jama'a al Islamiiya (Egypt). Because of their intrusion into an already unstable political process, Westerners tended to see the groups as simply political, revolutionary, or terrorists, downplaying their religious dimension. They have often been difficult to distinguish religiously as they fade imperceptively into the larger Muslim milieu. Then, at the end of the 1980s, a new revivalist group known simply as The Base (Al Qaeda) would emerge.

The emergence of Al Qaeda is very much tied to the career of its founder. Osama bin Laden grew up in Saudi Arabia, the son of a wealthy Saudi businessman (a pious Wahhabi Muslim) and his Syrian wife. He attended King Abdu Aziz University, where the conservative Wahhabi perspective was reinforced. There he met one of the key people in his life, Abdullah Azzam (1941–1989), a Jordanian Islamist leader who had joined the University faculty and who introduced him ideologically to Islamism and its program for establishing Islamic political power. Also on the faculty was no less a personage than Sayyid Qutb's younger brother Mohammad. Islamism provided the lens through which bin Laden saw the events of 1979 that changed his life: the Iranian revolution, the taking of the mosque in Mecca by a group of Muslim dissidents, and the Soviet invasion of Afghanistan. In 1980, he moved to Afghanistan, where he became reacquainted with Abdullah Azzam. In 1984, they established a center in Peshawar (on the Pakistani side of the Khyber Pass) as a logistics base for the anti-Soviet forces. During this time, he built a vast international network of support for the fight.

Then in 1989, as the Soviets gave up the fight in Afghanistan, Iraqi forces suddenly invaded Kuwait. In response, bin Laden offered his services to the Saudi government. That the Americans were invited to liberate Kuwait in his stead appears to be the start of bin Laden's real disillusionment with Saudi Arabia. The non-Muslim Americans coming to Saudi Arabia and leaving a military force behind after the Gulf War was cited as the primary issue in the initial fatwa (legal declaration) issued by bin Laden in 1996. As he noted, "The latest and the greatest of these aggressions incurred by the Muslims since the death of the Prophet (Allah's blessings and salutations be upon Him) is the occupation of the land of the two Holy Places, the foundation of the house of Islam, the place of the revelation, the source of the message and the place of the noble Ka'ba, the Qiblah of all Muslims, by the armies of the American Crusaders and their allies."

In 1990 bin Laden aligned himself with Hassan Al-Turabi, the leading Islamist advocate in Sudan who had supported the military takeover of Sudan in 1980; Al-Turabi believed that the fall of Saddam Hussein could become the catalyst for the establishment of Islamic governments coming to power throughout the whole Muslim world. It was then that bin Laden really established Al Queda and opened the first centers for the training of people in guerilla warfare and terrorism. During his six years in Sudan, bin Laden also ingratiated himself to the new Taliban rulers of Afghanistan, and in 1996 he relocated Al Qaeda to their territory. Along with funds for arms, he supported the Taliban with money to build new mosques. Among those who would join in this new phase of Al Qaeda's work would be Ayman Al-Zawahiri, another important ideological tie to the Islamist past. Al-Zawahiri was a former leader of the Egyptian Jihad group that grew out of the Muslim Brotherhood and was linked to the assassination of Egyptian president Anwar Sadat in 1981.

In 1998, Al Qaeda activated the core of its network to issue the now famous fatwa, the "Ruling against the Jews and Crusaders [Americans]." He charged the United States with various sins beginning with the continuing affront, that "for over seven years the United States has been occupying the lands of Islam in the holiest of places, the Arabian Peninsula, plundering its riches, dictating to its rulers, humiliating its people, terrorizing its neighbors, and turning its bases in the Peninsula into a spearhead through which to fight the neighboring Muslim peoples." The fatwa cited the Qu'ran and various Muslim sources to legitimize the position taken in light of the Muslim tradition, and the World Islamic Front called upon Muslims everywhere to join the fight. So there would be no misunderstanding of his intention, the fatwa concluded, "The ruling to kill the Americans and their allies – civilians and military – is an individual duty for every Muslim who can do it in any country in which it is possible to do it, in order to liberate the Al-Aqsa Mosque [in Jerusalem] and the holy mosque [in Mecca] from their grip, and in order for their armies to move out of all the lands of Islam, defeated and unable to threaten any Muslim."

Contextualizing Al Qaeda

The investigation of Al Qaeda in its Muslim context has just begun. This book considers a set of issues emerging from a look at some extreme cases of violence, the events of September 11 now extending the list of cases. Various contributors have, for example, highlighted factors that have been found in many new religions, such as charismatic leadership and totalistic organization, both of which on cursory examination appear to apply equally to Al Qaeda. Much attention was also paid to the role of apocalyptic narratives in predisposing new religions to violence. However, at this point, Al Qaeda (and the related Taliban) appear to have a different narrative, holding to a more postmillennial worldview (sometimes referred to as developmental millennialism). New religions also both challenge the larger social context and seek various levels of accommodation when tension arises. The different groups of the Islamist revival form a spectrum of social/cultural responses from the accommodationist Muslim Brotherhood, which has become a significant political party in Jordan, to Al Qaeda, which has continually raised the stakes in its challenge to the social order.

Most importantly, this set of analyses suggests that incidents of religious violence involve interactive exchanges between movements and societal institutions. In the case of Al Qaeda, this exchange has been on a global level. The future of Al Qaeda, the Taliban, and the other Islamist movements will very much depend on the strategies adopted by those agencies entrusted with the prevention of future terrorist incidents. It is our hope that this study will provide meaningful and helpful information for the various government agencies and another reference point base from which future studies of this most recent incident can proceed.

It will be most helpful to enlarge our understanding of Al Qaeda within the flow of the new Muslim religious movements that heretofore have been analyzed primarily as political or criminal groups. Such a fresh perspective could add much to our knowledge not only of the workings of Al Qaeda, but of the unique forms taken by new religious movements in the larger Muslim world. To apply what we have learned over the last generation in our study of new religions in the United States and the West to the larger world is now an obvious priority.

JGM & DGB

References

bin Laden, Osama. "Jihad against Jews and Crusaders." Posted at http://www.fas.org/irp/world/para/docs/980223-fatwa.htm. Accessed November 1, 2001 (also posted at other sites).

bin Laden, Osama. "Ladenese Epistle: Declaration of War." Posted at http://www.washingtonpost.com/wp-dyn/articles/A4342-2001Sep21.html. Accessed November 1, 2001.

Burke, Jason. "The Making of Osama bin Laden." *The Observer* (November 1, 2001). Posted at http://www.salon.com/news/feature/2001/11/01/osama_profile/index.html. Accessed November 12, 2001.

Gwynne, Rosalind. "Al-Qacida and al-Qur'an: The 'Tafsir' of Usamah bin Ladin." Posted at http://web.utk.edu/~warda/bin_ladin_and_quran.htm. Accessed November 12, 2001.

Jansen, Johannes J. *The Dual Nature of Islamic Fundamentalism.* Ithaca, NY: Cornell University Press. 1996.

Jansen, Johannes J. *The Neglected Duty: The Creed of Sadat's Assassins and Islamic Resurgence in the Middle East.* New York: Macmillan Company. 1986.

Mawdudi, Sayyid Abul Al-Mawdudi. *A Short History of the Revivalist Movement in Islam.* Delhi: Markazi Maktaba Islami. 1972.

Qutb, Sayyid. *Milestones.* Beirut, Lebanon: The Holy Koran Publishing House. 1978.

Rashid, Ahmed. *Taliban: Militant Islam, Oil, and Fundamentalism in Central Asia.* New Haven, CT: Yale University Press, 2001.

I

VIOLENCE AND RELIGION
IN PERSPECTIVE

DAVID G. BROMLEY AND J. GORDON MELTON

The relationship between religion and violence has been a subject of rapidly growing interest and concern to social scientists studying a broad range of religious groups and traditions. Violent acts and relationships are extremely diverse, of course, and so it is not surprising that the burgeoning literature on religion and violence incorporates analyses of numerous types of violence, groups, and contexts. A number of distinctions are conventionally drawn in distinguishing forms of violence. Violence is variously conceptualized as an act, a process, or a relationship. Violence may involve individual actions, as in the personal murder of one member of a religious group by another, an outsider by an insider, or an insider by an outsider. It may also involve collective action by or against a group, as in the cases of war, revolution, repression, and terrorism. Violence may or may not explicitly invoke religious objectives. For example, an individual who is a member of a religious group may simply be the perpetrator or victim of an act of violence, with no connection to a religious purpose, or violent acts may have a specific religious goal, such as assassination of a spiritual leader or execution for heresy. Violence may occur within the confines of a group, as in the case of schismatic conflict; it may also occur across institutional boundaries, as when the religious group is the target of political repression or the instigator of an attack against societal institutions. And violence occurs at different levels of injuriousness, with extensive loss of life being a limiting case. It is clear, then, that studying the connection between religion and violence involves a variety of distinct issues and relationships that require invocation of very different types and levels of theoretical explanation.

In this volume we approach violence from a specific perspective, focus on a particular form of violence, and are concerned with a specific set of groups. We treat violence as relational and processual rather than as simply social action. We shall argue that the violent outcomes analyzed in this volume are the product of an interactive sequence of movement–societal exchanges, and these qualities mean that ultimate outcomes remain contingent through the interactive sequence. Each of the four episodes that are the primary focus of analysis moved through several distinguishable phases of movement–societal tension that culminated in a moment of violent resolution. The structure of the movement–societal relationship can be described at various tension levels, but the emphasis throughout the book is on the processual nature of violent relationships. From this perspective, it is important to examine how violent relationships moderate as well as how they escalate.

With respect to forms of violence, we are concerned here with violence that is collective in nature. This means that even if violent acts are committed by individuals, they are undertaken in the name of the movement or control agent, and the violence is legitimated in terms of some organizational purpose. Collective action does not presume consensus, however, and dissent within both movements and control agencies may well occur in the course of violent exchanges. Since violence is relational, either the movement or the social order may be the instigator or the target at various points in the process; in most cases, causality is not unilateral precisely because violent relationships are interactive and contingent. It also follows that violence may be directed either inward or outward – suicide or homicide, to invoke legal terminology.

Finally, the focus of our analysis is on violence involving a particular kind of religious group, the kind referred to by scholars as "new religious movements." New religious movements constitute particularly important cases. These groups not only offer radical resistance to the dominant social order, they also sacralize that resistance. The challenge these movements pose is therefore fundamental in nature, as they threaten the logic and organizational forms through which the dominant social order is maintained. At the same time, these movements typically possess few allies and consequently are vulnerable to imposition of social control. Given the challenge posed by the movements, on the one side, and the imperative to maintain the existing social order, on the other side, the likelihood of tension and conflict is considerable.

The question of how new religious movements and societal control organizations come to be involved in violence is significant from both a theoretical and a public policy standpoint. There have been relatively few cases of collective violence of the kind we are examining. Benchmark cases in the second half of the twentieth century consist of the Manson Family murders in 1969, the Peoples Temple murder-suicides at Jonestown in 1978, the

Branch Davidian murder-suicides at Mount Carmel outside Waco in 1993, the Solar Temple murder-suicides in Switzerland and Canada in 1994, the Aum Shinrikyô murders in Tokyo in 1995, and the Heaven's Gate collective suicide in California in 1997. We have elected to maintain a tight focus by concentrating on the four major episodes of the 1990s, which continue to be at the forefront of both recent social scientific analysis and the formulation of public policy. In the conclusion to this volume we briefly review the murder-suicides in the Movement for the Restoration of the Ten Commandments in Uganda, but insufficient information prevents us from conducting a meaningful analysis of that case. There are a few other cases that have moved in the direction of the kind of collective violence we examine. These include the biological agent attacks on the local community by followers of Bhagwan Rajneesh, which led to the flight and arrest of Rajneeshee leaders; the growing tension between the Church Universal and Triumphant and federal authorities, which was defused through negotiation before reaching a critical juncture; and the confrontation between federal agents and The Covenant, the Sword, and the Arm of the Lord, which led to surrender by the movement. But even if all of these cases are combined, they constitute only a tiny proportion of the over 2,000 religious groups in the United States and the much larger number across Europe, Asia, and Africa.

It is important to understand the dynamics of these extreme cases of violence; it is equally important not to treat them as templates from which direct translations can be made to other groups and events. In our view, the cases at hand constitute extreme outcomes on a continuum of movement–societal conflict. The analytic task is to interpret these groups and events in terms of patterns and processes that characterize many other religious and nonreligious groups while at the same time illuminating the distinctive developments that produced climatic violence. In other words, we reason from the mundane to the exceptional rather than the reverse and resist invocation of novel theories or special explanations unless established theoretical understandings prove inadequate. This approach is particularly important in light of political campaigns that have been triggered by violent episodes involving religious movements. There have been initiatives in a number of nations to distinguish a subset of religious groups as "cults," "sects," or "destructive/dangerous groups" and to create profiles of their characteristics. These distinctions have then been linked to various kinds of legislation to broaden state sanctioning power. In our view, constructive public policy requires continuous effort to advance both our theoretical sophistication and further empirical investigation of a broad range of violent episodes.

We have chosen to begin the process of building an understanding of religious movement–societal violence with a twofold strategy comprising theory advancement and interpretive case study. The objective of the theory advancement chapters is to specify more clearly the social conditions under which movements or established institutions become involved in violent episodes. The interpretive case study chapters work from specific episodes toward that same objective. Therefore, in Chapters 2 and 3, we develop a general theoretical framework through which to interpret specific cases and then challenge some common misconceptions about the relationship of religion and violence. Chapters 4 to 7 of the volume presents theoretical analyses of critical elements of movement and societal organization that are frequently identified as contributing to violent outcomes. Specifically, contributors examine the link between violence and two pivotal internal characteristics of religious movements – high-demand organization and charismatic leadership dynamics – and two external characteristics of societal organization – governmental control agency operation and oppositional movement strategies. Attention then shifts in Chapters 8 to 11 to the four recent instances of movement–societal violence – the Branch Davidians, Heaven's Gate, Solar Temple, and Aum Shinrikyô. These episodes are considered in chronological order since earlier incidents influenced the occurrence of and reaction to later ones. We conclude in Chapter 12 with observations about the implications of these cases for theorizing about movement–societal violence and for the formation of appropriate public policy.

Contributions to the Analysis of Religion and Violence

In the opening chapter of the book, "Dramatic Denouements," David Bromley creates a general theoretical framework for integrating the occurrence of what he terms "Dramatic Denouements." Bromley argues that climatic moments during which a final project of ultimate moral reckoning is undertaken must be understood historically, processually, and interactively. He identifies three levels of disputation that represent increasing breadth and seriousness of claims-making: (1) Latent Tension, in which the foundational logic and organization of movement and society stand in contradiction to one another, although there may not be direct engagement; (2) Nascent Conflict, in which emergent bilateral conflicts are not articulated in ideological terms, future adversaries have not mobilized organizationally, and parties orient toward one another as "troublesome"; and

(3) Intensified Conflict, in which there is heightened mobilization and radicalization of movements and oppositional groups, entry of third parties, and orientation by parties toward one another as "dangerous." Intensified Tension creates the basis for Dramatic Denouements, in which polarization and destabilization of dangerous relationships lead to orientation by parties as "subversive" and to projects of final reckoning intended to reverse power and moral relationships. While the level of movement–societal disputation may escalate and Dramatic Denouements are possible, conflicts may be resolved at every level of dispute since accommodative and retreatist rather than contestive options may be selected. Once an intensified level of conflict is reached, Bromley argues, movement toward Dramatic Denouements is fueled by progressive polarization. To the extent that parties in conflict possess a cohesive ideology and organization that stands in contradiction to those of the other, the parties become subversive to one another. Factors promoting polarization include actions and symbolic designations by either side that threaten the other and internal radicalization that moves a party in a more extreme direction. The instability of polarized relationships can be accentuated by secrecy, organizational consolidation/fragmentation, and elimination of third parties. At some point in the polarization process, one or both sides may reach a point of last resort and launch a project of final reckoning.

In their chapter, "Challenging Misconceptions about the New Religions–Violence Connection," J. Gordon Melton and David Bromley challenge four major misconceptions about the connection between new religious movements and violence that have influenced both social scientific theory and public policy formation: (1) violence involving new religions is pervasive, (2) new religions are violence prone, (3) new religions provoke violence, and (4) violence by new religions cannot be averted. Together these misconceptions create an image of religious movements as inherently unstable, volatile, dangerous, and violent. Melton and Bromley contend that this image of religious movements is based on a relatively few historical cases of movement–societal conflict, treating these extreme cases as typical, and failing to recognize the interactive nature of most violent episodes.

The next four chapters that address critical elements of movement and societal structure that influence the occurrence of violent episodes. Thomas Robbins seeks to identify structural characteristics of religious movements that are associated with volatility in his chapter, "Sources of Volatility in Religious Movements." He categorizes factors that have been linked to violence into two major dimensions, social/cultural and exogenous/endogenous. In this chapter his focus is on endogenous factors, but he strongly affirms the role of exogenous factors as well and of the interplay of the two sets of factors in actual conflict situations. Robbins analyzes one endogenous cultural factor, apocalyptic worldviews, and one endogenous social factor, totalistic organization. His objective is to refine these broad categories and specify more precisely the elements of apocalypticism and totalism that may be linked to violence. This analytic specificity is critical since a large number of movements exhibit apocalyptic ideologies and totalistic organization. With respect to apocalypticism, Robbins identifies "catastrophic millennialism," a highly dualistic ideological system, in which the existing social order is perceived as evil and rapidly degenerating, as a particularly volatile orientation. Qualities of totalistic organization that are more likely to be associated with extreme volatility include the following: certain modes of commitment building, such as performance of irreversible acts and shared risk taking; attenuation of outreach and conversions, which produces greater social isolation and reality encapsulation, suppression of negative feedback, and boundary tensions; and charismatic authority, when such leadership involves increasing totalistic control, crisis mongering, objectification of followers, and absence of critical feedback.

In "Crises of Charismatic Legitimacy and Violent Behavior in New Religious Movements," Lorne Dawson explores the relationship between charismatic authority and violent episodes involving new religious movements. He identifies pivotal attributes of charismatic leadership that he argues are ubiquitous across a range of religious and nonreligious organizational realms. Given the pervasiveness of charisma, Dawson asserts that it is not charismatic leadership itself that creates the potential for danger but rather the "mismanagement of certain endemic problems of charismatic authority that are rooted in the problematic legitimacy of charisma." Because charismatic leaders each constitute their own unique traditions, charisma by its very nature requires continuous legitimation. Their problem is preserving the balance between asserting too much and too little dominance, with too much dominance being associated with violence. Dawson identifies four specific charismatic management problems: (1) maintaining the leader's persona, (2) moderating the effects of the psychological identification of followers with the leader, (3) negotiating the routinization of charisma, and (4) achieving new successes.

Stuart Wright explores the role of governmental agencies in cases of violence involving religious movements in "Public Agency Involvement in Government–Religious Movement Confrontations." Wright begins with the observation that the religious movements are extremely diverse on almost every dimension and goes on to argue that violence is better understood as a product of polarization between two contrasting forms of authority, charismatic and rational-legal. The concept of polarization permits the impetus toward distancing to be initiated by either the movement or the governmental agency. One of the most powerful forces producing polarization is designation by the movement and the agency of the other as subversive. Given that the agency and the movement are likely to polarize, the question is why collective violence is relatively rare. Wright presents evidence that while conflict between religious movements and the state is common, violent confrontation is rare. He argues that the likelihood of violence is sharply reduced by the "intervening influences initiated by intermediate groups," which serve to reduce polarization. Intermediate groups may be effective in two ways, by preempting aggressive state actions and by creating confidence among movements that they possess legal recourse.

Eileen Barker examines how different types of what she terms "cult watching groups" influence religious movement–societal conflicts in her chapter, "Watching for Violence: A Comparative Analysis of the Roles of Five Types of Cult-Watching Groups." She identifies the five types as (1) cult-awareness groups, (2) countercult groups, (3) research-orientated groups, (4) human rights groups, and (5) cult-defender groups. The pivotal characteristic that distinguishes the five types is the underlying issue that each group addresses in its cult-watching activities. The typology constitutes an argument against treating cult-watching groups as a unitary set. Rather, Barker argues, each type possesses a different organizational objective and occupies a distinct social location. These attributes, in turn, are significant determinants of their access to and influence on governmental, judicial, law enforcement, and media institutions. She cautions that while certain types of cult-watching groups have been relatively influential in western societies during recent decades, there is no reason to treat that particular political configuration as a template for the future or for other parts of the globe. In the cases examined in this volume, it has been primarily the cult-awareness and research-oriented groups that have been most influential. The former have been more influential in achieving popular acceptance of "dangerous cult" imagery, while the latter have gained political influence on the basis of professional expertise. Barker argues that movement–societal relationships become particularly dangerous when there is a mutual definition in terms of a subversive "other." This kind of polarization is likely to lead to deviance amplification, a process that research-oriented groups are more likely than anti-cult groups to discourage.

The next four chapters of this volume present case studies of the four major episodes of religious movement–societal violence during the 1990s. In "Mass Suicide and the Branch Davidians," John Hall analyzes the Branch Davidian confrontation with federal law enforcement agencies and draws comparisons with the earlier episode involving the Peoples Temple. Hall argues that both movements were predisposed toward conflict with external organizations but that this does not account for the ensuing confrontations. He carefully traces the emergence of an alliance between an oppositional movement of former members and relatives, the media, and various governmental agencies. As the Bureau of Alcohol, Tobacco, and Firearms (BATF) became involved in pursuing evidence of weapons violations, the agency's perception of the Davidians and ultimately its "dynamic entry" strategy both were significantly shaped by the "mass suicide" narrative promoted by the oppositional movement that finds its roots in the Jonestown episode. The failure of the BATF raid then produced the extended standoff and subsequently the second assault on the Davidians, during which the compound was destroyed and most of its residents died.

Massimo Introvigne and Jean-François Mayer analyze the murder-suicides in 1994 in Switzerland by the Order of the Solar Temple in their chapter, "Occult Masters and the Temple of Doom: The Fiery End of the Solar Temple." The authors examine several explanations offered for the episode – the brainwashing explanation propounded by anticult organizations, an illicit economic organization masquerading as a religion explanation, which was supported by a number of media sources; a psychological pathology explanation, which held favor in some academic circles; and a fragile millennial group explanation, which has been proposed by a number of scholars. The authors favor the last and have extended this explanation by delineating factors related to movement fragility. They offer a combination of four factors as explanations for the episode: an apocalyptic ideology, perceived external opposition, internal dissent and apostasy, and crumbling charismatic authority. They conclude with a comparison of the Solar Temple, Peoples Temple, and Heaven's Gate episodes that yields several important parallels between the three movements: a sense among members that (1) they did not belong to this world but rather in a different realm; (2) they were becoming increasingly estranged from this world; (3) they were targets of a powerful conspiracy determined to destroy their respective movements; and (4) they were no longer bound by the rules of contemporary society. These factors, Introvigne and Mayer contend, are significant elements of millennial group fragility that lead in the direction of climactic violence.

In his chapter, "Dramatic Confrontations: Aum Shinrikyô Against the World," Ian Reader examines the transformation of Aum from a peaceful meditation and healing group to the embattled movement that in 1995 placed nerve gas in the Tokyo subway system. Reader attributes Aum's violent end to a combination of internal factors – the leader's personality, the movement's world-rejecting orientation, extreme ascetic practices, and a variety of internal problems – and external factors – opposition from the media, the government, and the families of converts. The conflict with various elements of Japanese society led to what Reader refers to as a "persecution complex," such that the movement viewed itself as the target of a vast conspiracy. Given its polarized position and apocalyptic ideology, the actual opposition it faced fitted neatly into this persecution complex, which the movement continued to foster to sustain its boundaries, solidarity, and rejection of conventional society. Violence was first directed internally and only later involved outsiders. Once initiated, however, violence begat further violence and spiraled out of control. Thus there was a complex interplay of internal organizational and external oppositional dynamics that led to a moment of confrontation and destruction.

Robert Balch and David Taylor have been studying Heaven's Gate since shortly after its inception in 1975. In their chapter, "Making Sense of the Heaven's Gate Suicides," they argue that the "transit" was the result of a plan that developed slowly over the movement's two-decade history and was not the product of external provocation. The authors identify seven phases in the movement's developmental history that led to the 1997 transit. During the "awakening" period, the movement's apocalyptic ideology was formulated and its separation from conventional society was initiated. The "chrysalis" phase was characterized by the abandonment of old identities, the creation of new ones compatible with the "next level" of existence, and the pruning of group membership to a smaller core group. The creation of strong commitment to the movement within this small, tightly organized core group was the hallmark of the "classroom" period. The "crisis and uncertainty" phase was pivotal as charismatic authority increased, the movement began to regard itself as the target of conspiratorial forces, and the belief that physical death would be necessary for salvation began to emerge. In the "reaching out" period, the movement perceived its range of options narrowing and undertook more extreme actions. During the "searching for new options" phase, an alternative line of action was developed that called for suicide rather than physical transportation as a means of reaching the next level. The "final exit" phase, during which the transit was undertaken, was the product of synchronicity that propelled the movement through its prior phases. Balch and Taylor argue that each phase of the group's history established the basis for later developments, and they divide the factors leading to the suicides into three categories: (1) conditions that predisposed the group to radical action, (2) situational factors influencing the assessment of options, and (3) precipitating events that transformed suicide from an option into a reality. These factors moved the group through a series of phases that collectively involved a progressive disconnection from the phenomenal realm and an increasing connection with a transcendent realm, the next level, that made the transit an increasingly compelling strategic option.

In the concluding chapter, the editors elicit some of the main themes from the theoretical and case study chapters and identify key issues to advance this area of study, ponder the prospects for future violent events that parallel those examined in the volume, and assess the political consequences of the occurrence of violent episodes. In brief, implicitly or explicitly, each of the contributors acknowledges the likelihood that future violent episodes will occur. The combination of conditions that result in such events is exceptional but not unique. The violent episode in 2000 in Uganda involving the Movement for the Restoration of the Ten Commandments is compelling confirmation of that probability. Under these circumstances, it is important to construct interpretive frameworks that permit understanding of such episodes but not use them as templates to impose on a much broader range of movement–societal conflicts. The chapters as a whole also make a strong case for a contextual and interactive interpretation of violence as opposed to attributing causality to inherent characteristics of either movements or control agencies. There is a collective sense that specifying more closely the interactive factors that precipitate violent episodes should be the immediate objective of future work in this area. The theoretical significance of this objective is underscored by the political reaction to recent episodes of violence. Particularly in Europe, but elsewhere as well, governments have sought to formulate legislative criteria that would distinguish "legitimate" from "illegitimate" religion and to increase surveillance and control over groups placed in the latter category. The battle over these initiatives rages at this writing and promises to continue for some time. The political stakes are high for a range of groups caught up in this conflict, as well as for the longer-term balance between state and religion as countervailing sources of social legitimation.

2

DRAMATIC DENOUEMENTS

DAVID G. BROMLEY

The objective of this volume is to develop a sociological explanation of what I term "Dramatic Denouements." Dramatic Denouements transpire when a movement and some segment of the social order reach a juncture at which one or both conclude that the requisite conditions for maintaining their core identity and collective existence are being subverted and that such circumstances are intolerable. These relational moments are most likely to occur when the relationship between movement and society is characterized by polarization and destabilization. Parties on one or both sides thereupon undertake a project of final reckoning under the aegis of a transcendent mandate to reverse their power positions and to restore what they avow to be the appropriate moral order. This project is holistic in the sense that it is undertaken by the entire movement or social order or, alternatively, some segment thereof that acts in the name of the larger whole. Several definitions and assumptions are necessary to extend and clarify this argument.

First, the argument is historically grounded. The cases that are the focus of analysis here occurred in a specific historical context. Although parallels with other historical moments can plausibly be developed, the combination of social factors and their interactive dynamics would certainly vary in important ways. For heuristic purposes, I shall identify four levels of historically situated disputation that describe the increasing breadth and seriousness of claims-making in these episodes: (1) Latent Tension, in which the foundational logic and organization of movement and society stand in contradiction to one another, although there may not be direct engagement; (2) Nascent Conflict, in which emergent bilateral conflicts are not articulated in ideological terms, future adversaries have not mobilized organizationally, and parties therefore orient toward one another as "troublesome"; (3) Intensified Conflict, in which there is heightened mobilization and radicalization of movements and oppositional groups, entry of third parties, and orientation by parties toward one another as "dangerous" (Sarbin 1967); and (4) Dramatic Denouement, in which polarization and destabilization of dangerous relationships lead to orientation by parties as "subversive" and to projects of final reckoning intended to reverse power and moral relationships (Emerson and Messinger 1977; Emerson 1981).

Second, dispute escalation is an interactive, contingent process. Outcomes are myriad and complex since dispute escalation involves interactive, reflexive action; a variety of response options are available; disputes may be resolved at any point in the escalation process; strategies may involve multiple shifting responses; and apparently unrelated events may impact dispute dynamics. Indeed, participants become engaged in a nondeterministic, historically situated process in which they may or may not anticipate impending events to which they are contributing. Again, for heuristic purposes, I delineate three response options – contestive, accommodative, and retreatist – that are available at each dispute level (Grottanelli 1985). Here I am concerned with broad response *patterns*, which are likely to be the product of both internal and external dynamics, rather than specific actions, which may be varied and even inconsistent. Retreatist responses include various types of withdrawal that involve severing connections between parties. Movements may withdraw physically and socially through migration or isolation. Correspondingly, the dominant social order may marginalize and ignore them. Accommodative responses include different modes of adjustment on one or both sides that involve constructing coordination-style connections between parties. The social order may shift normative boundaries toward greater inclusiveness, or at least ignore practices that could be contested, and movements may find ways of creating specific rapprochements with established institutions or adopt more broadly conformist lifestyles. Contestive responses include numerous kinds of disputation that share in common constructing conflict-oriented connections between parties. Contestation may assume diverse forms – from symbolic posturing, to ritualized disputation, to violent combat.

As the level of disputation escalates, retreat and contestation both constitute modes of radical conflict and rejection of the alternative form of social order. Each also is a demonstration of power. In Dramatic Denouements these two responses assume their most extreme forms, Exodus and Battle. Exodus involves an orchestrated withdrawal from the locus of the order that is being opposed through which a participant in the conflict reasserts the moral superiority of its position, rejects the existing social order, and totally separates itself from that order. Battle is organized combat through which a participant in the conflict reasserts the moral superiority of its position, rejects the alternative social order, and launches a coercive campaign to replace that order with its own vision of an appropriate social order. Each constitutes a fundamental repudiation of the alternative social order; continued mutual existence or at least existence in the same space is rejected. Given the asymmetrical power relationship between movement and social order, it is clear that movements are more likely to choose accommodation or retreat and that contestation is a more viable response from dominant institutions.

Finally, the analytic posture adopted here departs from conventional wisdom concerning violence involving religious movements in an important respect – the Dramatic Denouement argument reverses the anomaly to be explained. The depiction of religious movements as inherently unstable, authoritarian, and predisposed to violence or control agencies as disposed to repression and aggression renders anomalous cases in which extreme outcomes are somehow avoided. I argue the reverse based on two premises. One is that, as in many other types of conflict, low to moderate levels are common and extreme levels are infrequent. Indeed, most movement–society disputes are contained or resolved in some fashion. The anomalous cases, then, are the Dramatic Denouements that do actually occur and that are the focus of this book. The other is that *either* movement or social order may play the *primary* role in precipitating a moment of Dramatic Denouement. If outcomes are the product of interactive dynamics rather than inherent characteristics, then specific resolutions may be the result of varying degrees of influence from either side. Indeed, the cases at hand vary distinctly in terms of whether internal or external forces were pivotal in triggering a Dramatic Denouement.

In order to develop the Dramatic Denouement argument, I trace the religious movement–societal conflict through three levels of disputation – Latent Tension, Nascent Conflict, and Intensified Conflict. I then identify conditions associated with the occurrence of Dramatic Denouements. The chapter concludes with a rehearsal of the four focal cases in terms of the Dramatic Denouement framework.

Latent Tension

The movement–societal conflict process, as I shall describe it, involves a particular kind of group and conflict grounded in a specific sociohistorical context. There is a long history of religious innovation and schismatic divisions in western societies. However, the prophetic movements with which we are concerned in this volume constitute a cohort of groups that have appeared at the same historical moment in a number of western societies in response to the same structural conditions (Bromley 1997). There is continuing Latent Tension between these prophetic religious movements and the dominant social order, as both incorporate foundational sources of authorization for social relations. This tension occurs on several dimensions. The state and economy serve as central sources of individual identity and social authorization for the full range of public sphere institutions. These institutions collectively naturalize the existing social order as embodying the minimum conditions requisite for a viable society. Prophetic movements stand in resistance to the established social order. They challenge its legitimacy by creating a vision of an alternative order; they reject its institutional arrangements and replace them with social forms that model a new order. The alternative order may take the form of "a state within a state" or a transnational organization that supersedes the state; either constitutes a direct challenge to state primacy. The dispute is foundational, as each offers ultimate authorization by sacralizing its ideology and organizational forms. For their part, prophetic movements sacralize their ideologies as spiritual revelation, their missions as a transcendental mandate, and their organizations as representations of ultimate reality. The result is a fundamental dispute over the moral standing of the existing social order.

Commitment to dominant institutions is premised on sociocultural continuity. A temporal linkage is created between a sacred past through which the current social order becomes the legitimate heir to that tradition. By contrast, prophetic movements are energized by sociocultural discontinuity, a conviction that there is a profound disjunction between the way the world is and the way it must be. The temporal linkage is between the present and an impending future that legitimates resistance to the current social formation. The effect of these two opposed orientations is either to stabilize or destabilize confidence in the continuation and security of the current social order. The stability of the current social order, in turn, influences the degree of individual investment in its institutional auspices. Prophetic movements legitimate adherents' severing commitment to the existing order and transferring loyalty to the quest for a new order. The degree of moral claims-making by prophetic movements is qualitatively greater than for established institutions given the former's urgent imperative to carry out its transcendent mission. These differences create the basis for disputes over the viability of the current order and individual loyalty to it.

The rituals of prophetic movements and the established social order likewise pull individuals in opposite directions. A number of the pivotal institutional processes for sustaining the social order, such as electoral voting and jury trials, are heavily ritualized observances of symbols values (democracy, equality, liberty, justice). These rituals serve to legitimate the existing social order and to embed individuals within that order. The rituals of prophetic movements have precisely the opposite objective: to detach individuals from the existing order. These rituals seek to maintain a constant connection with the transcendent. The effect is to locate both adherents and the movement as a whole in a liminal position between the phenomenal and transcendent realms, poised for the advent of the impending transformative moment. Because movement and social order occupy and espouse very different realities, communication and coordination become problematic.

Finally, the expansion of the state, along with the twin processes of secularization and differentiation, have diminished the public authorization capacities of religion, moved the religious institution to the private sphere, and expanded state regulatory activity. Where mainstream churches do participate in the public sphere, they play a supportive role that Williams and Demerath (1991) term "civic religion." State regulatory functions have multiplied rapidly, which creates the potential for a host of new societal–movement conflicts, most notably those related to individual rights. Prophetic movements, by contrast, seek to reverse the process of secularization and to move religion to the center stage of the social order as the primary source of authorization for social relations. Elevating the role of religion threatens the carefully constructed boundaries between societal institutions and between the public and private spheres, thereby creating the basis for an array of boundary disputes.

The dominant social order and prophetic movements thus face potential conflict on a number of dimensions. Movement and social order both offer foundational sources of authorization for social relations but from diametrically opposed premises. Further, the two are inextricably interrelated. The social order constitutes the sociocultural conditions against which prophetic movements mobilize; the movements, in turn, draw their energy, ideology, organizational forms, and membership from the social order. In sum, Latent Tension is inherent in the relationship between prophetic movements and the established social order.

If the potential for conflict is so high, the anomaly is the infrequency rather than the frequency of conflict escalation. Currently there are hundreds of religious movements of various types and scores more throughout history, but perilous conflicts are infrequent. Case histories suggest that accommodation and separation have been the most common responses, and contestation has typically been delimited and nonviolent. For example, throughout history radical communal groups have routinely distanced themselves from the established social order by migrating to isolated rural locations. The dominant social order often has responded by defining such groups as outsiders and studiously ignoring them. Both sides retreat to a position of minimal contact. Accommodation also has been and remains a likely response, as the influential church-sect model predicts. Numerous contemporary movements accommodated early in their histories or discovered niches as separatists, utopians, principled opposition, or eccentrics that diminished tension. For example, of the myriad Jesus Movement groups that appeared at the same time as The Family, most maintained their connections to the conservative Christian community and organized in ways that were defined as zealous but not heretical. A number of internal organizational dynamics as well as the real costs of movement–society tension have propelled groups toward accommodation and a more settled lifestyle. On the social order side, religious liberty and tolerance norms combined with limited state regulatory apparatus yield at least a nominally accommodative societal stance. Even where contestive relationships have developed, these often have been narrow and focused, with institutional auspices available for dispute resolution and little potential for dispute broadening. For example, the Branch Davidians were in open, continuous conflict with the Seventh-Day Adventists, but disputation was largely symbolic and the privatization of religion prevented public sphere involvement. Dispute escalation, therefore, has not been a product of latent tension, prophetic movement characteristics, or limited contestation.

Nascent Conflict

The emergence of Nascent Conflict is attributable to several key factors that set the stage for Intensified Conflict. Chief among these factors were the number of movements mobilizing during the same period, the development strategies they adopted, the availability of potential converts to the movements in certain social locations, the potential for opposition that was created by the appearance of the groups, and the vulnerability of the social

order to challenge during this crisis period. Nascent Conflict was characterized by emergent disputation; neither movements nor oppositional groups
had mobilized organizationally and ideologically. Disputes therefore tended
to be limited and bilateral, and many movements avoided conflict through
retreat and accommodation.

The root causes of what developed into the 1970s cult controversy can
be found in the major structural crisis that I have described elsewhere as a
shifting balance between contractual and covenantal forms of social relations
(Bromley 1997). This crisis increased both the vulnerability of the dominant
social order to challenges from prophetic movements and the appeal of those
movements at various locations within the social order. The proximate
causes of religious movement growth are to be found in three developments
that were not directly related to religion at all. The rapid growth and
concentration of young adult populations in colleges and universities created
a large pool of potential recruits. The subsequent emergence of the youth
counterculture produced a pool of individuals already in resistance to the
social order who later became available to religious movements in the wake
of countercultural decline. The rescinding of tight restrictions on oriental
immigration resulted in the appearance of a number of oriental religious
groups that critiqued the dominant social order from an eastern perspective.
What emerged was a broadly based resistance that ranged from rebellion
within the Christian tradition, as in the Jesus Movement, to a sudden
surge in the number of eastern religious movements. From a historical,
structural perspective, then, what became the cult controversy emerged out
of specific unique circumstances, none of which were inevitable but all of
which probably were necessary for the conflict that ensued. Further, the
specific groups that initiated conflict significantly shaped the direction that
the conflict was to take.

The first glimmerings of conflict began with The Family (originally the
Children of God) and soon broadened to include the Unificationist and
Hare Krishna movements. However, the dispute emerged only gradually,
and trouble remained inchoate for a time. The Family was only one of
many Jesus Movement groups seeking to bring youthful members of the
counterculture to Christ. There is little evidence that Moses David Berg's
early coffee house ministry generated any substantial opposition. Indeed,
the Jesus Movement provided a safe haven for youth who might otherwise
have been involved in more risky ventures. At its inception, the movement
was small and lacked an identity (even a formal name), Berg's charismatic
claims had yet to emerge, and the organizational structure remained quite

fluid. On these counts, the movement did not appear to pose any obvious threat to families or other institutions. Parents who did oppose the religious zealousness of their offspring often initially employed informal, low-level settlement techniques (e.g., containing, moderating, tolerating) to deal with noncompliant behavior. Where conflict did occur, it was between family members and the movement. Since families facing similar situations initially were not in contact with one another, opposition remained unorganized and common grievances were not articulated.

The inception of The Family was soon followed by the emergence of the Unificationist and Hare Krishna movements. Both of the latter movements also began with a small coterie of members, loose-knit organization, and charismatic claims-making that was gradually developed and slowly divulged. And opposition was quite limited. During his early speaking tours across the United States, for example, Rev. Sun Myung Moon was treated as an oriental evangelist, and his calls for the United States to assume its divinely mandated role drew a polite, if sometimes quizzical, reception. Similarly, Prabhupada was received as one in a series of Eastern spiritual figures who became fashionable as gurus among upper-middle-class Americans. All three of these movements exhibited an optimistic, if naive, conviction that their beliefs would be readily accepted if given an open hearing. The appearance of these movements did not immediately trigger conflict. The movements themselves slowly built organizational momentum, and there was no active control coalition. As a result, the movements did not manifest some of the radical characteristics that would be so prominent just a few years later, and relations between movement and society were not particularly contentious.

At this juncture the movements occupied the morally ambiguous status of "troublesome," in contrast to the morally discredited status of "dangerous" or "destructive" that soon followed. Events were underway, however, that would intensify the conflict between prophetic movements and the social order. The appearance of multiple movements simultaneously broadened the base of potential opposition, and the geographic dispersion of the movements created national visibility for the emergent dispute. The movements drew heavily on societal resources by adopting proselytization, which divided families, rather than procreation as a growth strategy. Appeals to middle-class young adults yielded a substantial pool of families occupying a similar class position from which an oppositional coalition could be formed.

The conflict trajectory that occurred was not inevitable, however. Arguably, had The Family been the only group at issue, the pool of converts small and more marginal socially, or the movements simply regional, conflict escalation might not have ensued. Likewise, had the movements recruited within dominant traditions, the conflict might have remained more circumscribed, as it has for groups like Orthodox Judaism or Opus Dei. In this instance, however, two of the three movements were from outside the dominant Christian tradition, which facilitated characterizing the problem as an external subversive threat. The conflict might also have taken quite a different tack had Christian Identity movements that pose a more direct challenge to the state been the initial focus of controversy. As it was, the three movements that triggered conflict adopted persuasive rather than coercive strategies, which limited the grounds for invoking state sanctions and moved the oppositional coalition in the direction of a privatized, self-help movement.

The movements, the emergent countermovement, and the few governmental agencies involved in the Nascent Conflict exhibited all three response alternatives. Most notable perhaps was the retreatist response by movements. From its inception, for example, The Family has reacted to conflict by exiting the situation, as evidenced in the "flee bags" that Moses David Berg instructed his followers to have packed at all times. In the wake of modest conflict, The Family adopted a communal migratory style and then emigrated from the United States to Europe by 1971. Heaven's Gate followed a similar course just a few years later. When early recruitment success engendered opposition, the movement went underground and maintained a communal, migratory lifestyle for many years. There was also limited contestation. The Unificationists and Hare Krishna both developed mobile fund-raising and recruitment teams that came into conflict with local municipalities over the balance between community and movement rights. These movement–society clashes were sometimes symbolic in character. The Branch Davidians and The Family both challenged the legitimacy of established churches, on occasion interrupting church services and decrying their spiritual corruption. The Family conducted marches in a number of cities, and the Unificationists organized rallies to condemn the irreligiousness of modern life. In response, political leaders, sometimes in concert with aggrieved families, orchestrated legislative hearings that served as public degradation ceremonies at which complaints against movements were aired.

Amid these various disputes, there were some accommodation initiatives as well. For example, the Unificationists and groups of parents sought to establish a mediation process under the auspices of the National Council of Churches in order to resolve movement–family disputes, and mobile Unificationist and Hare Krishna solicitation teams sometimes sought to negotiate mutually acceptable terms for fund-raising rules with local officials. Since the conflict was not particularly intense at this juncture, none of these various responses, conflicts, and resolutions attracted widespread notice. Conflict would shortly intensify with rapid movement and counter-movement mobilization as well as the intervention of regulatory agencies. It is noteworthy in this regard that *none* of the movements that initiated the escalating conflict ultimately became involved in a Dramatic Denouement episode. Each found a means for accommodating and lowering tension levels.

Intensified Conflict

Several key developments transformed Nascent Conflict into Intensified Conflict. Chief among these were a continuous expansion in the number of prophetic movements, heightened mobilization and radicalization of these movements, mobilization and radicalization of oppositional groups, and the entrance of third-party control agencies into the conflict. These developments resulted in an accumulation of disputes, linkages between those disputes, and coalition formation on both sides. In this circumstance, both the movements and elements of the social order began to orient toward one another as "dangerous," that is, as engaging in organized, ideologically directed activity constituting a direct threat to the other. Conflict remained loosely coupled, however, because coalitions were transitory and unstable, and neither movements nor oppositional groups were able to gain a decisive victory. As a result, Intensified Conflict did not in itself yield the polarization associated with Dramatic Denouement.

The internal mobilization of movements involved organizational development and radicalization, both of which contributed to conflict escalation. As they mobilized, many movements developed apocalyptic/millennial ideologies that elevated the sense of urgency within their ranks and legitimated a more radical course of action. Prophetic revelations of an impending transformative moment enhanced charismatic authority. Communal or other high-demand organizations, often accompanied by geographic mobility, simultaneously strengthened internal relationships and weakened external ties. Such developments together pushed the movements toward greater liminality and a sense of playing a pivotal role in unfolding cosmic events. Even while they radicalized, a number of movements also became more formidable as they rapidly built membership, economic, and organizational bases. Roughly the same sequence of initial radicalization, organizational development, and environmental opposition characterized the experience of many, although by no means all, movements that appeared during the 1970s.

Opposition to the prophetic movements followed closely on the heels of movement mobilization and also moved rapidly in more radical direction. Families of converts began banding together upon confronting a movement–member alliance that rejected their claims to loyalty and authority. The anticult movement developed its own apocalyptic ideology, which created the specter of a proliferation of rapidly growing, destructive cults that were accumulating economic and political power (Shupe and Bromley 1980). The key elements in this ideology were "cults" and "brainwashing" that permitted the linking of diverse movements and organizational practices. The countermovement overcame its early balkanization and fashioned a national coalition that raised its visibility and influence. Countermovement ranks swelled as a result of an increase in the number of religious movements and their membership growth. The anticult movement also undertook various forms of direct action, most notably attempting to reverse the effects of what it regarded as cult programming of adherents through a ritual of deprogramming. Movements responded to countermovement tactics by distancing further, heightening surveillance, and challenging countermovement initiatives. The countermovement, in turn, expanded its control measures to include legislative initiatives to repress movements as organizations and civil litigation to seek redress for putative abuse of adherents.

One important outgrowth of radicalization in movement and countermovement ranks was a tendency to miscalculate the power and solidarity of the other. For example, both continued to misassess the depth and permanence of member affiliations despite the fact that each clearly exhibited low recruitment rates and high turnover rates. These erroneous perceptions encouraged even more radical postures and were used as leverage in enlisting coalitional partners. The end result was a growing conviction in both camps that their opponents were extremely dangerous.

Mobilization by movement and countermovement groups was accompanied by the entry of third parties, which reshaped the nature of the conflict. Most important was the entry of a range of governmental units representing all three branches and levels of government; the media were also an important force in creating a public definition of the conflict. The intervention of governmental agencies changed the nature of the conflict in two ways. The agencies pursued their own regulatory agendas rather than grievances on either side. They also constituted attractive coalition partners, as they controlled access to legitimate sanctioning power and had the imprimatur of neutrally dispensed justice. Each side initially had sought third-party regulatory status for itself. Anticult associations attempted to position themselves as civic watchdog organizations. They identified cultic characteristics, practices, and groups that distinguished between legitimate and illegitimate religion and also pursued independent sanctioning capacity, most notably through conservatorship powers that would grant families legal custody of offspring affiliated with cultic groups. For their part, religious movements created a series of nominally free-standing groups positioned as religious liberty protection organizations. They asserted broad principles of religious rights and tolerance such that their movements would fall under the mantle of legitimate religion and invoked constitutional free exercise and establishment provisions to trump oppositional control initiatives. When such regulatory status proved elusive, both sides actively sought alliance with governmental agencies and the media.

Beyond the mobilization and radicalization of movements and their opponents and the activation of control agencies, several other factors contributed to the structure of Intensified Conflict. Both the formation of new movements and the development of existing movements created additional sources of dispute and a sense that there was an endless array of disruptive groups. Changes in the targets and priorities of regulatory agencies and the anticult movement produced a comparable effect for movements embroiled in new or unanticipated controversies. Since organizational apparatus and interpretive frames were now in place, conflicts surrounding emerging movements often escalated rapidly rather than developing incrementally. Emergent public issues also created new bases of conflict. For example, a number of movements became embroiled in child abuse allegations both because the movements had begun to produce a second generation and due to expanded child welfare regulatory activity. And specific incidents involving one religious movement in some cases increased the level of tension surrounding others. The Peoples Temple tragedy in the United States and the Solar Temple episode in Europe both increased public apprehension and control initiatives for a time.

There was also mounting frustration on all sides as movements, countermovements, and control agencies alike were unable to achieve a final, decisive triumph. While some movements did attain membership and economic viability, none created the kind of social transformation that they envisioned. In no case have their millennial expectations been realized or their moral claims honored; for most movements, membership turnover has been massive; they have faced mounting opposition rather than acceptance; and few have established significant social or political alliances. Correspondingly, the anticult movement has been unable to achieve the status of a regulatory unit with access to sanctioning power, and its alliances with governmental units have been mercurial. Perhaps the anticult movement's greatest success was the cultural diffusion of the cult/brainwashing symbols that became the lens through which a diverse array of groups and events were thematized. For their part, governmental agencies frequently were limited in their capacity to control movements. Although certain agencies did exercise sanctioning power, no lasting coalition developed among various agencies or levels of government of the kind currently witnessed, for example, in China's campaign against Falun Gong. For a time during the 1970s and 1980s in the United States and during the 1990s in Europe, a coalition comprised of anticult and governmental agencies made headway in implementing a control agenda, but all of these initiatives have yielded mixed results. Movements have been able to evade governmental controls not only through legal protections accorded religious groups but also through transnational organization that often has placed them beyond the reach of national governments. The anticult movement was able to muster support from government agencies in some cases, but in other cases movements were protected from government and countermovement control efforts by appellate courts.

Intensified Conflict, a relationship in which parties become dangerous to one another, was thus a product of several factors: (1) growth in the number of movements, which multiplied the number of disputes; (2) mobilization and radicalization of both movements and a countermovement, which made each more formidable and threatening to the other; (3) entry of third parties, which created coalitional partners for both sides as well as the potential for independent regulatory initiatives; and (4) involvement of various parties in multiple disputes simultaneously, which contributed alternatively to a perception of a serious "cult problem" or a "religious repression problem." Frustration on all sides at their inability to achieve a clear or lasting victory also contributed to more confrontive stances. Although intense, the level of conflict fluctuated as a result of the impact of particular incidents as well as unrelated events in the social order that washed over into the cult controversy. The degree of unpredictability therefore remained high as movement mobilization presented new sources of conflict, and as shifting priorities for oppositional and regulatory groups created unexpected challenges to movements. Despite this intensification, however, conflict remained loosely coupled. Movements rarely formed more than temporary alliances with one another, the coalitional base of the anticult movement remained quite narrow, and governmental agencies usually did not act in concert. For the conflict as a whole, then, there never has been a polarization into two unified camps that would ultimately lead to a decisive moment of conflict resolution.

Because the structure of conflict has been loosely coupled, the full range of response options remained available despite the intensification of conflict. While in many cases movements, opponents, and regulatory units have been involved in a series of specific encounters, the emphasis here is on overall response patterns. In many respects, the most striking response pattern has been accommodation by the religious movements within a relatively brief time period in response to both internal pressures toward a more settled lifestyle and contestation by oppositional and regulatory groups. For example, the three movements initially at the forefront of the cult controversy – Unificationism, the Hare Krishna, and The Family – adopted more settled, conventional lifestyles within two decades. Unificationists reduced their isolation, held conventional jobs, and began establishing an alliance with conservative political groups. The Hare Krishna broadened its membership by appealing to immigrant Hindus, sanctioning segments of the movement that engaged in illegal activity, and acknowledging and reforming abusive childrearing practices. The Family renounced most of the radical sexual experimentation that had been a primary source of contention. Other movements followed a similar course. The Church Universal and Triumphant initiated discussions with federal officials to defuse mounting tension and subsequently engaged in a thorough reorganization process. The Messianic Communities reduced its isolation and opened dialogue with a range of community groups. Among governmental institutions, the most significant accommodation occurred through the judicial system, where appellate courts repeatedly blunted efforts by oppositional and regulatory groups to sanction religious movements. These decisions prevented extreme economic and coercive measures from being carried out. For example, the Unificationist Movement was involved in over 2,000 legal cases involving public fund-raising, winning virtually all of them on appeal. The result of these cases, and many more involving the Hare Krishna, was a stabilization of the conflict that both reaffirmed movement rights and tightened regulations.

Some movements chose retreat in the face of contestation. For example, in the face of growing public controversy, the Dawn Horse Communion acquired a South Pacific island to which the movement leader and a coterie of followers relocated. For a time The Way International was a major anticult target. In response to both internal turmoil and external opposition, the movement virtually cut off external ties, secluding itself in several movement enclaves. Some groups, such as the Church of the Living Word and the Glory Barn, secluded themselves following a period of conflict and simply dropped out of the controversy. Synanon, which began as a respected drug treatment program, subsequently moved steadily toward an isolated communal lifestyle. The Peoples Temple also initially employed a retreatist strategy in its migration to Guyana. Correspondingly, it has been rather common for local communities to erect social barriers to movements. In essence elements of the community (churches, businesses, municipal governments) withdraw socially, leaving a movement enclave that is *in* but not *of* the larger community.

Movements, oppositional groups, and regulatory agencies all have initiated contestive relationships. However, there are remarkably few cases of movements beyond the Black Muslims and Scientology selecting a persistently contestive stance. The Church of Scientology is the preeminent example of a movement that has continued to sustain contestive relations with oppositional and regulatory groups. The movement publicly renounced illegal activity after an armed raid by federal agents and the imprisonment of several leaders. It has nonetheless continued to mount aggressive campaigns against formidable opponents, including both the Internal Revenue Service (IRS) and the anticult movement. For its part, the IRS has gained a reputation as the most consistently aggressive federal regulatory agency, using its authority to deny or revoke the tax-exempt status and bringing tax evasion charges against a number of movements. Examples include the imprisonment of Reverend Moon on tax evasion charges and the contesting of the tax-exempt status in the cases of The Way International, The Music Square Church, the Church Universal and Triumphant, Synanon, and the Church of Scientology. The Immigration and Naturalization Service (INS) also became involved in disputes with a number of movements whose membership included a substantial number of immigrants. The deportation of Rajneesh was the most visible of these cases. The anticult movement has continued to launch campaigns against movements, often by enlisting a regulatory unit as an ally. Child welfare agencies have been frequent allies, as in the cases of The Family and Messianic Communities, where large numbers of children have been taken into custody amid allegations of child abuse.

Intensified Conflict set the stage for Dramatic Denouements. Movements, oppositional groups, and regulatory agencies all were mobilized, and the interpretive frameworks legitimating further escalation were put in place. As a result of the loosely coupled nature of conflict at the level of Intensified Conflict, however, Dramatic Denouements have been discrete episodes. They also have been infrequent. Few conflicts even at the level of Intensified Conflict have escalated into Dramatic Denouement. Intensified Conflict may remain stable as long as the parties engage through narrow, focused disputation, conflict resolution structures are in place, and there are means available for reducing or evading conflict. Additional dynamics are necessary for Dramatic Denouement to occur.

Dramatic Denouement

I have argued that Dramatic Denouements are rare events and that almost all have involved single movements. Dramatic Denouements are rare because both movements and control agents have at their disposal various means of settlement through which to diminish movement–societal tension. They involve single movements because the structure of Intensified Conflict has not involved preexisting, mobilized, polarized coalitions. Rather, each episode emerges somewhat independently, even if each occurrence may shift the probabilities and course of future events. At the same time, there is a significant probability that some cases will reach the level of Dramatic Denouement because at the level of Intensified Conflict ideologies and organizational forms have radicalized to the point where the stage has been set for the moment of final reckoning to occur.

Dramatic Denouements as relational moments are most likely to develop out of a structure of Intensified Conflict that establishes the context for an escalation of conflict. This moment is reached through progressive polarization. Polarized relationships involve a combination of distance and connection between parties who are rooted in the same social formation but organized on fundamentally incompatible premises. To the extent that each possesses a cohesive ideology and organization that stand in contradiction to those of the other, the parties become subversive to one another. Factors promoting polarization include actions and symbolic designations by either side that threaten the other and internal radicalization that moves a party in a more extreme direction. The instability of polarized relationships can be accentuated by secrecy, organizational consolidation/fragmentation, and elimination of third parties. At some point in the process, one or both sides reach the point of last resort and launch a project of final reckoning.

Movement toward polar positions usually is precipitated by a change in the level and form of the conflict relationship that makes it more menacing. This occurs through some combination of relational and internal dynamics. On the one hand, either or both parties may apply symbolic designations or engage in organizational actions that threaten the other. On the other hand, either or both parties also may engage in internal ideological or organizational activity that creates a more radical stance internally. These two kinds of dynamics also are interactive, of course, as a threatening stance from opponents may produce internal reactions within the threatened group and radical internal changes may be threatening to outsiders. In addition, there is a tendency for each set of dynamics to become more radical. Parties that engage in relational threats against opponents that they deem subversive are likely to heighten their own sense of endangerment in the process and to undertake more forceful control actions against them. It is also the case that internal radicalization frequently requires containment and control actions to deal with any dissension that, in turn, yields even more radical outcomes. These complex interactive dynamics result in a highly volatile situation that is vulnerable to destabilization and escalation.

The relationship between polarized parties may be destabilized by secrecy, organizational consolidation/fragmentation, and elimination of moderating third-party influence. Secrecy generally produces greater volatility and unpredictability in conflict situations. Given that the parties already assess one another as engaged in subversive conduct, secrecy renders presumably hostile intentions and actions opaque. The party discovering covert actions becomes apprehensive that even more subversive conduct may remain concealed; the concealing party becomes anxious as time passes and the amount of undiscovered clandestine activity mounts. A second destabilizing influence is control centralization or fragmentation. Control centralization increases the potential for radical action by formally or informally placing power in the hands of a small organizational cadre. Indeed, most of the radical practices that led toward Dramatic Denouements were initiated by relatively small subgroups, usually secretively at first. In movements, centralization of control may occur as a result of heightened charismatic claims, but there usually is an inner circle that supports those claims. In the case of regulatory units, centralization of control involves shifting authority to a single agency or a subunit within the agency. Paradoxically perhaps, control fragmentation also may have destabilizing effects. Organizational divisions and defections create the potential for more radical actions by the core organization, which finds itself confronting opposition from former allies. For movements, charismatic deterioration also may heighten movement instability when the leader's physical or psychological condition deteriorates. As parties on either side move in polar directions, fewer parties occupy moderate positions, and the remaining moderates are likely to possess less influence. From a coalitional standpoint, therefore, polarized parties become more isolated even as their positions become nonnegotiable. A reduction in the number and viability of moderating influences makes radical initiatives more probable and more easily consummated. If various constituencies within the social order are forced to choose between polar positions, the prospects for challenging movements are distinctly unfavorable given the enormous advantage control agencies have in enlisting coalitional partners.

The impetus toward Dramatic Denouement begins at a moment of last resort when all existing avenues for redress have been pursued unsuccessfully. In this moment, one or both sides conclude that the current situation constitutes an intolerable threat to their legitimacy and viability and a final resolution must be reached. Dramatic Denouements thus become moments of destiny. Response options assume their most extreme forms under these circumstances. Partial accommodations will no longer suffice. The only acceptable form of accommodation becomes Capitulation, in which one party accedes totally to the demands of the other. Correspondingly, simply continuing contestation over narrowly drawn issues is insufficient; only a Battle through which one party dominates or destroys the other is acceptable. And merely stepping back from the brink and achieving separation is unsatisfactory. The solution must be Exodus, in which one party moves outside the opponent's realm of control. The asymmetrical power relationship between movement and social order becomes critical in determining the options available to each party. The social order or its representatives will not withdraw; this is not a revolutionary moment in which the movement will subsume the society. Nor will the society Capitulate. By contrast, all three responses from the challenging movement remain possible. Under these circumstances, a few of the logical possibilities are the most probable. If the movement initiates a Dramatic Denouement, the most likely scenario is Exodus or Battle; Capitulation is most likely where one of the other two options fails. By contrast, control agencies are more disposed to initiate Battle, to which the movement may respond in kind or by Capitulation or Exodus.

Battle and Exodus both are organized as projects of full and final reckoning that are intended to reorder an unacceptable situation "once and for all." Their key attributes are transcendent legitimation, holistic action, and moral accounting; where possible, these projects culminate in "sealing actions." In polarized relationships, each party moves to defend the core elements of its ideology and organization, which are privileged with transcendent status. At this juncture, therefore, the deliberations and actions of both parties are orchestrated in terms of transcendent mandates. In the case of control agencies, transcendent mandates are those that naturalize the dominant social order. Officials seek to discern, for example, what law, justice, or community security requires. Prophetic movements are likely to be engaged in ongoing interactions with transcendent forces or entities that shape their perception of acceptable lines of action. In this sense, what had previously been bilateral exchanges now involve a third-party intermediary. Exodus and Battle projects are intended to demonstrate transcendent power, and it is this power upon which the parties' utter confidence in ultimate success rests. In the case of movement Exodus, the transcendent force serves as a guide and protector as the journey to another realm is undertaken. In the situation of Battle, the transcendent force is a powerful ally that ensures ultimate victory, even if in another realm. For either type of project, the termination of mortal existence is not likely to be the yardstick by which success or failure is measured, as these actors occupy a cosmic stage. Projects are holistic in the sense that they are undertaken on behalf of and in the name of the movement or social order; united action is therefore essential. However, particularly where control has been assumed by a subgroup within a movement or control agency, the "consensus" upon which actions are premised may be the product of coercion or manipulation as well as of informed, voluntary agreement. The demand for a final reckoning lends these projects a quality of moral imperative; they are undertaken with a profound sense of righteousness. The requirement for ultimate resolution means that parties on both sides have a sizable stake in ensuring that the moral ledger is balanced at this moment. Since the parties are morally polarized, this accounting will involve at least a total repudiation of, and often an unleashing of wrath against, dissenters and enemies. Apostates are particularly likely to be targets since they have knowingly betrayed the sacred cause. To the extent that circumstances permit, the parties are also likely to engage in sealing actions designed to ensure that the final reckoning will not be subject to further revision. Such actions typically involve eradicating any evidence, material or human, that would undermine the legitimation for the Dramatic Denouement project.

Contemporary Episodes

The four cases that are the focus of analysis each reveal the dynamics associated with Dramatic Denouements. In each case the movement initially was relatively small, nonvisible, and in low tension with the larger society. However, all these movements developed during a period of intensive conflict, which meant that symbolic categorizations, regulatory apparatus, and coalition links were available. This meant that developing conflicts could escalate rapidly, as key elements of the conflict infrastructure were already in place. The trajectory of each episode varied, with a key difference being the mixture of internal and external factors that moved the group toward Dramatic Denouement. The Branch Davidians represent the best example of the primacy of external factors and Heaven's Gate the clearest illustration of the primacy of internal factors. Whichever set of factors predominated, the conflict between movement and social order at some point escalated qualitatively and moved toward a moment of Dramatic Denouement. The key processes involved in reaching this moment were polarization and destabilization that led to a point of last resort and the launching of a project of final reckoning.

The Branch Davidians

The Branch Davidians offer the best illustration of a Dramatic Denouement episode in which there was substantial external precipitation. The movement had a long history as a small, reclusive, schismatic offshoot of Seventh-Day Adventism; tensions with the surrounding community were low, with the exception of the Adventists, from whom the Davidians actively recruited members. The Davidians began to resemble the other groups typically categorized as new religious movements when David Koresh joined the movement in the late 1970s. While Koresh was involved in a struggle with a competitor for movement leadership during the 1980s that involved a violent clash, the movement did not exhibit any tendency toward externally directed violence. However, the movement did take a more radical direction internally under Koresh's leadership by the later 1980s. Koresh identified himself as *a* (as opposed to *the*) messiah who offered his disciples an assured route to salvation by following him as he carried out the opening of the Seven Seals contained in Revelations. He also taught that the world had already entered the period of tribulation preceding Armageddon and the Second Coming. He increased the movement's sense of threat and urgency by amending an earlier teaching that placed the onset of Armageddon in Israel and announcing that it would begin instead in the United States with an attack on the Davidians. Koresh also created a more tight-knit, hierarchical organization. He separated male and female followers and created an inner circle within each group where individual status was contingent on the closeness of the relationship to him. Within the women's group by 1987 he began secretly initiating sexual relationships with "spiritual wives," a practice that soon created serious problems internally and externally. Within two years Koresh had promulgated his "New Light" doctrine that established the "House of David." Koresh was to initiate a new lineage of God's children from his own seed; the children created through these unions would erect the House of David and ultimately rule the world. Opposition to the House of David created internal divisions, as sexual jealousies were aroused and some parents rebelled at the involvement of their young daughters, and the basis for external intervention, as child welfare agencies were mobilized by reported sexual relations with girls under the age of legal consent.

Beginning in 1989, an oppositional coalition formed that gathered strength over the next several years, and by 1992 conflict had reached an intense level. Family members disturbed about reports of young girls being inducted into the House of David, and sexual partners who rebuffed Koresh or were rebuffed by him banded together into an apostate group under the leadership of Marc Breault, who was repulsed by Koresh's relationships with young girls and fearful that his new bride would soon become a candidate for the House of David. This group was successful in cultivating allies, eliciting interest from a television station, which produced an exposé, as well as state Child Protective Services (CPS), which opened an investigation. Initial contacts also were established with the FBI. The BATF became interested as well when a delivery service reported a shipment of empty hand grenade casings to the Davidians. None of the initial investigations resulted in any sanctions, but they did establish a network from which continued pressure and, ultimately, official actions emanated. Just as importantly, the failure of these investigations created frustration, particularly within CPS, over an inability to confirm illicit activity officials were convinced was taking place. The sequence of events also increased the sense of threat within the Davidian community. It was at this juncture that Koresh began arming his followers and calling members abroad back to the Mount Carmel compound. A mutually threatening situation was created. David Koresh's sexual relationships with females under the age of legal consent constituted a direct challenge to child welfare agencies mandated to detect and prevent abuse. Correspondingly, welfare agency investigations of those sexual practices constituted an explicit challenge to the House of David, a central Davidian mission to establish a divinely authorized lineage through its messianic leader. In addition, both sides undertook additional actions that elevated the other's suspicions. For example, the Davidians were forced to falsify birth records to protect the House of David, and the BATF gained secret access to the Davidians through an undercover agent, whose identity was subsequently discovered by Koresh.

The BATF finally assumed responsibility for direct action against the Davidians apparently for several reasons – its mandate to control weapons violations, a concern that weapons might be used against the surrounding community, and a need to defend its organizational budget and even survival amid governmental reorganization proposals – but it also received significant information and support from CPS and the apostate group. It was from these nonbureau sources that the mass suicide scenario surfaced, as well as allegations of widespread child abuse. There was little evidence to support these claims, but they were instrumental in gaining Department of Justice approval for the initial raid in February 1993 and for employing the "dynamic entry" tactic as opposed to other alternatives.

The misguided and mismanaged February raid profoundly altered the conflict calculus for the FBI, which assumed control of the situation in the wake of the BATF debacle. The raid, and in particular the death of federal law enforcement officers, moved the conflict to a qualitatively different level and severely constricted the range of solutions available. In each side's scenario the other played a demonic role, and each calculated its position in terms of a transcendent mandate. For government officials, although a peaceful conclusion was preferable, no goal could supersede bringing those responsible for the homicides to justice and ending what had become an armed insurrection. They awaited Battle or Davidian Capitulation. For their part, the Davidians were now confronted by the prospect that endtime events had indeed been set in motion and that the police at their gates were the forces Koresh had prophesied.

Still, the die was not cast on either side; there was an appeal to last resorts during a prolonged standoff. The FBI tried a contradictory combination of increased pressure and isolation interspersed with sometimes conciliatory negotiation to dislodge the Davidians; Koresh led the Davidians in continuing to unlock the Seven Seals and await divine instruction on the proper course to follow. It appears that the Davidians may have hoped to avoid a stark Battle or Capitulation choice by producing a revelatory message for the world before surrendering, thus salvaging some semblance of victory. For a variety of reasons, federal agents perceived, perhaps incorrectly, that neither conciliation nor duress would succeed and that continued flouting of legitimate authority could not be tolerated. A CS gas assault on the compound was launched; residents died in the fire, by their own hand, and at the hands of their compatriots. Given the rapidity of events, there was little opportunity for the kind of ritualistic organization that characterized the final scene in the Solar Temple, Peoples Temple, or Heaven's Gate episodes. As a result, the extent to which the fire and Davidian deaths represented sealing actions when it was clear that the battle was lost will remain an unanswered question. The almost immediate bulldozing of the scene constitutes more compelling evidence of sealing actions by federal agents. In the end, however, neither set of sealing actions was successful. The indeterminate circumstances surrounding their deaths left the Davidians without a clear symbolic legacy, and the actions of law enforcement agents will forever link them to the Oklahoma City bombing.

The Solar Temple

The roots of the Order of the Solar Temple (OTS) can be traced to Joseph Di Mambro's membership in a Rosicrucian group during the mid-1950s and a communal group, La Pyramide (later the Golden Way), that he formed in the 1970s. The relationship between OTS leaders Di Mambro and Luc Jouret dates to the mid-1970s, and the founding of the precursor organization to OTS occurred in 1984. These early ventures by Di Mambro and Jouret appear to have engendered little public notice. However, during the 1980s OTS mobilized rapidly, and tension with the social order intensified. Secrecy was at the very core of OTS organization, which regarded itself as the successor to a thousand-year-old secret Templar order. Di Mambro and Jouret created a multilayered set of organizations in which the outer ring, the Amenta Club and the Archedia Club, were relatively conventional and accessible. However, these clubs also served as recruitment vehicles for the higher-demand, clandestine OTS. In the latter there were, for example, vows of secrecy, hidden ritual chambers, and a mysterious group of "Ascended Masters" with whom movement leaders were in regular communication. Another degree of layering within OTS involved three "degrees" of membership leading to a select inner circle that controlled the movement. Arguably, yet a third level of secretiveness involved the production of technological magic by a small group within the inner circle through which the images of Ascended Masters were created at OTS rituals. This secrecy created dual sources of tension as members lived double (secular and occult) lives that had to be carefully partitioned, and some of the movement's most compelling qualities were based on the fabricated illusions that had to be concealed from members and nonmembers alike.

The seclusiveness of OTS headed off escalation of tension with host societies for several years, and membership expanded steadily until the late 1980s. At this juncture, a new level of conflict between OTS and its host societies began to develop. Both internal and external developments created extreme polarization. OTS ideology became increasingly apocalyptic in its prophecy of an impending environmental apocalypse, and the organization began planning to establish a base in Canada that would offer refuge from the looming cataclysm. The movement also began aligning itself with a postapocalyptic world by inaugurating a new lineage through nine "cosmic children" who would constitute the first generation of the New Age. The first of these children, Emmanuelle, was believed to be the product of an immaculate conception by Di Mambro's mistress and the avatar who would preside over the inauguration of the New Age. Other radical practices were instituted that expanded both leadership authority and requisite membership commitment. Most notable were the "cosmic marriages" through which Di Mambro and Jouret restructured marital relationships among members. Internal radicalization resulted in external social control reactions. As the apocalyptic message of the movement became public knowledge, the OTS faced a precipitous decline in the fortunes of its clubs, invitations for Luc Jouret's speaking engagements, and recruitment of new members. The movement received its first taste of media hostility and anticult castigation when Rose Marie Klaus, whose marital relationship had been superseded by a cosmic marriage, went public with her complaints.

Secrecy proved to be a major source of destabilization for OTS because it was so fundamental to the movement's ideology and organization. When revelations that the compelling appearances of Ascended Masters in OTS rituals were simply carefully orchestrated illusions, commitment to the movement began to unravel. Di Mambro's son distanced himself from the movement upon learning of the chicanery. More potentially threatening was the distancing of Antonio Dutoit, the technician who produced the illusions; his disillusionment raised the specter of a particularly dangerous apostate who could discredit the movement. Moreover, Dutoit and his wife appear to have indirectly challenged Di Mambro's authority by appropriating the identity of the movement's avatar in naming their son Christopher Emmauel. Di Mambro responded by declaring the Dutoit child the Antichrist, which only inflamed hostility further. There were also threats to leadership stability from several sources. Di Mambro was afflicted with several potentially life-threatening illnesses, tensions emerged between Jouret and Di Mambro when the former lost control over the Canadian branch of OTS, and Di Mambro's opulent lifestyle and deceptions led to a succession of defectors who demanded reimbursement of their monetary contributions. OTS leaders thus faced internal threats to their leadership as well as the prospect that divisions within the movement might lead to public disgrace.

It appears that events in the spring of 1993 triggered a conclusion by movement leaders that the only remaining resort was Exodus. Ironically, the impetus toward Exodus was augmented by an extraneous event when the group was mistakenly suspected of having issued a terrorist threat. As a result of the investigation that followed, police discovered that movement's members had purchased illegal weapons. The weapons prosecution brought additional negative publicity to OTS, triggered investigations in other nations, and convinced movement leaders that OTS was the object of a vast and powerful conspiracy. The movement found itself in public disrepute, and its recruitment and financial bases both were seriously eroded. It was during this period that the movement began receiving cosmic messages that a "Transit" was necessary and that the Transit would not involve a corporeal trip aboard a spacecraft but an incorporeal voyage following termination of their mortal existence.

The core leadership then launched a project of Exodus in the form of an interstellar Transit. The project was carefully arranged and premised on the assumption of an alliance with transcendent powers who would receive and protect those embarking on the Transit. The holistic nature of the project is revealed in the orchestration of the final scene to include committed members and dissidents. Dissidenters and former members who were judged to have betrayed the movement were executed in an act of moral reckoning. Members who were sympathetic to the Transit but unable to end their corporeal existence were "helped" across the cosmic threshold, joining the committed members who initiated their own transits. The project included an elaborate sealing action that involved coordinating events in widely separated locations, leaving messages interpreting the group's position and excoriating its critics, luring dissident members to the Transit sites for execution, and setting pyrotechnic devices to destroy all physical representations of the movement and thereby to preserve its secrets and its purity.

Aum Shinrikyô

Aum Shinrikyô moved from a state of relatively low tension to engaging in Battle against Japanese society in a little over one decade, with events escalating rapidly after 1990. The movement's founder, Asahara Shôkô, left the Agonshû movement in the early 1980s to establish the organizational predecessor to Aum Shinrikyô in 1984. Aum assumed a more radical form over the next few years as Asahara began predicting Armageddon for 1993 in the form of nuclear war, and the core membership became full renunciates living communally and distancing themselves from society. Asahara claimed for himself messianic status as the figure who would usher in an ideal spiritual kingdom on earth and, more ominously, asserted the right of a guru to order the death of a person for whom that was karmically advantageous (*poa*). Still, the movement maintained an optimistic orientation by virtue of its prediction that cataclysm could be averted by eliminating negative karma if a sufficient number of converts could be won and Aum centers could be established around the world before 1993. Individuals were taught that they could gain spiritual liberation for themselves and even attain superhuman capacities through the teachings and rituals of Aum.

By the late 1980s, movement–societal conflict had intensified. Families of recruits who became full renunciates organized and went public with their complaints, there were allegations of expropriation of members' financial resources, and the movement was believed to be involved in very austere purification rituals that placed participants in serious physical jeopardy. Aum also adopted much more radical beliefs and practices that heightened tensions. The movement achieved neither its recruitment nor its dispersion goals, which made the expectation of a nonviolent transition to the new world problematic. Asahara then began narrowing the ranks of those who could be saved from the coming apocalypse. Most significantly, the movement became involved in criminal activity as it first concealed the death of an adherent during a ritual and then murdered another adherent who was on the verge of defecting and revealing the details of the first death Although several years passed before evidence of these events was discovered, the movement faced the increasing likelihood that its actions would be revealed.

At the beginning of the 1990s a new level of movement–societal conflict was reached. Perhaps the turning point was the entry of Aum members, including Asahara, into national elections that produced a political debacle and public humiliation for the movement. The public had resoundingly rejected Aum, thereby confirming Asahara's judgment that there was no longer any hope of saving humanity. It appears that this constituted a moment of last resort for the movement. Asahara announced to his followers that the movement could not endure the present state of affairs. It appears that, for a moment at least, consideration was given to both Exodus and Battle, with the latter position soon prevailing. From that time forward, the movement turned inward and distanced itself from Japanese society by building communes in remote areas. Members were urged to engage in increasingly extreme purification rituals. Several additional members died in 1994, and their deaths also had to be concealed. Force was employed to prevent defection and reclaim wayward members, and indeed it appears that a number of members may have been killed during this period in the belief that they were spies for the forces Aum believed to be arrayed against it. The date for Armageddon was repeatedly revised so that the end became ever more imminent. The movement compiled an enemies list and avowed a vast conspiracy that included both the Japanese and U.S. governments. As the outside world came to be regarded as the ultimate evil, restraints upon what the movement regarded as reprisal for its unwarranted persecution dwindled. Control of the movement increasingly shifted to an inner circle of 100–200 Asahara loyalists. This contingent of the movement then began secretly preparing for Battle. Laboratories were built in which biological and chemical weapons and delivery systems could be developed. In June 1994 the authority of the state was challenged when Aum established an array of agencies paralleling those of the state, and in that very month the first experimental attacks were launched in Matsumoto. At the same time, police agencies that had long been suspicious about Aum's involvement in a range of illegal activities were moving toward action against the movement.

By 1995 Aum faced an increasingly desperate situation. The movement perceived itself to be the target of a conspiracy by the Japanese and U.S. governments. The likelihood of imminent police intervention against Aum grew. An attorney working for an anti-Aum parents group had discovered that key charismatic claims made by Asahara were demonstrably false. Asahara then ordered the murder of the attorney and his family, as well as the kidnapping and murder of another dissident member. The brother of a movement member who threatened to initiate an external investigation of the movement was kidnapped and killed. When the movement learned that a police raid was impending, the March 20, 1995, sarin gas attack in the Tokyo subway system was launched with only minimal preparation. This attack was intended to preempt the imminent government incursion against Aum and perhaps to trigger the moment of Armageddon that Aum had predicted. The mismanaged attack failed to produce a disaster on the scale that might have occurred, and police agencies proceeded with the raid on Aum centers two days later. In this episode, the Battle that Aum initiated ended abruptly and left no opportunity for a sealing action, as neither the anticipated societal breakdown nor apocalyptic events materialized.

Heaven's Gate

Heaven's Gate emerged out of a spiritual quest by Marshall "Herff" Applewhite (Do) and Bonnie Lu Nettles (Ti) that began in early 1973 and evolved into a loosely organized movement two years later. Within a year of the time that Do and Ti began proselytizing, conflict intensified and the group almost immediately retreated from public view. The severing of contact with conventional society occurred after early recruitment successes resulted in a state police investigation, an attempt by outsiders to "rescue" a member, and complaints by a former member that were aired in the media. The group then adopted a highly seclusive, migratory, communal lifestyle that was oriented around cultivating the personal attributes required for life at the Next Level and replicating its social forms as closely as possible in an earthly setting. The movement had created an organizational style that thoroughly rejected conventional society and thereby stood in heightened tension, but the tension generated existed almost exclusively within the movement due to its small size and subterranean existence. As a result, Heaven's Gate escaped the conflicts that engulfed more visible religious movements.

Conflict reached a new level beginning in the mid-1980s as the movement began to organize itself in a fashion that rendered conventional society increasingly subversive to its core logic and mission. The conflagration at Waco raised apprehensions within the movement about the implications for its own future, and there were suspicions about ongoing police surveillance of the movement; however, there was no direct conflict with control agencies. Rather, it was primarily internal radicalization that propelled the movement toward greater polarization. Ti's death in 1985 was a unforseen occurrence that undermined the movement's longstanding belief that entry to the Next Level would be achieved with a corporeal body. The ideology was subsequently reformulated to define the human "vehicle" as simply a "container" that could be jettisoned. This revision severed a key link with the existing social order in a circumstance where that link was already tenuous; it also created the option for the movement to assume the initiative in organizing an Exodus to the Next Level at any time by simply abandoning mortal containers. The movement's ideology also began shifting in a decidedly more apocalyptic direction. In particular, the positing of evil space aliens who kept humans in bondage through religion and sexuality rendered the conventional order fundamentally subversive to the movement's goal of reaching the Next Level.

The group also continued to shift its organizational forms, rejecting those indigenous to the existing social order and replacing them with forms appropriate to the technologically superior Next Level. For example, members conducted their day-to-day lives as an "Away Team" in a physical environment designed to replicate the craft that would transport them to the Next Level and in a fashion designed to inculcate personal traits consonant with their future lives; and more traditional occupations were abandoned in favor of website design so that members spent much of their time in cyberspace. Similar distancing occurred sexually. When the group's efforts to expunge any vestiges of sexual desire through such means as grooming and dress failed, some members arranged their own castration as an ultimate solution. Much of the movement's time appears to have been spent attempting to connect with the Next Level and to ascertain the timing and conditions of its interstellar Transit through Do's revelations. Heaven's Gate generated polarization through these internal developments, but the movement undertook no threatening action against the larger society beyond rejection of it. The only publicly visible opposition mustered by the movement was a largely invisible campaign to challenge what it regarded as misinformation and misconceptions that had been part of its public identity for more than a decade.

And so, at this juncture, the movement was perched at the very edge of the phenomenal realm. Membership attrition had reduced the group to a small core of long-term, aging adherents who had little remaining connection to the society outside its cloister. The movement's precarious perch was destabilized by the deterioration in Do's health. Given that the group oriented itself through Do's prophetic persona and revelations, the uncertainty about his personal future rendered the movement's collective future on this planet even more uncertain. Heaven's Gate now had reached a point of last resort and undertook its "last chance" appeal and accompanying recruitment campaign. The indifference and ridicule in response to the movement's messages and campaign were taken as signs that their "classroom" preparation was finished. Heaven's Gate then launched a project of final reckoning. Some indecision remained as the group considered doing Battle with the police and explored various relocation sites on this planet. When the movement concluded that these alternatives were untenable, consensus emerged around an Exodus strategy.

The appearance of the Hale–Bopp comet in 1995 was interpreted as a sign that the time for departure had arrived. The movement then proceeded with all deliberate speed to organize its Exodus in an orderly and purposeful fashion. Goodbyes were said, debts paid, and responsibilities completed. Members even undertook one last sojourn into conventional society as a final test of their Exodus decision. Heaven's Gate had now fulfilled its moral responsibility by revealing the truth and gathering those willing to be saved. The Exodus constituted a final rejection of a moribund social order that soon would be "spaded under" and a demonstration of the power of the movement to transcend the impending Apocalypse. The organization of the departure site and the video messages left behind were designed as a sealing action. The attire of members symbolized their status as members of the Away Team returning home; the immaculate condition of the departure site bespoke planning, order, and purpose. The tapes communicated their eager anticipation of the voyage and sought to refute the attributions of suicide that were likely to follow. Those who failed to make the Transit probably would also fail to understand it, but the Away Team could no longer be responsible for path others had chosen.

Conclusions

In this chapter, I have developed an historically grounded structural explanation for what I term Dramatic Denouements. I have argued that Dramatic Denouements are most likely to occur during periods of intensive conflict. They transpire when a movement and some segment of the social order reach a juncture at which one or both conclude that the requisite conditions for maintaining their core identity and collective existence are being subverted and that these circumstances are intolerable. The key development leading toward Dramatic Denouement is polarization of the movement–society relationship. In a polarized relationship in which each side possesses a cohesive ideology and organization that stand in contradiction to those of the other, the parties become subversive to one another. In this circumstance, several factors – secrecy, organizational consolidation/fragmentation, and elimination of moderating third parties – are likely to destabilize an already volatile situation. Parties on one or both sides may thereupon undertake a holistic project of full and final reckoning to reverse their power positions and to restore what they avow to be appropriate moral order. At this point response options narrow, and the selection of options is determined by the transcendent mandates to which the parties are committed.

Dramatic Denouements are important to understand because they constitute those rare moments when human groups seek extraordinary, climactic clarity and closure. Most of the processes involved are also found in more mundane forms of social relations. It is the context and combination in which these processes occur that create the distinctive form. I have termed Dramatic Denouement. An understanding of the dynamics of Dramatic Denouement has implications both for understanding radical forms of human organization and for policy initiatives designed to avert catastrophic situations.

References

Bromley, David G. "A Sociological Narrative of Crisis Episodes, Collective Action, Culture Workers, and Countermovements." *Sociology of Religion* 58 (1997): 105–140.

Emerson, Robert. "On Last Resorts." *American Journal of Sociology* 87 (1981): 1–22.

Emerson, Robert, and Sheldon Messinger. "The Micro-Politics of Trouble." *Social Problems* 25 (1977): 121–134.

Grottanelli, Cristiano. "Archaic Forms of Rebellion and Their Religious Background." In *Religion, Rebellion, Revolution*, edited by Bruce Lincoln. New York: St. Martins Press, 1985: 15–45.

Sarbin, Theodore. "The Dangerous Individual: An Outcome of Social Identity Transformation." *British Journal of Criminology* 7 (1967): 285–295.

Shupe, Anson, and David Bromley. *The New Vigilantes*. Beverly Hills: Sage, 1980.

Williams, Rhys, and N. J. Demerath III. "Religion and Political Processes in an American City." *American Sociological Review* 56 (1991): 417–431.

3

CHALLENGING MISCONCEPTIONS ABOUT THE NEW RELIGIONS–VIOLENCE CONNECTION

J. GORDON MELTON AND DAVID G. BROMLEY

The expansion of religious diversity in the West over the last half century, and particularly the rise of what have been termed "new religious movements," has produced a a major scholarly reassessment of the place of religion in the social order as well as a strong public reaction to the beliefs, practices, and leadership of a number of the new movements. The conservative wing of the Christian community has repudiated what it regards as deviation from the true Christian tradition by publishing hundreds of theological exposés of cultic heresy. Parents of converts to new religious movements have banded together to form an anticult movement that has rejected the religious legitimacy of the groups and affiliations with them. In their wake, a critical cult-awareness movement led by members of the legal and psychological professions has arisen to call attention to groups believed to be physically or psychologically harmful to their members and to the public at large. An array of governmental agencies have come into conflict with religious movements over issues ranging from tax-exempt status to immigration regulations to church–state boundary issues. Media portrayals of these various conflicts have created the specter of a public menace by employing the designation "cult" as a common link that homogenizes religious movements. Scholars have mounted a major research program to interpret the religious meaning and social significance of the movements and generally have resisted the invariant and obfuscating cult appellation.

The categorization of religious movements as cults has been based on a number of putative characteristics, most notably what have been termed "brainwashing" practices. More recently, "abuse" and "violence" have performed a similar function in distinguishing "dangerous" or "deviant" religious groups (Melton 1992; Singer with Lalich 1995: 88–89). Violence is a particularly potent symbolic designation given public fears about the extent of violence in a variety of social contexts and the potential for invocation of state sanctions in response to acts of violence. The primary objective of this book is to explore the conditions under which religious movement–societal violence occurs; one important component of developing a more sophisticated understanding of that relationship is the challenging of facile, formulaic connections between religious movements and violence. The linking of violence to new religious movements through the model of cults as dangerously unstable and predisposed to internally or externally directed collective violence constitutes a model founded on formulaic logic and facile reasoning. Indeed, if there is a single overarching theme that bridges the chapters in this volume, it is the complex, interactive nature of movement–societal violence. As a postscript to the preceding chapter and a prelude to those that follow, we challenge four widely shared misconceptions concerning the relationship between new religions and violence. These include assertions that (1) violence involving new religions is pervasive, (2) new religions are violence prone, (3) new religions provoke violence, and (4) violence by new religions cannot be averted.

Violence Pervasiveness

The central misconception concerning new religions and violence, and the one from which others most often derive, is that violence involving new religions is commonplace. Implicit in this view is a contrast between new and established religions, with the latter being depicted as more pacific. There are a number of grounds for challenging the violence pervasiveness thesis.

First, there are few truly new religions. Most movements labeled as new in fact borrow major ideological and organizational elements from long-established religious traditions that are accorded social legitimacy. For example, Hare Krishna derives from Bengali Hinduism; Aum Shinrikyô from Buddhism; the Church Universal and Triumphant from Theosophy; the Branch Davidians from Adventism; the United Order from Mormonism; Happy, Healthy, Holy from Sikhism; Mahikari from Shintoism; and ECKANKAR from Sant Mat. In short, the criteria for distinguishing newness are much more complex than can be conveyed through any simple dichotomy.

Second, as we observed in the introduction to this volume, there are many forms of violence, and these various types of violence may or may not be connected either to a religious group or to a religious purpose. However, violent incidents, such as personal murder and suicide, are much more likely to be connected to an individual with a new religious affiliation than to a member of an established church. Further, violent incidents involving new religions are much more newsworthy if they involve one of these movements. The aggregation of all types of violence involving members of new religions, attributions of acts to "cultic" qualities, and the high-profile publicizing of such incidents creates the impression of pervasive violence. By contrast, violent or criminal acts by members of mainstream religions usually are not attributed to their religious affiliation and, as the current revelations concerning pedophilia in the Catholic Church illustrate, violations of massive proportions are necessary to link religious organization and deviant behavior. With respect to the connection between new religions and violence, the reality is that since the murders committed by the Manson Family some thirty years ago, only twenty groups can be implicated in violent incidents involving multiple homicide or suicide. And most of these bear little resemblance either to the cases discussed in this volume or to the stereotypical violent cult.

Third, the number of religious groups that have formed in recent decades is extraordinarily large. As Melton's compilation of religious groups reveals (Melton 1998), more than half of the 2,000 religious groups now functioning in the United States were established since 1960. And these figures do not include the even larger number of movements, such as New Age groups, that are quasi-religious in nature (Melton, Lewis, and Kelly 1990; Greil and Robbins 1994). This means that the base on which any rate of violence involvement is calculated has become much larger and, given the relatively small number of violent incidents, the proportion involved in collective violence may be smaller. Whatever "age" is designated as the criterion for newness, it might be the case for the last half-century at least that the association of newness and violence actually is inverse. A similar conclusion can be reached for Africa, where more than 5,000 new religions have appeared over the last seventy years. The massive loss of life in the 2000 episode involving the Movement for the Restoration of the Ten Commandments was horrific, but it was also a very rare event.

Fourth, even if schismatic religious groups and movements that constitute syncretic blends of several traditions are accepted as new, the comparative standard against which violence pervasiveness is measured is highly problematic. Even a cursory examination of the extent of religiously inspired violence around the globe reveals the untenability of distinguishing new from old religions in terms of their connection to violence. For example, at this writing there is ongoing violence between Protestants and Catholics in Northern Ireland, Israelis and Palestinians in the Middle East, Muslims and Hindus in India, Muslims and Christians in the Sudan, Christians and Muslims in Indonesia, and Tutsi and Bantu tribes in Rwanda.[1] And this list could easily be extended. One reason that the comparison between new and established religions with respect to violence is elusive is that conflicts involving the latter tend to be treated as political in nature, while those involving the former tend to be defined as simply deviant or criminal. However, it would seem more insightful to interpret the resistance that new religious movements offer to the established order as political, albeit through a religious format. Viewed from this perspective, mainline churches in the United States, for example, currently are in a pacific period during which their political alliance with the state and other major institutions is relatively strong, supportive, and stable. However, the histories of many denominations are replete with much more confrontive stances involving resistance and repression. And as conflicts in recent decades over issues like race relations, abortion, and governmental authority indicate, religious groups that appear settled may quickly reassume a more confrontive posture.[2]

In sum, the violence pervasiveness thesis is rooted in problematic definitions of newness and violence that load the argument in the direction of its confirmation. It tends to be based on the visibility given to deviant activity by new religions. And finally, it gains support by largely ignoring or redefining the violence in which established religions have been and are involved.

Violence Proneness

The argument that violence by new religions is pervasive leads naturally to the question of why this might be so. The answer is often traced to the

---

[1] There is a vast literature on contemporary violence involving major religious communities around the world. As a beginning, one might consult Marshall (1997) or the State Department report *International Report for International Religious Freedom for 1999* (2000), posted in full at *http://www.state.gov/www/global/human_rights/irf/irf_rpt/1999/index.html*. As the twenty-first century begins, fresh religious violence has emerged in Ireland and, in a very similar situation, in Nigeria. The level of continuing religious violence worldwide is often misunderstood in secular contexts, where religion is dismissed as a seemingly unimportant aspect of human life.

[2] The conflicts between what would now be considered the major religious bodies in the United States and both the government and other religious groups constitute a history of religious intolerance that includes the Congregationalist killing of Quakers, periodic outbursts of anti-Catholicism, anti-Hindu riots along the West Coast at the beginning of the twentieth century, and the burning and bombing of African American churches during the civil rights movement. See Raab (1964), Myers (1960), and Hurley (1962).

premise that these movements are inherently violence prone. By this logic, a "tendency toward violence" becomes a defining characteristic of new religions and is attributed to instability and pathological organizational and leadership qualities (Stark 1991). Two of the most commonly cited characteristics of new religions that putatively produce violence proneness are millennial/apocalyptic ideologies and charismatic leadership. Both are posited as sources of movement instability that creates a tendency toward violence.

Fresh outbursts of charisma always pose a threat to established social patterns, and at the same time charisma is a potent form of authority that can generate intense commitment. As a result, there are countervailing pressures to preserve and routinize its effects in many religious traditions. Because charisma can easily outflank institutional control mechanisms, traditions in which charisma is an important resource recount cautionary tales of its dangers and abuse. In the Christian tradition, accounts of the pathological, in this case violent, religious leader can be traced to sixteenth-century Germany during a period of developing hostilities between Roman Catholics and Lutherans. Two radical movements of the time, one led by the priest Thomas Münzer and the other by the prophet Jan Bokelson at the town of Münster, took up arms against civil authorities; both movements were crushed and their leaders executed. However, in both Roman Catholic and Lutheran retelling of these sagas, Munzer and Münster came to symbolize the dangers of charismatic leadership and of following such leaders (Williams 1962). In these cases, of course, we lack the detailed historical records necessary to determine the extent of instigation and provocation on either side, but it is clear that a small number of historical cases have been invoked to confirm the connection between charismatic leadership and violence. In the present era, Jim Jones and Charles Manson (despite the contested status of the Manson Family as a religious group) serve as comparable cultural landmarks.

The problem with selecting specific instances in which charismatic leaders may have provoked their followers to violent confrontations, of course, is the prevalence of charisma in religious and nonreligious settings alike (Weber 1968; Bird 1993). Since a high proportion of new religious movements begin with a charismatic leader and a small band of followers, and since most established religious groups often preserve a measure of charismatic authority, it is problematic to assert a direct causal relationship between charismatic leadership and violence. For example, a number of religious leaders associated with established religious groups have been regarded as extremely charismatic – Billy Graham (Southern Baptist), Oral

46

Roberts (United Methodist), Fulton Sheen (Roman Catholic), and Jimmy Swaggart (Assemblies of God). Some are respected and others reproved, but they are not immediately presumed to harbor violent tendencies. Further, the presence of charismatic leadership does not establish a causal link to specific outcomes. For example, in the cases of both the Peoples Temple and Rajneesh, it was organizational lieutenants who were pivotal in the initiation of violence, the high profile of Bhagwan and Jim Jones notwithstanding (Carter 1990; Maaga 1998). In the cases considered in this volume, there is little doubt that charismatic authority was a significant factor in the development and trajectory of the movements. However, the authors of the theoretical and case study chapters argue for a contextual, interactive rather than a decisive, determinative role for charisma in episodes of violence. Attributing organizational outcomes to the personality of a single individual, even a powerful charismatic leader, usually camouflages much more complex social dynamics.

The relationship between millennial ideology and violence is even more problematic. Again, there are a few historical cases of millennial groups that are invoked to demonstrate the violence potential of unrestrained millennialism. For example, the Fifth Monarchy Men, a British movement of the mid-1600s, came to believe that the end of the rule of Charles I signaled the imminent Second Coming of Christ. After waiting a few years, some members grew restive and provoked riots in London. Authorities responded by arresting and executing the group's leaders. However, there are good reasons to dispute a causal connection between millennialism and violence. One is that nonmillennial groups have been studied far less extensively than their millennial counterparts. Religious groups such as the Church of the Lamb of God and the Nation of Yahweh have been involved in violence but have received relatively little popular or scholarly attention. But the more important issue is that millennialism is an integral element of Western theologies and as such is expressed in various forms in many Christian traditions. Given the pervasiveness of millennialism in Christian thought, it would be difficult indeed to identify it as a cause of violence. Indeed, there is little evidence that even relatively extreme forms of millennialism yield a proclivity for violence. For example, the nineteenth-century biblical interpretation system referred to as "dispensationalism" that found an institutionalized form in early-twentieth-century fundamentalism places current humanity in the dispensation of grace that will lead imminently to the personal reign of Christ or kingdom of God. Most fundamentalist groups are peaceful even while rejecting societal secularization.

Perhaps an even more compelling illustration is found in the nineteenth-century Millerite movement, which also draws on this theological tradition. When William Miller's prophecy that Christ would return in 1843 was not fulfilled and successive predictions also failed, the movement experienced a crisis. Over the next decades, the movement splintered into numerous factions with different interpretations of what had happened. Over 100 different churches were formed, each of which developed its own variation on Miller's original theme, including two major international movements, the Seventh-Day Adventists and the Jehovah's Witnesses. Today, millions of conservative Evangelical church members in the United States are dispensationalists, and prophecy books remain extremely popular at Evangelical bookstores. What is striking about these large, diverse millennial movements is the lack of violence associated with them. Only after a 150 years did violence find its way to an Adventist group, the Branch Davidians.[3] Given the history and the excesses of various Adventist groups, it is difficult to base an explanation of the Davidians' last days on its apocalyptic beliefs.[4]

Violence Provocation

If new religions are dangerously unstable and violence prone due to some combination of maniacal leaders, fanatical followers, and mercurial organization, then they are presumptively the likely source of violence provocation. According to this reasoning, two probable scenarios are that such movements will engage in acts of collective implosion (suicide) or explosion (homicide). There are a small number of violent episodes throughout American history that appear to fit one of these types, but they actually do not match either scenario very closely. For example, during the nineteenth century there were well-documented incidents of violence such as the Mountain Meadows massacre of settlers by the Mormons and the battle between federal troops and the spirit dancers at Wounded Knee. A more recent and less publicized case involves Ervil LeBaron's Church of the Lamb of God. Following the establishment of his church in 1970, LeBaron unilaterally announced his leadership over all of the many polygamy-practicing groups that had emerged from the Church of Jesus Christ of Latter-Day

---

[3] The Branch Davidian movement had existed in peace for sixty years in Texas, and there are several other branches of the movement that have never been associated with violence.

[4] It is the case, of course, that a characterization of the Branch Davidian belief did play a part in the Bureau of Alcohal, Tobacco, and Firearms decision to make their dramatic entry at Mt. Carmel.

Saints throughout the twentieth century. When the other groups ignored his self-proclaimed leadership, several of his lieutenants initiated a campaign of coercive consolidation. It began with the murder in 1972 of his own brother, Joel LeBaron, who had founded the Church of the First Born of the Fullness of Times. Rulon Allred, leader of the Apostolic United Brethren, was murdered in 1977. Additional members of both groups were killed, as were people who resigned their membership in the Church of the Lamb of God. Deaths of other polygamy group members and former members of Ervil LeBaron's church continued throughout the late 1980s; (Bradlee and Van Atta 1981; LeBaron 1981). Another example is the former Nation of Islam under the leadership of Eiljah Muhammad (as distinguished from the reorganized Nation of Islam now led by Louis Farrakhan), which also carried out a variety of murders against members of revival Muslim organizations. Finally, there is the nameless drug-smuggling group in Matamoros, Mexico, that employed elements of Palo Mayumbe ritual as organizational devices to orchestrate the murders of a number of its competitors. In the former cases, however, the incidents were part of long-running battles between minority groups and the dominant social order, while the latter incidents were internecine warfare, with carefully planned strikes against rival groups. None of these episodes involved unstable groups imploding or exploding into violence. Even in the recent case of the Movement for the Restoration of the Ten Commandments in Uganda, it is not clear how unstable the movement actually was. It appears that internal conflict emerged in the movement following failed prophecy, and movement leaders chose mass murder of disciples, and perhaps their own deaths as well, rather than abdicate power. If this interpretation is correct, the Movement for the Restoration does not closely resemble either the cases discussed in this volume or the pathological cult model. The Manson Family may be one of the best cases of a dangerously unstable movement that ultimately undertook a violent campaign, and that may be why it continues to serve as a cultural landmark decades after its demise. To offer these distinctions between different types of violence is not to offer legitimation for any of them, of course, but rather to argue for distinctions that are analytically productive.

The image of provocatively violent cults is sustained not only by the invocation of dubious parallels with present and past groups but also by a steady flow of rumors and distorted reports. For example, in recent years there has been a succession of new items in which religious groups were reported to be planning mass suicide. These groups included the Chen Tao, a Taiwanese millennial group located in Garland, Texas, for a time; La Luz del

Mundo, an international Pentecostal group headquartered in Mexico; the Concerned Christians based in Denver, Colorado; the Isis Holistic Center, a German New Age organization; the Stella Maris Gnostic Church, based in Cartagena, Colombia; and the Dios con Nostros, a Pentecostal church in Lima, Peru.[5] La Luz del Mundo, the Stella Maris Gnostics,[6] and Dios con Nostros were victims of fraudulent reports by ideological enemies; the others were victims of the feigned fears of anticult spokespersons.[7] In none of these cases was there any credible supporting evidence, but the initial press releases received much greater attention than the silence or retraction that followed.

Another source of such reports has been unsupported accounts provided by former members. For example, during the 1970s there were persistent reports with ominous undertones of "suicide training" in the Unification Church (Carroll and Bauer 1979) and allegations that The Way International and the International Society for Krishna Consciousness were arming themselves, presumably for provocative action. As one social scientist wrote, "Ex-members have stated that while in their respective cults, they were prepared to kill another person, to kill their parents, or to take their own lives if so ordered" (Appel 1981: 183). The largely rhetorical function of these allegations is evidenced by the fact that it in fact has not been the large, visible groups like the Unification Church and Hare Krishna, labeled violence prone, that have become most likely to initiate violence. Rather, it has been the reverse; small, obscure groups have been more likely to become embroiled in violent episodes, albeit usually not as a result of provocative actions.

While a handful of cases in which movements have initiated violent incidents can be identified, the much more likely scenario is that new

---

[5] "Taiwan UFO cult suicide watch!!" posted at *http://members.tripod.com/~tokyoboiardwalker/ UFO.html*; "Spanish police state they prevented mass suicide by Alma (Isis Holistic) Center cult," posted at *http://www.stelling.nl/simpos/isis.htm*; "UFO cult disappears in Colombia" (Reuters, July 9, 1999); "Doomsday group, leader missing/Cult watchers say mass suicide possible" (Associated Press, October 16, 1998), posted at *http:// www.showmenews.com/19998/Oct/16/News/199810161/.html*; "Rechazan Iglesias Promover Suicidios," *Reforma* (April 3, 1997).

[6] On the Stela Maris case, see Alan Murdie, "Stella Maris Cult 'Disappearance" (July 1999), posted at *http://www.xmo85.dial.pipex.com/colombia.htm*.

[7] One of the more horrendous reports of cult suicides concerned an unnamed cult led by one Ca Van Liem of Te He, Vietnam. It was widely reported that he had led a mass suicide of village followers in October 1983. In June 1984 the truth finally came out. The Vietnamese Army had killed most of the village residents, who were unhappy over changes instituted in the region by the government.

religions are the targets of violence or provocation. In most of these cases the movements have responded by seeking reduction of tension or remedial action through the judicial system. For example, a number of new religious centers have been the targets of bombing attacks: the W.K.F.L. Fountain of the World center in the San Fernando Valley of California in 1958, the Rajneesh center in Portland in 1984, the Hare Krishna temple in Philadelphia in 1984, and the Unification Church center in Paris in 1996 (Melton 1992: 361–393). In other cases, new religious groups have been the targets of provocative police actions. For example, the predawn raid by dozens of armed state troopers on the Messianic Communities at Island Pond, Vermont, during which all of the community children were taken into custody, was met by the movement initially with redress through the courts and later with a program to reduce isolation and build bridges with the local community (Bozeman and Palmer 1997; Swantko 1998; Palmer 1999). Likewise, the response by The Family to dozens of raids by police and military personnel on their homes and seizure of their children around the world has been uniformly nonviolent and has resulted in legal exoneration in almost every case. The widespread use of coercive deprogramming by anticult activists on behalf of family members with relatives during the 1970s and 1980s, sometimes with the knowledge and tacit support of law enforcement and judicial officials, has almost always been redressed through civil and criminal judicial proceedings rather than physical reprisal.[8] In the aforementioned case of Ervil LeBaron, it is notable that none of the groups LeBaron attacked or threatened responded to his acts beyond cooperating with authorities in their efforts to track him and his confederates. The current case of Falun Gong suppression in China is the most recent instance of continued nonviolent resistance despite large-scale imprisonment of members and a steadily mounting death toll.

Finally, the case of the Church Universal and Triumphant provides an illustration of a movement that worked proactively to head off confrontation rather than act provocatively. The movement migrated to Montana in the mid-1980s, and by the early 1990s a strongly apocalyptic ideology emerged on top of a previously well-developed survivalist stance, which led to the building of bomb shelters and acquisition of weapons for defense

---

[8] By far the most visible instance of a church relying on the courts to redress its grievances rather than resorting to violence is the case of the Church of Scientology, which has built a reputation as an extremely litigious organization. In light of the issues being discussed here, however, its success in court has been a major guarantee that it has developed a nonviolent program of response to the issues it continues to face.

during the anticipated possible impending cataclysm. Opposition to the movement by anticult groups, local media, environmentalists, and former members intensified following the move to Montana and the development of its more radical stance. Publicity about the acquisition of weapons expanded opposition by drawing the attention of the Justice Department and the Internal Revenue Service. Cognizant of its increasingly embattled position, the movement over the next several years undertook a number of initiatives to reduce external conflict – hiring external consultants to analyze its church organization, organizational reform that included separation of the church's prophetic and administrative roles, environmental protection projects, reintegration of children into the local public schools, and reduction in the size and isolation of the community.

New religious groups arguably distinguish themselves by constructing ideological and organizational systems that challenge existing social arrangements, and contentiousness between movement and established social order is not uncommon. In that sense, new religions intend to be "dangerous." They view the future of the existing social order and their own futures as endangered. The contrast between the way things are and the way they might be is what energizes challenging movements of all kinds. As Rodney Stark (1984) has pointed out, if a new religion does not have a bite, if it is not in tension with existing spiritual understandings, then it is unlikely to attract adherents. In a similar vein, Dean Kelley (1972) has argued, it is those groups that challenge, that do not compromise, that call their adherents to a higher cause that are likely to be more successful. However, there is a significant difference between contentiousness and rebellion, on the one hand, and violence, on the other hand. The historical record and current events suggest that new religions are much more likely to engage in fierce rhetoric than violent action. In fact, for a number of the movements that precipitated the controversy over cults, the striking pattern is not how intransigent they have remained but rather how rapidly they have adopted relatively settled, accommodative lifestyles.

Violence Predetermination

The violent cult model leads to the conclusion that cult-precipitated violence is virtually predetermined, and that in fact it will be frequent given the predisposition of cults to violence and an increase in the number of cultic groups. If violence is inevitable and unacceptable, then it follows implicitly or explicitly that more extensive social control measures are necessary to reduce the likelihood of violence. There are several reasons to be skeptical of this conclusion. As we have observed in our commentary on historical and contemporary violent episodes, there have been a limited number of episodes of collective violent events during various historical periods. However, the number of such episodes has been nominal during most periods and minimal relative to the number of groups in existence at that moment. Further, in a number of instances the groups involved have been small and obscure, and a violent act was the means through which they achieved visibility. The probability of any reasonable surveillance or control measures being effective under such circumstances is remote. More importantly, protest is more likely when conditions are experienced as repressive, so an increase in social control apparatus may well have the effect of increasing violent incidents. As the current episode involving the Falun Gong suggests, strong state sanctions may produce precisely the opposite of the results intended.

At the same time, a complete absence of any social control is unlikely to prevent violence either. In virtually every case, both movement and social order are implicated in violent episodes, if for no other reason than that movements constitute challenges to the existing social order that typically are met with resistance, and coercion is a response that occurs from one or both sides when voluntary compliance is not forthcoming. As the cases in this volume illustrate, the degree to which movement or social order fuels the shift toward violence varies, but an abdication of all social control would in all probability yield some cases in which movements would tend in a violent direction largely on the basis of internal dynamics. If both movement and social order contribute to most violent episodes, then avoiding formulaic interpretations and seeking to identify the complex dynamics that result in extreme events is the most useful approach to both understanding and averting collective violence.

Preconception and Reconception

In this chapter we have challenged four widely shared misconceptions concerning the relationship between new religions and violence – pervasiveness, proneness, provocativeness, and predetermination – that together have created a stereotypical conception of the "violent cult." Our objective in taking on these misconceptions is to create the basis for reconceptualizing the analysis of movement–societal relationships in more productive terms. We argue that definitions of newness and violence tend to load the argument in the direction of confirming assertions of pervasiveness and disregarding violence involving established religions. The violence proneness premise derives primarily from linking millennial/apocalyptic ideologies and charismatic leadership to violent episodes. But both millennialism and charisma are commonplace in a number of religious traditions, so a far more nuanced understanding of the impact of these phenomena is necessary. Images of religious movements as provocative, we argue, are attributable to the invocation of dubious parallels with present and past groups, as well as to a steady flow of rumors and distorted media reports. In fact, while there are a limited number of cases in which movements have initiated violent incidents, the more likely scenario is that new religions are the targets of violence. For the most part, the movements that precipitated the controversy over cults are more noteworthy not for how intransigent they have remained but rather for how rapidly they have adopted relatively settled, accommodative lifestyles. Finally, it is probably the case that there will be future episodes of violence involving religious movements. The likelihood seems to be, however, that such cases will involve some of the myriad small, obscure groups that dot the religious landscape. One implication is that increasing surveillance and control runs the risk of producing limited prevention dividends while possibly heightening movement–societal tension levels. But it is just as true that eschewing any claim to social control under the banner of religious liberty runs the risk that some groups will engage in destructive activity that might have been prevented. Under such conditions, it is important to abandon formulaic conceptions of violent cults in favor of pursuing a sophisticated, multidimensional understanding of movements, control agencies, and movement–societal interactions simultaneously. It is this objective that informs each of the chapters that comprise the remainder of this book.

References

Appel, Willa. *Cults in America: Programmed for Paradise*. New York: Holt, Rinehart and Winston, 1981.

Bird, Frederick. "Charisma and Leadership in New Religious Movements." In *The Handbook on Cults and Sects in America*, edited by David Bromley and Jeffrey Hadden. Greenwich: JAI Press and the Association for the Sociology of Religion, 1993: 75–92.

Bozeman, John M., and Susan J. Palmer. "The Northeast Kingdom Community Church of Island Pond, Vermont: Raising Up a People for Yahshua's Return." *Journal of Contemporary Religion* 12 (1997): 181–190.

Bradlee, Ben, Jr., and Dale Van Atta. *Prophet of Blood*. New York: G. P. Putnam's Sons, 1981.

Carroll, Jeffrey, and Bernard Bauer. "Suicide Training in the Moon Cult." *New West* (January 29, 1979): 62–63.

Carter, Lewis. *Charisma and Control at Rajneeshpuram: The Role of Shared Values in the Creation of a Community*. New York: Cambridge University Press, 1990.

Greil, Arthur, and Thomas Robbins. *Between Sacred and Secular: Research and Theory on Quasi-Religion*. Greenwich: JAI Press and the Association for the Sociology of Religion, 1994.

Hurley, Mark. *The Unholy Ghost: Anti-Catholicism in the American Experience*. Huntington, IN: Our Sunday Visitor, 1962.

Kelley, Dean M. *Why Conservative Churches Are Growing: A Study in Sociology of Religion*. New York: Harper & Bros, 1972.

LeBaron, Ross W. *The LeBaron Family*. Lubbock, TX: Author, 1981.

Maaga, Mary M. *Hearing the Voices of Jonestown*. Syracuse: Syracuse University Press, 1998.

Marshall, Paul. *Their Blood Cries Out*. Dallas: Word Publishing, 1997.

Melton, J. Gordon. *Encyclopedia of American Religions* (6th edition). Detroit: Gale Research, 1998.

Encyclopedic Handbook of the Cults in America (revised edition). New York: Garland, 1992.

Melton, J. Gordon, James R. Lewis, and Aidan A. Kelly. *New Age Encyclopedia*. Detroit: Gale Research, 1990.

Myers, Gustav. *A History of Bigotry in the United States*. New York: G. P. Putnam's Sons, 1960.

Palmer, Susan J. "Frontiers and Families: The Children of Island Pond." In *Children in New Religions*, edited by Susan J. Palmer and Charlotte E. Hardman. New Brunswick: Rutgers University Press, 1999: 153–171.

Raab, Earl. *Religious Conflict in America: Studies of the Problems Beyond Bigotry*. Garden City, NY: Doubleday Anchor, 1964.

Singer, Margaret Thaler, with Janja Lalich. 1995. *Cults in our Midst*. San Francisco: Jossey-Bass.

Stark, Rodney. "Normal Revelations: A Rational Model of 'Mystical' Experiences." In *New Developments in Theory and Research*, edited by David Bromley. Greenwich: JAI Press and the Association for the Sociology of Religion, 1991: 239–252.

"How New Religions Succeed: A Theoretical Model." In *Future of New Religious Movements*, edited by David Bromley and Phillip Hammond. Macon: Mercer University Press, 1984: 11–29.

Swantko, Jean A. *An Issue of Control: Conflict Between the Church in Island Pond and State Government*. Palenville, NY: Author, 1998.

U.S. Government. *International Report for International Religious Freedom for 1999*. Washington, D.C.: U.S. State Department, 2000.

Weber, Max. *On Charisma and Institution Building: Selected Papers*. Edited by S. N. Eisenstadt. Chicago: University of Chicago Press, 1968.

Williams, George H. *The Radical Reformation*. Philadelphia: Westminster Press, 1962.

4

SOURCES OF VOLATILITY
IN RELIGIOUS MOVEMENTS

THOMAS ROBBINS

There are several factors operating with respect to novel, noninstitutional-ized religious movements that tend to enhance volatility and the potential for violence. Some of these factors are fairly easy to enumerate (e.g., Robbins and Anthony 1995; Robbins and Palmer 1997; Dawson 1998: 128–157). However, such enumerations do not at this time allow us to *predict* which militant sects and esoteric cults will become involved in episodes of mass suicide, or mass murder, or in violent confrontations with authorities. Movements such as the Peoples Temple, the Branch Davidians, Aum Shinrikyô, Heaven's Gate, and the Order of the Solar Temple, which have become in-volved in sensational episodes of extreme violence, do tend to share certain characteristics. Unfortunately, many other movements that have heretofore been nonviolent also share many of these elements and even share some of the *combinations* of elements that have been identified in certifiably tumultuous groups.

The vast majority of unconventional and relatively noninstitutional-ized "alternative religions" or "cults" are not explosively violent. The most that can probably be said at this time is that certain ideological, organiza-tional, and tactical features of a movement such as apocalyptic worldviews, charismatic leadership, or a "totalistic" milieu (and particular variations on these features) may represent necessary but not sufficient conditions for the more spectacular kinds of violent altercations (Robbins and Anthony 1995; Dawson 1998). Other things being equal, these elements may enhance the likelihood of violence, but they certainly do not ensure such violence and may indeed be quite compatible with a definite absence of conspicuous instability.

If we look at the factors that have been identified as enhancing the likelihood of extreme violence involving religious movements, we find that they can be categorized in terms of two dimensions: social versus cultural factors and exogenous versus endogenous factors (Robbins and Anthony 1995; Dawson 1988).

"Social" factors refer largely to structural and organizational patterns such as patterns of leadership, communal structures, social control practices, and so on. "Cultural" factors pertain mainly to ideological and orientational modalities, that is, group beliefs and attitudes. Obviously the distinction between social (or structural) factors and cultural (or ideological) factors is not watertight; for example, charismatic leadership and its constitutive messianic-prophetic mystiques may entail both structure and culture. Beliefs are also entailed in social control.

There are also ambiguities with regard to the distinction and relationship between internal or "endogenous" factors pertaining to apparently intrinsic properties of movements, such as ideology, organization, and leadership, and external or "exogenous" influences arising from the environment to which movements must adapt. Environmental exigencies can shape the emergence and transformation of internal properties of religious movements. Thus some scholars have stressed the dynamic factor of external *opposition and persecution*, which accentuates the paranoid potential of movements' millennial and apocalyptic visions and thereby encourages extreme behavior, for which the sinister cults are held exclusively responsible by society (Richardson 1981; Lewis 1994; Kaplan 1997; Hall and Schuyler 1998; Wright 1999). Such writers have criticized the notion that certain ideological or organizational properties of esoteric movements are "causes" of extreme violence involving alternative religions (Richardson and Kilbourne 1983; Melton 1985; Tabor and Gallagher 1995; Hall and Schuyler 1998). This "relational" perspective on violence and deviant religious movements has deepened the study of "cult violence," but it has sometimes been taken to extremes, and it can operate as an apologetic, as the present writer has noted in a mild critique (Robbins 1997). Some groups appear to erupt in extreme violence in a context characterized by rather limited or even largely nonexistent opposition and provocation (Mayer 1999; Balch and Taylor this volume).

Perhaps the most significant article in the genre that highlights the exogenous, relational dimension of religious movement violence is the recent study "Apostasy, Apocalypse, and Religious Violence" by Hall and Schuyler (1998), which presents a tentative model of "apocalyptic religious conflict" and applies it to episodes of collective violence associated with the Peoples Temple at Jonestown, the Branch Davidians at Waco, and the 1994 Solar Temple incidents in Quebec and Switzerland. (For a more complex and advanced model see Hall this volume; Hall, Schuyler, and Trinh 2000.) Hall and Schuyler propose that extreme collective religious violence does not emerge from an intrinsic property of esoteric groups themselves. They locate "the genesis of such violence in social conflicts *between* utopian religious movements on the one hand, and on the other, ideological proponents of an established social order, who seek to control 'cults' through loosely institutionalized, emergent oppositional alliances" (Hall and Schuyler 1998: 142). The oppositional coalition is generally composed of recriminating *apostates*, sensationalist *media*, and modern *governments* posing as the champions of cultural legitimacy against dangerous deviance.

The consequence of prolonged apocalyptic religious conflict may ultimately be to *unravel or destabilize the religious sect*. The group's capacity to continue functioning in its own terms is undercut, and extreme violence arises as "both a vehicle of aggression against detractors and affirmation of a principle of self-determination within the apocalyptic community" (Hall and Schuyler 1998: 148). Thus, "extreme religious violence is the result of the interaction between a complex of factors typically set in motion through apostasy and anti-subversion campaigns" (1983: 142).

Hall and Schuyler acknowledge that *certain kinds of movements may be particularly prone to violence*: movements with distinctly apocalyptic worldviews, charismatic leadership, tight internal social control, and intense communal solidarity, with strong social boundaries isolating the group from the broader society. The endogenous violent potential of such groups, however, is actualized only under certain interactional conditions. The authors acknowledge that the spectacular example of mass suicide among Heaven's Gate devotees in April 1997 may pose a problem for their model since the violence at the Heaven's Gate settlement "was not directed outward and seems to have lacked any significant apocalyptic basis in external conflict" (Hall and Schuyler 1998: 144).

The authors also concede that the external pressures on the Solar Temple were considerably less than the pressures on the Peoples Temple or the Branch Davidians, that is, there was no armed incursion of government agents, as at Waco, or even a visit by a high official with an entourage, as at Jonestown. Nevertheless, the capacity of critics, antimovement activists, and officials to destabilize a movement and thus "set the stage for an apocalyptic denouement [does] not necessarily depend on direct spatial confrontations" (1998: 167). The Solar Temple did experience agitation by apostates and anticult activists, negative media attention, and a governmental investigation prior to the violence. The authors believe that such opposition may have pushed the Templar leaders to accelerate the "transit" of devotees to a higher plane of existence beyond Earth that the Templars had originally anticipated (see also Hall and Schuyler 1997).

It might be noted, however, that while the Solar Temple did experience *some* degree of apocalyptic religious conflict prior to its violent events, it faced much *less* opposition, apostate activism, media sensationalism, and governmental hostility than has been experienced by controversial movements such as Scientology, the Unification Church, or The Children of God. Stigmatized by anticult crusaders as classical "destructive cults," these latter groups have *not* been embroiled in extreme violence. By implication there would seem to have been some endogenous element pertaining to the worldview, organization, or leadership of the Temple that rendered it more susceptible to a violent response to social conflict compared to other (even more) controversial movements.

Obviously, endogenous and exogenous factors will generally interact to produce egregious violent outcomes. Social and cultural factors will interact to produce the endogenous potential for violence. Its flaws notwithstanding, Hall and Schuyler's original model of apocalyptic religious conflict is on the cutting edge because it has implications for understanding the way in which internal modalities such as an apocalyptic worldview interact with external conflicts to produce an explosive outcome. The Hall–Schuyler model is presently evolving and becoming more complex (Hall this volume; Hall et al. 2000).

In this chapter, we will be concerned primarily with two broad classes of internal variables: factors pertaining to "apocalyptic worldviews" and factors related to "totalistic organization" (including extremely charismatic leadership). These factors appear to represent predisposing endogenous conditions that enhance volatility and the likelihood of violence, although the latter may be strongly affected by exogenous influences. We will, however, attempt to refine these variables and thus subdivide broad notions such as "apocalypticism" and "totalism" into more specific subconditions. Are some varieties of apocalyptic or millennialist orientations particularly potent in terms of a group's susceptibility to violence? We will also flag some more complex and interactive formulations that have implications for advancing scholarly analysis beyond the mere specification of individual predisposing conditions related to violence.

Apocalypticism

Hall and Schuyler (1998) identify "apocalyptic expectations" or visions of an imminent total transformation of the world, as a key factor characterizing spiritual movements involved in extreme violence. Such visions provide a basis for extrapolating environmental tension in a paranoid direction. "In each of the instances of mass religious violence involving NRMs [new religious movements]," notes Lorne Dawson, "apocalyptic beliefs – beliefs about the ultimate end of human history – have played a crucial role in structuring and motivating the acts of the people who died either by their own hands or at the hands of others" (Dawson 1998: 132).[1]

Apocalyptic worldviews have definitely characterized the recent cults that have become embroiled in spectacular mass violence such as the Peoples Temple (Hall 1987; Chidester 1988; Jones 1989; Lifton 1999), the Branch Davidians (Boyer 1993; Anthony and Robbins 1997; Gallagher 2000), the Order of the Solar Temple (Hall and Schuyler 1997, 1998), Aum Shinrikyô (Mullins 1997; Watanabe 1998; Reader 2000), and Heaven's Gate (Balch and Taylor this volume). Conspicuously violent sects in history have also tended to manifest apocalyptic expectations of an approaching final End, as instanced by the self-immolating Russian Old Believers in the seventeenth and eighteenth centuries (Crummey 1970; Robbins 1986, 2000), the early Mormons (Underwood 2000), the extremist Circumcellion Fringe of the Donatist "Church of Martyrs" in North Africa in late antiquity (Knox 1950), and the radical Anabaptists, who seized Münster and briefly established "New Jerusalem" and a reign of terror in seventeenth-century Germany (Cohn 1961; Boyer 1993).

Why should there be an association between apocalypticism and extreme violence? If the "last days" are unfolding and the putatively corrupt society is doomed, its rules and conventions may not appear compelling. Indeed,

---

[1] We will not deal here with formal definitions of apocalypticism, millennialism, millenarianism, etc. (see Robbins and Palmer 1997). We note that some writers have distinguished between "millenarianism" (or "millennialism"), which focuses on the utopiate end state or goal of apocalyptic transformation, and "apocalypticism," which focuses on the catastrophic transformative *process*. Apocalypticism has been deemed more volatile (Bromley 1997; Lee 1997; Robbins and Palmer 1997).

millennialists often anticipate a future order that *reverses* the present order such that "the last shall be first" and present elites will be unpleasantly disposed of (Lebra 1972). Apocalyptic visions thus "have definite antinomian implications" (Robbins and Anthony 1995: 239), which are likely to be actualized to the degree that the millennial community demands actual operational *autonomy* from the discredited and dying sociopolity. Apocalyptic sectarians, moreover, sometimes view themselves as a spiritual vanguard of "saints" or the "elect," whose destiny to survive the transitional turmoil may entail a legitimation of ruthless conduct toward the less favored worldlings, whose otherness to spiritual grace inhibits consideration for them at least in endtimes, when apocalyptic push comes to shove (Knox 1950; Robbins and Anthony 1995). Apocalyptic visions may thus *isolate* devotees from the norms and values of the broader society.

Groups with apocalyptic expectations are likely to anticipate that the imminent last days will be suffused with violence and persecution, which will be particularly directed against the saints. The latter must survive to inherit the world or at least to keep the light of Truth shining. They must therefore see to the defense of their sacred enclave. They must stockpile weapons and train themselves in their use. To the degree that real or imagined threats to the group are perceived as associated with an endtimes scenario, "enemies" will be demonized and perceived as representing Satan, the Antichrist, or some other eschatological dark horse. His minions may be violently resisted.

A case in point entails the Branch Davidian tragedy at Waco. The Bureau of Alcohol, Tobacco, and Firearms (BATF) conducted a militarized raid on the Davidian compound with over eighty armed agents, helicopters, and so on. "From the perspective of the Branch Davidians, then, surely the Anti-Christ and his minions were at the door, dressed in the tactical combat gear of the BATF and the FBI. The prophecies of the apocalypse were coming true!" (Dawson 1998: 136). Thus apocalyptic fervor and blundering provocation by officials may interact to precipitate a violent holocaust in a manner delineated by Hall and Schuyler's (1998) relational model. Nevertheless, as Hall and Schuyler acknowledge and as Robbins (1997) emphasizes, in a number of cases the provocation or confrontational stimulus presented by authorities or other enemies may sometimes be substantially milder than the militarized BATF raid at Waco. The provocation may even appear to be practically nonexistent, as in the case of the Heaven's Gate suicides and largely created (or wildy extrapolated) through the prophetic imagination of leaders such as Asahara Shôkô of the Aum

Shinrikyô movement or Joseph Di Mambro of the Solar Temple (Mayer 1999; Reader 2000).

Apocalypticism-millennialism is a key cultural factor related to episodes of extreme cult violence. There are presently many (and possibly a growing number of) apocalyptic-millennialist groups in the United States. However, very few of them have become involved in extreme violence, and many – perhaps most – would not do so even in the face of strident activist opposition, unfair persecution, or even an armed raid by officials. However, subvarieties of apocalyptic worldviews may enhance a group's susceptibility to both controversy and persecution and to a violent response to such vicissitudes.

Catherine Wessinger (1999, 2000) has recently formulated the idea of "catastrophic millennialism." Catastrophic millennialists see evil "as being rampant, and things are believed to be getting worse all the time. Therefore to eliminate evil and achieve the earthly salvation, the world as we know it has to be destroyed and created anew by God (or a superhuman power)... the catastrophic destruction is *imminent*" (Wessinger 1997: 49). Catastrophic millennialism is generally associated with a "pessimistic evaluation of human nature and society." The latter must be destroyed because humanity cannot transform it and create utopia or the millennium by itself. Catastrophic millennialism is also rooted "in the pervasive human tendency to think in dualistic categories.... This dualistic thinking, the 'us' versus 'them' mentality, which leads to the belief in the necessity of battling evil located in the demonized 'other,' is the conceptual basis of warfare" (Wessinger 1997: 50). Citing Tabor and Gallagher (1995), Wessinger notes that "The 1993 confrontation between the Branch Davidians and Federal law enforcement agents involved dualistic thinking on both sides – the Branch Davidians regarded their attackers as agents of satanic 'Babylon,' and the BATF and FBI agents regarded David Koresh as a demonic criminal and con man" (Wessinger 1997: 50; see also Anthony and Robbins 1995, 1997).

Because of its association with dualistic thinking, and more particularly because of the expectation of looming chaos and violence, catastrophic millennialism tends to render movements particularly volatile and paranoid. Various movements that ultimately became involved in extreme violence such as Aum Shinrikyô (Mullins 1997; Lifton 1999; Reader 2000), early Utah Mormonism (Underwood 2000), the lethally violent fringe of the antiabortion "rescue" movement (Kaplan 1995), a violent subgroup of the ecology movement "Earth First" (Lee 1997), the Russian Old Believers (Robbins 1986, 2000), and the Peoples Temple community at Jonestown

(Hall 1987; Maaga 1998) tended, prior to their violence, *to evolve their worldview in the direction of a more catastrophic version of millennialism*. In these movements (and in other movements such as the Manson Family), violent episodes appeared to be preceded by a shift of attitudes on the part of the leaders and followers toward a more catastrophic millennial orientation often entailing a more intense preoccupation with violent apocalyptic visions and a greater expectation of violence and chaos.

On the other hand, external hostility and persecution tend to intensify a group's preoccupation with catastrophic apocalyptic visions. Catastrophic millennial visions appear especially meaningful to people who are experiencing persecution (Underwood 2000; Wessinger 2000). When a marginal group makes an accommodation to its society and receives an accommodation permitting it to develop stable institutions, catastrophic apocalyptic beliefs may still persist, but the intensity of apocalyptic rhetoric and the urgency of catastrophic imagery will likely diminish (Robbins 1986, 1999; Underwood 2000; Wessinger 2000). A symbiotic relationship thus appears to exist between catastrophic millennialism and persecution. The dualistic worldview of millennialists is likely to be reinforced and appears to be validated by experiences of hostility and persecution (Underwood 2000, Wessinger 2000). If left more or less to themselves, millenarian movements such as early Mormonism often evolve stable institutions and deemphasize catastrophic apocalypticism. However, this process may engender volatile schismatic offshoots that accentuate the wild apocalyptic prophecy (Robbins and Palmer 1997).

It must also be noted that the apparently symbiotic relationship between catastrophic millennialism and persecution may conceal a chicken–egg conundrum. Grim apocalyptic expectations may sometimes precede and help produce persecution, especially when the former become associated with radical separatism, antinomianism, and a movement's demand for absolute social and legal *autonomy* vis-à-vis the doomed society. In modern complex and interdependent societies in which the state has a broad regulatory agenda, the suspension of normal rules on behalf of a messianic group will be resisted. The example of Jim Jones and the Peoples Temple is instructive here. Jones and his devotees fled California for the Guyana jungle partly to maximize utopian autonomy, only to find that they could neither maintain total autonomy nor cope effectively with tropical agricultural and health problems. Growing anxiety and despair coupled with an escalating conflict with antimovement activists, as well as the personal deterioration of the prophet, set the stage for a gigantic tragedy of mass suicide and homicide, which was precipitated by a dramatic inspection by a suspicious U.S. congressman (Johnson 1979; Hall 1987; Maaga 1998).

Catastrophic millennialism may appear to some observers as simply *millennialism or apocalypticism per se*, or as a more intense level or a greater degree of millennialism. Alternatively, a categorical variable may be implicated, such as O'Leary's distinction between "tragic" (catastrophic, deterministic) and "comic" (noncatastrophic, indeterminate) modes of apocalypticism (O'Leary 1994). Wessinger (1997) contrasts catastrophic millennialism with "progressive millennialism," which envisions a more gradual, sedate millennial transformation and entails the belief that humans can themselves construct utopia or the millennial kingdom by working in harmony with the divine plan, cosmic modalities, or history (Wessinger 2000; see also Lamy 1997: 217–252). Originally applying this idea to Annie Besant and the early Theosophists, Wessinger initially (1997) inferred that optimistic progressive millennialists are less likely than catastrophists to become violent. Nevertheless, her most recent conception (2000), with its emphasis on a progressive view of history and the role of human agency in world transformation, has led several writers to view violent and dualistic "secular" millennialisms such as Marxism–Leninism (Ellwood 2000), Maoism (Loewe 2000), and the ideology of the Khmer Rouge (Salter 2000) as progressive millennialism. However, such "revolutionary" visions of total and violent political transformation might alternatively be deemed catastrophic even in the context of a progressive view of history. Wessinger's distinction may ultimately be *multivariate* and entail subcomponents that do not neatly align along two poles; for example, violent, catastrophic visions may sometimes be compatible with a premise of human agency, as in Marxism–Leninism and Maoism. In any case, dualistic thinking, particularly "exemplary dualism," in which contemporary sociohistorical entities such as communism, New Age occultism, or the Jewish people are transmogrified into polarized eschatological categories, has often been viewed as linked to extremism, violence, and sinister scapegoating and has been identified in the meaning systems of various notorious cults (Anthony and Robbins 1978, 1995, 1997; Jones 1989; Robbins and Anthony 1995; Dawson 1998: 138–139).

Wessinger's catastrophic millennialism can be viewed as a generalized version of the Protestant prophetic category of fundamentalist "premillennialism," which refers to the idea that the Second Coming of Christ must precede the Millennium because humankind is too sinful to bring in the millennial kingdom by itself. Christ must first return to defeat the

Antichrist at Armageddon. Wessinger's progressive millennialism evokes evangelical "postmillennialism," which envisions a gradual christianization of culture until the world more or less segues into the Millennium. Humanity, or rather the church, brings in the Millennium. Bromley (1997), Robbins and Palmer (1997), and others have viewed premillennialism as more volatile than postmillennialism because of the former's expectations of chaos, violence, and catastrophe in the "Great Tribulation" or reign of the Antichrist prior to Christ's return. Yet most premillennialists "commonly combine intense expectation of the End with quietism" (Gorenberg 1999: 21).

Contemporary premillennialists are divided over whether the "saints" will have to endure the harsh Tribulation (post-tribulationism) or whether they will be "raptured" up to join Jesus before the tribulationist oppression commences (pretribulationism). Most fundamentalist churches are pretribulationist and affirm the "rapture" such that the faithful *will not have to endure the rule of the Antichrist*. This belief may operate as a safety valve, reducing volatility by inhibiting expectations of lethal endtimes persecution and thereby downgrading actual opposition to a sub-eschatological level. Pretribulationists generally perceive endtimes events as *imminent but not as occurring right now*. Such a view inhibits both dramatic disconfirmation of prophecy and "eschatological paranoia" in which the troubles of the group are presumed to be literally tribulationist or otherwise deeply eschatological (O'Leary 1994; Rosenfeld 1995; Barkun 1997; Robbins and Palmer 1997). Eschatological paranoia overtook the most extreme and suicidal of the fiercely persecuted Russian Old Believers, who came to believe that *the tsar was the Antichrist* (Robbins 2000). Under military assault, the Branch Davidians may have become eschatologically paranoid and concluded that their immediate demise at the hands of the "Babylonians" was inescapable qua "the slaughter of the Lamb" in the Last Days (Robbins 2000).

Apparent *disconfirmation of prophecy* has often been viewed as destabilizing for a millennial movement (Stone [Jacqueline] 2000). Continual disconfirmations of prophecy may have destabilized the Heaven's Gate group (Gorenberg 1999). But apparent *confirmation* of dark visions may also be unsettling by way of eschatological paranoia. David Koresh and his followers at Waco may have perceived the BATF raid and/or the FBI assault as a confirmation of their "midtribulationist" expectation that they would be slaughtered during the rule of the Antichrist. Koresh may also have felt threatened by a possible disconfirmation of prophecy under humiliating and *trivializing* circumstances – the messiah surrenders and retires to prison

(Anthony and Robbins 1995, 1997). This is hard for a messianic leader – the "Lamb" – to accept. By definition, the Apocalypse does not peter out!

Apocalyptic movements that *demonize the state* may be particularly volatile. Jurgensmeyer (1997) has compared Aum Shinrikyô to groups such as the militant Islamics who blew up the World Trade Center in New York City. Such movements denounce the godless, secular state and detest its worldly, compromising elites. They strike at conspicuous symbols of state power and secular modernity.

Finally, there is the issue of millenarians' perception of their own role in the final transformation. Believers may be more likely to act violently to destroy the corrupt Babylon if they assume that *they can influence eschatological and/or historical events* (Rapoport 1988; Rosenfeld 1995). But this is a tricky issue. A premise of efficaciousness may enhance the likelihood of "revolutionary" violence directed outward, while the self-perception of a group's helplessness on earth can motivate a suicidal "exiting" on the model of the Solar Temple or Heaven's Gate, whose devotees saw their destiny as leaving a doomed world (Mayer 1999). Yet the Old Believers (and possibly the Branch Davidians) thought that their incendiary suicides could be magically effective in hastening the final End (Robbins 1999). Aum Shinrikyô and, earlier, the Manson Family thought that their outward homicidal violence might spark a larger apocalyptic social war (Lifton 1999). We might also consider contemporary Christian Reconstructionists, neo-postmillennialists who anticipate that Christians can actually accede to power – perhaps imminently – and bring in the millennial Kingdom (Shupe 1997). Will this orientation, which encourages confident political activism and undercuts fatalist armageddonism, encourage or inhibit violence?

Totalism, Encapsulation, and "Mind Control"

Shortly after the Heaven's Gate collective suicides, *New York Times* columnist Frank Rich (1997) quoted a well-known "cult expert" to the effect that "The whole debate over the beliefs and theologies of Heaven's Gate or any other suspected cult group is a red herring. What makes a cult a cult is not its religion ... but the practice of mind control techniques, usually by a charismatic leader, that robs members of their 'independence of thought."

On its face, this is at least a partly flawed statement. Just as there are many more groups with apocalyptic or catastrophic millennial beliefs than there are violent or highly volatile groups, the same can be said for groups manifesting mind control features such as authoritarian, charismatic leadership, strong internal pressures for conformity, communal totalism, and experiential rituals alleged to enhance suggestibility. Groups with such elements are not uncommon, yet few such groups are violent. The present writer has been a critic of brainwashing and mind control concepts (Anthony and Robbins 1992); nevertheless, there is a kernel of truth to activists' rhetoric about mind control. There are, as Anderson (1985) notes, an array of "deceptive" and "coercive" practices within various movements that have the effect of enhancing the power of the leadership over the followers such that aggressive or unbalanced prophets will encounter less internal resistance in instigating violence. Groups with significant elements of deceptive and coercive patterns may bear watching because they have a *potential* for destructiveness related to the absence of accountability and institutional restraint on the leadership, although this potential may never be actualized (Anderson 1985).

Instead of employing the sensational rhetoric of mind control and brainwashing, there may be greater heuristic value in referring to "total institutions" that are set off from the rest of society by stringent physical and/or psychological boundaries, and that isolate and *encapsulate* their members through various institutional and social psychological mechanisms that comprehensively regulate members' lives and insulate them from the normative expectations of conventional society (Goffman 1961; Lebra 1972; Dawson 1998). Total institutions or communal "totalism" and radical patterns of social organization are often associated with millennialist and world-transforming ideologies (Kanter 1968, 1972a,b; Bar Kun 1972). Indeed, the latter have sometimes been viewed primarily as instrumental vehicles for social mobilization and the formation of new radical totalist communities (Kanter 1972a).

It is not always clear whether totalism refers to a structural or cultural phenomenon. Robert Lifton's (1961) well-known concept of "ideological totalism" (including "religious totalism") appears to combine organizational components of institutional totalism such as milieu control with cultural and rhetorical elements of absolutist and totalist worldviews (Anthony and Robbins 1997). At least one orientational element of ideological totalism, the "dispensing of existence" (Lifton 1961: 435–437), may have clear implications for violence. Although it is rarely interpreted literally by sectarians, this idea embodies the view that the rights and claims of persons outside of the religio-ideological vanguard need not be respected in trying circumstances (Robbins and Anthony 1995). Asahara's extrapolation of *poa* as an enlightened being's proper but lethal compassion for someone who, if left alive, would become enmeshed in bad karma through evil actions (i.e., actions threatening to Aum Shinrikyô) may be viewed as an extrapolation of Lifton's notion (Watanabe 1998; Lifton 1999).[2] Knox (1950) discusses sectarian extrapolations of the idea that "dominion" presupposes grace, such that legitimate rights to rule, own, procreate, or even live pertain exclusively to the elect.

Totalistic social movements generally entail various patterns and mechanisms of resocialization and social encapsulation that operate to encourage participants to identify with the group and its leader and to monitor their behavior in terms of group norms rather than conventional expectations (Kanter 1968, 1972a,b; Lebra 1972; Dawson 1998: 148–155). As members' extragroup bonds and connections become attenuated, there is a "reduction of normative dissonance" (Mills 1982) within many movements that "sets the stage for more extreme, perhaps even violent behavior" (Dawson 1998: 153). The intensification of members' commitment may lead to an erosion of prior inhibitions against extreme behavior, at least if it is enacted at the behest of group leaders and/or directed against enemies. Thus, "as the commitment of members increases, along with their investment of time and money, their sense of responsibility is increasingly defined by the overall religious authority of the group, rather than by any values which they may have previously entertained" (Pye 1996: 265).

Totalism, like apocalypticism, may conceivably vary in *degree*. A communal movement might be deemed more totalist than a close-knit noncommunal sect. Mechanisms of control and encapsulation delineated by Kanter (1972a) and others might be counted. A combination of structural or institutional totalism and Lifton's absolutist ideological totalism may enhance the potency of either factor. Communal movements with the immediacy of a resident messianic leader (see later) may be more volatile than multicommunal movements with a distant or bureaucratic leadership (Galanter 1999).

All of the factors discussed up to this point do not indicate that totalistic organizations (or even extreme totalistic millennialist movements) are violent – most are not. Nevertheless, in such organizations, inhibitions against extreme behavior directed by the leadership may be lowered,

---

[2] According to Lifton (1999), the most dangerous cults combine a conception of altruistic killing-as-healing with other patterns including catastrophic apocalypticism, an obsession with weaponry, and a "totalized guruism" in which the leader is practically deified and followers aspire to become his "clones." Lifton sees the leaders of certain groups such as Aum and the Manson Family as inclined to "force the end" in the sense of employing symbolic violence to precipitate an anticipated apocalyptic scenario.

especially as the leader may directly or indirectly *purge* the group of re-
calcitrant, inner-directed, or dissident associates (Robbins and Anthony
1995). Some mechanisms of commitment building may have more intrinsic connections to crime and violence. In general, the millenarian totalist
movement has been said to differ from conventional and "official" total institutions such as mental hospitals in that "it tries to change the behavior of
individuals *against* the normative expectations of the larger society" (Lebra
1972: 211–212; emphasis in the original). Certain modes of commitment
building may even entail inducing members to perform *irreversible* acts that
may include crimes as well as relinquishment of wealth and kinship ties,
which constitute a decisive abandonment by the devotee of the received social order and which more or less "burn the bridges" of the convert (Kanter
1968, 1972a; Lebra 1972). Criminal, deviant, and violent behavior may
also be encouraged because it is *risky*. Shared risk is a bonding experience,
and by encouraging risky and deviant behavior, a movement leader may
raise the costs of commitment and thus render the latter more rewarding
for those who persevere (Baumgarten 1999).

Since many or most totalist millennialist movements are not violent, we
need to consider what conditions enhance the volatility of apocalyptic totalism. Marc Galanter's complex social systems model of totalist "charismatic
groups" may be significant here (Galanter 1999: 92–109; see also Robbins
and Anthony 1995: 249–251; Dawson 1998: 148–153). The basic "transformative" systemic function of a cult entails attracting and socializing new
recruits. An internal surveillance or "monitoring" function regulates and co-
ordinates system components. The "feedback" function informs the system
about the effectiveness of the performance of its transformative function as
well as its adaptive relation to its environment. This includes *negative* feedback, which is essential to the system's self-regulation in the long run but
may threaten the system in the short run by demoralizing participants and
even challenging beliefs. Finally, a "boundary control" function protects the
system from external threats. Leaders are continually tempted to suppress
negative feedback, although such suppression may ultimately impair the
system. One can imagine various exigencies, such as enhanced intragroup
conflict, conflict with outsiders, apparent disconfirmation of prophecy, or
a leader's failing charisma, that could lead to efforts to curtail negative
feedback. According to Galanter, both inhibition of negative feedback
and escalation of boundary tension (the proximate cause of most extreme
violence) may often reflect a deemphasis and/or lack of efficacy in *recruitment*

such that a communal system turns in upon itself and shifts its energy from the central transformative function to internal monitoring. Negative feedback will then tend to be suppressed, and penetration of system boundaries will be less tolerated. To put this differently, proselytization or interpersonal outreach must also involve *cognitive* outreach to persons whose ideas may not initially be identical with the group's. Attenuation of outreach will isolate the group more tightly in its "separate reality," which will be increasingly threatened by discrepant constructions of reality and thus by penetration of boundaries. Heightened tension at the boundary enhances the likelihood of conflict and violence.

Galanter applies his model to the Jonestown tragedy. Relocation of the movement from California to tropical Guyana implied a reduced emphasis on recruitment and a greater demand for group autonomy and insulation. Demands for commitment to Jim Jones's increasingly extreme beliefs intensified, as did concern with loyalty in response to traumatic key defections. As conflict escalated, some apostates crusaded against the group and found allies such as Congressman Leo Ryan. Critics were demonized, and apocalyptic doom was increasingly emphasized by the leadership. Ryan's unwelcome visit appeared to destroy the prospect of permanently guarding the cult's boundary and suppressing negative feedback. Therefore, "Jones chose to preserve ... [the movement's] identity in spirit if not in living membership" (Galanter 1999: 119). In the second edition of his book, Galanter applies his model to the Branch Davidians, Aum Shinrikyô, and Heaven's Gate (1999: 179–184).

Galanter (1999: 179–184) pinpoints four conditions that appear to be implicated in outbreaks of extreme cultic violence: (1) *isolation* of the group, which becomes encapsulated in its own idiosyncratic reality; (2) *grandiosity and paranoia* characterizing the leader's self-concept (which isolates him); (3) *absolute dominion* of the leadership over regimented devotees (who become isolated from extrinsic influences); and (4) *governmental mismanagement* of boundary conflict. The last may entail the hasty and blundering use of force by federal agents at Waco or the belated response of the Japanese police to the escalating criminality and violence of Aum Shinrikyô (yet it must be noted that there was no governmental role in the Heaven's Gate event). Galanter notes that administrative complexity may inhibit violence by providing a layer of "middle management" to mediate between the rank and file and a somewhat distant leader such as Rev. Sun Myung Moon (Galanter 1999: 117).

Dawson (1998: 149–150) also briefly applies Galanter's model to various notoriously violent cults. *The suppression of negative feedback is deemed crucial.* Encapsulated devotees of totalist groups such as Aum Shinrikyô, the Solar Temple, or the Branch Davidians lacked access to the reactions of outsiders and could not easily gauge the degree to which group behavior was becoming bizarre and maladaptive. Followers, feeling threatened, suppressed their doubts and weaknesses. The leader and his loyalist associates then became paranoid over possible penetration of the symbolic boundaries that guarded a jeopardized messianic construction of reality, which now had to be sustained at all costs. Rigid totalism, like catastrophic apocalypticism, tends to isolate devotees from conventional frameworks for interpreting reality.

Although Dawson (this volume) will treat charismatic leadership at length, we shall briefly look at this factor as a key element of totalist organization. Ideological-institutional totalism (and mind control) are often seen as going hand in hand with charismatic leadership (Rich 1997; Galanter 1999). It is often in behalf of protecting and absolutizing the authority of an inspirational leader with a grandiose self-concept that the institutional controls constitutive of an authoritarian totalist milieu are elaborated. Messianic-charismatic mystiques legitimate totalistic organization. Charismatic authority has also been cited as a general corollary of apocalyptic worldviews since "prophecies presuppose prophets" (Anthony and Robbins 1995: 245; see also Dawson 1998: 132), and prophets need expectations of transformation and turmoil to legitimate the abandonment of received authority (Wallis and Bruce 1986). Finally, apocalyptic movements have been said to be particularly volatile when encumbered by "'messianic' leaders who identify the millennial destiny of humankind with their own personal vicissitudes and demonize any opposition to their aspirations" (Robbins and Anthony 1995: 144). Thus charismatic totalism, apocalypticism, and volatility-violence may be interrelated, even though there are many totalist movements possessing apocalyptic-millennialist worldviews and charismatic-messianic leaders that are not notably violent.

Ideas about the linkage of violence to totalist millennial movements with grandiose charismatic leadership have now perhaps become a bit clichéd. The volatile Montana Freemen, who were besieged by the Federal Bureau of Investigation (FBI) in 1996, lacked a charismatic leader (Rosenfeld 1997), and the fragmentation of authority in a group may sometimes enhance the likelihood of violence (J. Rosenfeld personal communication). Nevertheless, charismatic leadership is often linked to group volatility because of its intrinsic *precariousness* (Wallis and Bruce 1986). Precariousness inheres in the absence of both institutionalized *restraints* to keep the leader in bounds and institutionalized *supports* to sustain the leader and stabilize his regime (Wallis and Bruce 1986; Robbins and Anthony 1995).

Charismatic leaders are freer than bureaucratic functionaries to act on impulse. The leader's authority is based on the (potentially ephemeral) subjective perception of the followers that the leader has a special "gift of grace." In the absence of immediate restraints and long-term supports, the leader often has both the capacity and the motivation to try to "simplify" the environment within the group by eliminating sources of dissension and normative diversity, including potential alternative leaders (Robbins and Anthony 1995). By enhancing the totalist quality of the movement's milieu, the leader not only bolsters his authority but also mitigates the cross-pressures that operate to inhibit devotees from accepting extreme demands made upon them by a wild leader (Mills 1982). A charismatic leader may also enhance volatility by "crisis mongering" in order to enhance his perceived indispensability (Bird 1993).

From a psychodynamic perspective (Oakes 1998), charismatic leaders may incline toward violence because, as narcissists, they perceive their followers as *extensions of themselves*, which may make them more willing to sacrifice their followers in a climactic confrontation or suicidal drama. Yet the orientation of the devotees to a charismatic leader may also have an element of narcissism (Anthony and Robbins 1995; Oakes 1998). Followers may tend to project their motives and aspirations onto the charismatic leader. Consequently, they can misread the leader's intentions and the direction in which he is taking the group. Volatility may thus be encouraged by both narcissistic leaders' objectification of their followers and the projective quality of the latter's identification with their prophet (Anthony and Robbins 1995, 1997). It follows that the personality dynamics of the devotees, as well as that of the leaders, may be distinctive and may contribute to volatility. Millennialist movements and other cults have both been described as refuges for alienated, disoriented persons, persons experiencing neurotic distress, and persons with latent hostilities that manipulative leaders may extrapolate and channel (Wright and Wright 1980; Young 1990; Anthony and Robbins 1995, 1997; Galanter 1999).

Finally, narcissistic leaders may lack intimate friends or equal associates who can criticize their wilder impulses and inspirations. They come to depend on reinforcement and adulation from uncritical devotees. This condition has two consequences: (1) high-level defections may traumatize the leader and enhance group volatility (this was clearly the case with the Peoples Temple, Aum Shinrikyô, and the Solar Temple), and (2) the grandiose leader may become more extreme, unbalanced, and paranoid over time (Storrs 1997; Maaga 1998; Lifton 1999).

Conclusion

It appears that various ideological and organizational properties of millennialist cults, as well as situational exigencies, may be accorded the status of almost necessary but not sufficient causes of extreme violence involving such groups. I say "almost" necessary because there is always a tragedy in which one or more of these elements does not appear to be present; for example, there was no controversy or persecution regarding Heaven's Gate in the 1990s or any governmental action leading up to the mass suicides of 1997. Nevertheless, the goal, as this author sees it, should be to develop models that interrelate various factors, and in particular, interrelate social and cultural elements as well as internal movement properties such as charismatic leadership or catastrophic millennialism and exogenous factors such as the intensity and quality of opposition to the group.

There are three formulations that appear to the writer to hold the most promise in this area – two of which have already been discussed. Galanter's social system model (1999), which implicitly specifies totalistic groups, has been applied to several groups and episodes. It has the advantage of being a very systematic formulation that, moreover, seeks to show how certain systems evolve in a manner that renders them particularly susceptible to explosive responses to external pressure. It pinpoints the interrelated developments of attenuated outreach (which can be a partly exogenous factor) and diminished tolerance for negative feedback as signs of possible trouble ahead. However, the model does not scrutinize the nature and degree of hostile external pressure. The boundary threat is just there, and the dynamic factors are mainly endogenous variables related to the malfunctioning or precariousness of the system.

Hall and Schuyler (1998) put primary emphasis on the dynamism of external agitation against a group. But to maintain this emphasis, they seem compelled to disregard huge variations in the intensity of opposition prior to violent outbreaks. Variations in different groups' vulnerability are not extensively treated, although Hall and Schuyler, unlike Galanter, specify an apocalyptic worldview as well as totalism as key factors. The model is evolving (Hall et al. 2000; Hall this volume).

Finally, a very recent formulation by Catherine Wessinger (1999, 2000) could be easily synthesized with both Galanter's and Hall and Schuyler's models. Wessinger presents a typology of millennial movements that have been involved in violence. She highlights "fragile" movements that, as a consequence of internal conflicts, disconfirmation of prophecy, conditions undermining the leader's charisma, or the conspicuous failure to achieve unrealistic goals set by a grandiose leader, are particularly susceptible to being destabilized by external pressure and are the least tolerant of boundary conflict. Wessinger applies this concept to the Solar Temple, whose most important leader, Joseph Di Mambro, was aging and incontinent; to Aum Shinrikyô, which had failed to become the political force envisioned by Asahara; and to the Jonestown settlement, which was failing in several respects and whose leader was deteriorating both psychologically and physically. In contrast, the Branch Davidians, as an "assaulted" group, did not, in Wessinger's view, manifest signs of substantial internal fragility but rather reacted violently to the provocative, militarized quality of the assault by federal agents. A third type, "revolutionary" groups such as the Montana Freemen, have forceful political and insurrectionary orientations. But since Fragile and Assaulted movements may have revolutionary aims, and since revolutionary or fragile groups can be assaulted, Wessinger's types are not mutually exclusive; moreover, Jurgensmeyer (1997) appears to treat Aum Shinrikyô as a revolutionary group.

Galanter, Wessinger, and Hall and Schuyler have developed somewhat complex models or typologies pointing to interactions between external pressures and endogenous features that produce emergent group volatility. This is surely the direction in which scholars should be moving.[3]

In general, apocalypticism, totalism, and the subvarieties that we have highlighted tend to enhance modes of *isolation*: isolation of the spiritual community from the standards of the broader society, and isolation of individual devotees from all influences competitive with the leader and with group norms. Isolation and encapsulation in a separate reality do not guarantee violence – one might conceive of an isolated pacifist or antiracist movement in a society such as Nazi Germany. But since most societies

---

[3] We also note Lifton's important study of Aum Shinrikyô (1999), in which certain patterns such as totalized guruism (see footnote 2) and certain developments such as high-level defections are viewed as interacting to increase the likelihood of violence.

disvalue a conception of disorderly violence such as lethal gas planted in subways, it may be organizationally and ideologically isolated and encapsulated groups that are most likely to engage in extreme, disvalued violence.

References

Anderson, Susan. "Identifying Coercion and Deception in Social Systems." In *Scientific Research on New Religions*, edited by Brock Kilbourne. Proceedings of the Annual Meetings of the Pacific Division of the American Association for the Advancement of Science jointly with the Rocky Mountain Division, Logan, Utah. AAAS, 1985: 12–23.

Anthony, Dick, and Thomas Robbins. "Religious Totalism, Exemplary Dualism and the Waco Tragedy." In *Millennium, Messiahs, and Mayhem*, edited by Thomas Robbins and Susan Palmer. New York: Routledge, 1997: 261–284.

"Religious Totalism, Violence and Exemplary Dualism." *Terrorism and Political Violence* 7 (1995): 10–50.

"Law, Social Science and the 'Brainwashing' Exception to the First Amendment." *Behavioral Science and the Law* 10 (1992): 5–30.

"The Effect of Detente on the Growth of New Religions: Reverend Moon and the Unification Church." In *Understanding New Religions*, edited by Jacob Needleman and George Baker. New York: Seabury, 1978: 80–100.

Barkun, Michael. "Millenarians and Violence: The Case of the Christian Identity Movement." In *Millennium, Messiahs, and Mayhem,* edited by Thomas Robbins and Susan Palmer. New York: Routledge, 1997: 247–260.

Baumgarten, Albert. "Betting on the Millennium." Paper presented at the annual meeting of the Society for the Scientific Study of Religion, Boston, 1999.

Bird, Frederick. "Charisma and Leadership in New Religious Movements." In *Handbook of Cults and Sects in America* (Vol. 3A, *Religion and the Social Order*), edited by David G. Bromley and Jeffrey Hadden. Greenwich, CT: JAI Press, 1993: 75–92.

Boyer, Paul. "A Brief History of the End of Time." *New Republic* May 17, 1993: 30–33.

Bromley, David G. "Constructing Apocalypticism." In *Millenium, Messiahs, and Mayhem*, edited by Thomas Robbins and Susan Palmer. New York: Routledge, 1997: 31–46.

Chidester, David. *Salvation and Suicide.* Bloomington: University of Indiana Press, 1988.

Cohn, Norman. *Pursuit of the Millennium.* London: Oxford University Press, 1961.

Crummey, Robert. *Old Believers in the World of Antichrist.* Madison: University of Wisconsin Press, 1970.

Dawson, Lorne. *Comprehending Cults.* Toronto: Oxford University Press, 1998.

Ellwood, Robert. "Nazism as a Millennial Movement." In *Millennialism, Persecution, and Violence*, edited by Catherine Wessinger. Syracuse, NY: University of Syracuse Press, 2000: 241–260.

Galanter, Marc. *Cults: Faith, Healing, and Coercion*. New York: Oxford University Press, 1999.

Gallagher, Eugene. "Theology Is Life and Death." In *Millenialism, Persecution and Violence*, edited by Catherine Wessinger. Syracuse, NY: University of Syracuse Press, 2000: 82–100.

Goffman, Erving. *Asylums*. Garden City, NY: Doubleday, 1961.

Gorenberg, Gershom. "Tribulations." *New Republic* June 14, 1999: 18–21.

Hall, John. *Gone from the Promised Land*. New Brunswick, NJ: Transaction, 1987.

Hall, John, and Philip Schuyler. "Apostasy, Apocalypse and Religious Violence." In *The Politics of Religious Apostasy*, edited by David G. Bromley. Westport, CT: Praeger, 1998: 141–170.

"The Mystical Apocalypse of the Solar Temple." In *Millennium, Messiahs, and Mayhem*, edited by Thomas Robbins and Susan Palmer. New York: Routledge, 1997: 247–260.

Hall, John, Philip Schuyler, and Sylvaine Trinh. *Apocalypse Observed*. New York: Routledge, 2000.

Johnson, Doyle Paul. "Dilemmas of Charismatic Leadership." *Sociological Analysis* 40 (1979): 315–323.

Jones, Constance. "Exemplary Dualism and Authoritarianism at Jonestown." In *New Religious Movements, Mass Suicide, and the Peoples Temple*, edited by Moore, Rebecca, and Fielding McGehee. Lewiston, ME: Edwin Mellen, 1989: 209–230.

Jurgensmeyer, Mark. "Terror Mandated by God." *Terrorism and Political Violence* 9 (1997): 16–23.

Kanter, Rosabeth. *Commitment and Community*. Cambridge, MA: Harvard University Press, 1972a.

"Commitment and the Internal Organization of Millennial Movements." *American Behavioral Scientist* 16 (1972b): 219–244.

"Commitment and Social Organization." *American Sociological Review* 33 (1968): 499–517.

Kaplan, Jeffrey. *Radical Religion in America*. Syracuse, NY: Syracuse University Press, 1997.

"Absolute Rescue." *Terrorism and Political Violence* 7 (1995): 128–163.

Knox, Ronald. *Enthusiasm*. London: Oxford University Press, 1950.

Lamy, Philip. *The Millennium Rage*. New York: Plenum, 1997.

Lawson, Ronald. "The Persistence of Apocalypticism within a Denominationalizing Sect." In *Millennium, Messiahs, and Mayhem*, edited by Thomas Robbins and Susan Palmer. New York: Routledge, 1997: 207–228.

Lebra, Takie Sugiyama. "Millenarian Movements and Resocialization." *American Behavioral Scientist* 16 (1972): 192–218.

Lee, Martha. "Environmental Apocalypse." In *Millennium, Messiahs, and Mayhem*, edited by Thomas Robbins and Susan Palmer. New York: Routledge, 1997: 119–138.

Lewis, James, ed. *From the Ashes*. Lanham, MD: Rowman and Littlefield, 1994.

Lifton, Robert J. *Destroying the World to Save It*. New York: Holt, 1999.

Chinese Thought Reform and the Psychology of Totalism. New York: Norton, 1961.

Loewe, Scott. "Western Millennial Ideology Goes East." In *Millennialism, Persecution, and Violence*, edited by Catherine Wessinger. Syracuse, NY: University of Syracuse Press, 2000: 220–240.

Maaga, Mary. *Hearing the Voices of Jonestown*. Syracuse, NY: Syracuse University Press, 1998.

Mayer, Jean. "Our Terrestrial Voyage Is Coming to an End: The Last Voyage of the Solar Temple." *Nova Religio* 2 (1999): 172–196.

Melton, J Gordon. "Violence and the Cults." *Nebraska Humanist* 8 (1985): 51–61.

Mills, Edgar. "Cult Extremism." In *Violence and Religious Commitment*, edited by Kenneth Levi. University Park: Pennsylvania State University Press, 1982: 75–102.

Mullins, Mark. "Aum Shinrikyô as an Apocalyptic Movement." In *Millennium, Messiahs, and Mayhem*, edited by Thomas Robbins and Susan Palmer. New York: Routledge, 1997: 313–324.

Oakes, Len. *Prophetic Charisma*. Syracuse, NY: University of Syracuse Press, 1998.

O'Leary, Stephen. *Arguing the Apocalypse*. Oxford: Oxford University Press, 1994.

Pye, Michael. "Aum Shinrikyô." *Religion* 26 (1996): 261–270.

Rapoport, David. "Messianic Sanctions for Terror." *Comparative Politics* 20 (1988): 195–213.

Reader, Ian. *Religious Violence in Contemporary Japan*. Honolulu: University of Hawaii Press, 2000.

Rich, Frank. "Heaven's Gate-gate." *New York Times* Op-Ed section, April 17, 1997:

Richardson, James. "Violence and the New Religions." Paper presented at the annual meeting of the Society for the Scientific Study of Religion, Baltimore, 1981.

Robbins, Thomas. "Apocalypse, Persecution and Self-Immolation." In *Millennialism, Persecution, and Violence*, edited by Catherine Wessinger. Syracuse, NY: University of Syracuse Press, 2000: 205–219.

"Religious Movements and Violence." *Nova Religio* 1 (1997): 13–29.

"Religious Mass Suicide Before Jonestown: The Russian Old Believers." *Sociological Analysis* 44 (1986): 1–20.

Robbins, Thomas, and Dick Anthony. "Sects and Violence." In *Armageddon in Waco*, edited by Stuart Wright. Chicago: University of Chicago Press, 1995: 236–262.

Robbins, Thomas, and Susan Palmer. "Patterns of Contemporary Apocalypticism." In *Millennium, Messiahs, and Mayhem*, edited by Thomas Robbins and Susan Palmer. New York: Routledge, 1997: 1–27.

Rosenfeld, Jean. "The Importance of the Analysis of Religion in Avoiding Violent Outcomes." *Nova Religio* 1 (1997): 72–95.

"Pai Marire, Peace and Violence in a New Zealand Millenarian Tradition." *Terrorism and Political Violence* 7 (1995): 83–108.

Salter, Richard. "Time, Authority, and Ethics in the Khmer Rouge." In *Millennialism, Persecution, and Violence*, edited by Catherine Wessinger. Syracuse, NY: University of Syracuse Press, 2000: 281–298.

Shupe, Anson. "Christian Reconstructionism and the Angry Rhetoric of Neo-Postmillennialism." In *Millennium, Messiahs, and Mayhem*, edited by Thomas Robbins and Susan Palmer. New York: Routledge, 1997: 195–206.

Stone, Jacqueline. "Japanese Lotus Millennialism." In *Millennialism, Persecution, and Violence*, edited by Catherine Wessinger. Syracuse, NY: University of Syracuse Press, 2000: 261–280.

Stone, Jon, ed. *Expecting Armageddon*. New York: Routledge, 2000.

Storrs, Anthony. *Feet of Clay: A Study of Gurus*. New York: Free Press, 1997.

Tabor, James, and Eugene Gallagher. *Why Waco?* Berkeley: University of California Press, 1995.

Underwood, Grant. "Millennialism, Persecution and violence: The Mormons." In *Millennialism, Persecution, and Violence*, edited by Catherine Wessinger. Syracuse, NY: University of Syracuse Press, 2000: 43–61.

Wallis, Roy, and Steve Bruce. "Sex, Violence, and Religion." In *Sociological Theory, Religion, and Collective Action*, edited by Roy Wallis and Steve Bruce. Belfast, Northern Ireland: Queens University, 1986: 115–127.

Watanabe, Manabu. "Religion and Violence in Japan Today." *Terrorism and Political Violence* 10 (1998): 80–100.

Wessinger, Catherine. "Interacting Dynamics of Millennial Beliefs, Persecution, and Violence." In *Millennialism, Persecution, and Violence*, edited by Catherine Wessinger. Syracuse, NY: University of Syracuse Press, 2000: 3–42.

How the Millennium Comes Violently. Chappaqua, NY: Seven Bridges Press, 2000.

"Millennialism with and without Mayhem." In *Millennium, Messiahs, and Mayhem*, edited by Thomas Robbins and Susan Palmer. New York: Routledge, 1997: 47–60.

Wright, Stuart. "Anatomy of a Government Massacre," *Terrorism and Political Violence* 11 (1999): 39–68.

Wright, Fred, and Phyllis Wright. "The Charismatic Leader and the Violent Surrogate Family." *Annals of the New York Academy of Sciences*. 347 (1980): 266–276.

Young, Thomas. "Cult Violence and the Christian Identity Movement." *The Cultic Studies Journal* 7 (1990): 150–157.

5

CRISES OF CHARISMATIC LEGITIMACY AND VIOLENT BEHAVIOR IN NEW RELIGIOUS MOVEMENTS

LORNE L. DAWSON

There is a marked tendency for the popular media to emphasize the role of supposedly "manipulative and mad" charismatic leaders in the tragic events surrounding the deaths of members of new religious movements. The focus on the role of the leader, perhaps the only member of the group about whom there is some information, reflects both our age-old desire to personify evil and the dramatic requirements of telling a good story. Clearly, there is some truth to the presumption that the powerful leaders of these groups were instrumental in bringing about the violence. Equally clearly, however, the focus on the greed, lust, or mental instability of the leaders fails to explain adequately why so many people were willingly to place their fates so completely in their hands. Why would the faithful follow these seemingly deranged leaders to their death? For decades, the answer to this question hinged on assuming that the followers were the victims of systematic programs of "brainwashing" or "mind control." But the empirical evidence acquired by scholars of religion has soundly discredited that assumption, so we must look elsewhere for answers (Dawson 1998: 102–127).

The dramatic and exceptional incidents of cult-related violence we have witnessed in the last several decades stem, as Robbins delineates in the previous chapter, from the convergence of many factors, both endogenous and exogenous. The impact of charismatic leaders is one of the constants of these incidents. The focal point for research and concern, though, should not be the sanity of the leader or the brainwashed condition of the followers, but rather the nature and the dynamics of the charismatic mode of leadership that almost all scholars agree is a hallmark of new religious life. As with the apocalypticism and totalism explored by Robbins, there is nothing intrinsically violent about charismatic leadership. All institutions (e.g., governments, businesses, the military) actively cultivate and reward its presence in some measure as an effective way to achieve their ends. It is a strong feature of all religious life – encouraged in pastors, preachers, and educators – and essential to the foundation of the great religions of the world. Yet, as is commonly recognized, charismatic modes of leadership are more volatile. Is this simply because they are more intense, emotional, and countercultural (even revolutionary)? Certainly that is part of the answer, but a more specific answer can be formulated. The true danger stems, I will argue, from the mismanagement of certain endemic problems of charismatic authority that are rooted in the problematic legitimacy of charisma. Four of these problems are identified and analyzed here: (1) maintaining the leader's persona, (2) moderating the effects of the psychological identification of followers with the leader, (3) negotiating the routinization of charisma, and (4) achieving new successes. When leaders, trying to preserve their authority, make the wrong choices in the face of these challenges, they can set off a cycle of deviance amplification that greatly increases the likelihood of violent behavior.

Charismatic Leadership: Insights into Its Nature

Defining Charismatic Authority

As classically formulated by Max Weber (1964: 358), the term "charisma" applies "to a certain quality of an individual personality by virtue of which he is set apart from ordinary men and treated as endowed with supernatural, superhuman, or at least specifically exceptional powers or qualities. These are such as are not accessible to the ordinary person, but are regarded as of divine origin or as exemplary, and on the basis of them the individual concerned is treated as a leader." For Weber, charisma is a term used to designate one of three modes of authority (i.e., legitimated forms of domination), the other two being traditional and rational-legal. Traditional leaders are granted authority by those they govern by virtue of custom, because certain kinds of people have always done so. With rational-legal authority, the right to rule is identified with certain offices that are legally constituted, no matter who may occupy those offices. The authority is invested in the position, not the person. Charismatic authority reverses this state of affairs. It is rooted in the display of exceptional abilities by an individual. In fact, in its historically most prevalent form, these abilities, as Weber stresses, are thought to be divinely (or supernaturally) granted or inspired. These are two of the four defining features of charismatic authority.

Regrettably, in defining charismatic authority, Weber refers to an individual's "personality." Popularly, charisma is presumed to be something people possess, an intrinsic feature of their nature. But as Weber further argues and as all scholars interested in the subject stress, charisma is really something that people attribute to someone. It is a quality that people perceive on the basis of certain identifiable behaviors. It is fruitless, most researchers conclude, to seek to delineate some universal set of "personality features" of charismatic leaders. As Ruth Willner dryly comments (1984: 14), "It is difficult to consider Gandhi and Hitler as cast in the same personality mold." The focus of research should be the charismatic relationship, the interactive process by which leaders displaying certain behaviors are perceived to be charismatic by followers, who in turn may share certain features. This focus has led to a wide consensus on the third and fourth defining features of charismatic authority.

The third defining feature of charismatic authority is that it rests on a relationship of great emotional intensity, which typically leads followers to place an extraordinary measure of trust and faith in their leader. Charismatic authority is highly personal in nature, even in instances where the person subject to that authority has little direct contact with the charismatic leader.

Fourth and finally, this near-absolute trust in the leader means that groups formed by charismatic authority tend to display unusually high levels of cohesion, value congruence, and task performance. Charisma is an extremely effective means of galvanizing commitment to a cause or an organization.

Prompting the Attribution of Charisma

So, what kinds of behaviors prompt the attribution of charisma to a leader? Biographies, case studies, and a growing body of empirical research suggest that people distinguish between charismatic and noncharismatic leaders on the basis of certain perceived abilities and interests (Willner 1984; Bass 1988; Conger and Kanungo 1988; Gardner and Avolio 1998). Charismatic leaders are deemed to be more visionary in their style of leadership and more emotionally expressive. In both regards, they are thought to display greater sensitivity to the deficiencies of the status quo and the needs of their followers. They become involved in the lives of their followers, at least in the early stages of their movements. They are also marked by their higher levels of activity and exemplary behavior. They are "high-energy" types who tend to lead, at least initially, by the example they set. This can often entail what seems to be a marked willingness to incur risk and to be unconventional. They make the sacrifices they demand from others and appear to be "more concerned with doing the right things than with doing things right" (Bass 1988: 40). They seem to exude self-confidence and determination, and as all commentators agree, they are equipped with superior rhetorical and impression management skills. The latter point is quite important. The leader's ability to create the impression that he or she has performed extraordinary and heroic feats, and possesses uncanny, even supernatural powers, acts as the catalyst for the attribution of charismatic authority. The leader's success is linked to his or her assimilation to one or more of the cultural myths of the society. Out of the mutual needs of the leader and followers, the charismatic leader is constructed and hence the charismatic bond established (Wallis 1982). But it is the leader who must understand, intuitively or otherwise, how to manipulate the shared cultural legacy to enhance his or her status. Often relatively small deeds of daring are made to appear much grander in scope and meaning through staged events and the artful and audacious use of scriptural and other mythical claims and analogies (Willner 1984; Gardner and Avolio 1998). Kets de Vries (1988: 240–241) observes that part of the appeal of charismatic leaders lies in the fact that they "facilitate the transformation of a historical or mythical ideal from a remote abstraction into an immediate psychological reality."

Of course, this latter point is paradigmatically the case with the founders of new religions. They are almost by definition successful *bricoleurs*, fashioning what often appear to be rather preposterous new religious teachings from existing ideas. The Solar Temple, for example, grew out of a very long and complicated tradition of secret neo-Christian mystical organizations based on ancient and medieval lore about the quest for the Holy Grail and the teachings and tragic fate of the Knights Templar. To this already eclectic mixture of beliefs and practices the Solar Temple added a variety of occult notions "ranging from Rosicrucianism to Egyptian thanatology to Luc Jouret's oriental folk medicine and ecological apocalypticism" (Palmer 1996: 305). Aum Shinrikyô even more strangely combined aspects of Indian and Tibetan Buddhism, which are not strictly compatible, with doses of Christian apocalypticism, oriental folk medicines, and New Age therapeutic practices (Reader 1996; Lifton 1999). In each of these groups, the popular mythology of reincarnation was invoked to legitimate further the special status and powers of the charismatic leaders and their lieutenants. The leaders and their most loyal followers are Moses, Jesus, or the Buddha reincarnated, or one of a host of lesser but no less exotic figures ranging from the Egyptian Pharaoh Akhnaton to the Comte de Saint-Germain (see, e.g., Hall and Schuyler 2000: 126).

The Psychology of Charismatic Attribution

Most discussions of why followers develop such intense emotional commit-ments to charismatic leaders – why they participate in the construction of charismatic relationships – rely on notions of unconscious need satisfac-tion and on the processes of projection and identification. There are several variants of this thesis. The most common approach takes Freud's specula-tions in *Group Psychology and the Analysis of the Ego* (1959) as its point of departure. Others call upon insights derived from the social psychology of Albert Bandura (Madsen and Snow 1991) or the psychoanalytic theories of narcissism of Heinz Kohut and elements of Durkheim's sociology of religion (Lindholm 1990; Oakes 1997). The conclusions reached, nonethe-less, are much the same. From the psychoanalytic perspective, followers attribute charismatic qualities and power to a leader as a way of resolving the unconscious conflict they are experiencing between their ego and their ego ideal. Projecting the ego ideal – the internalized sense of what society ideally expects of them – onto the leader, and then entering into a condition of deep personal identification with the leader, allows followers to satisfy vicariously the demands of the ego ideal, thereby relieving themselves of the profound psychological tension created by their actual failure to live up to the ego ideal (Downton 1973; Bass 1988: 50–52; Kets de Vries 1988: 242–245). The relief of transferring this responsibility can be quite eu-phoric, easily leading to the misattribution of the source of the relief to the leader and his or her movement. The release of the followers from the pangs of conscience also serves to weld a sense of close identity with others under-going the same experience – the other members of the leader's community. Each new conversion, in turn, reinforces the identification of the existing followers with the leader. A comforting group ego ideal emerges, for a time at least, with the charismatic leader as its symbolic focal point and primary mechanism of expression.

These psychological interpretations are helpful in understanding why the charismatic bond exists. But the general pattern of need, projection, and identification with the leader is an intrinsic aspect of the human con-dition, which only the most remarkably well adjusted among us can avoid altogether. So we must move beyond psychology to understand fully how these relationships sometimes become so deviant that they pose a physical danger to followers.

Charismatic Legitimation and Its Problems

The charismatic mode of authority is uniquely precarious. Charismatic leaders, more so than traditional or rational-legal leaders, must sustain their own legitimacy. They exist largely without the external support of custom and established institutions. Any particular traditional leader is essentially just the temporary embodiment of a set of ingrained cultural expectations, while any particular rational-legal leader is only a representative of an abstract set of principles, rules, and regulations. Alternatively, charismatic leaders are essentially a rule of custom or law unto themselves. Each of their actions either establishes, reinforces, or undermines their own authority. In fact, much of the authority of charismatic leaders stems from the very nature of the impressions they create in their daily interactions with others. As these patterns of interaction change, so do the very nature and viability of this authority. Charisma requires a kind of continuous legitimation work. Of course, this is true to a lesser extent with the rule of custom or law as well. Revolutions may happen when any particular manifestation of traditional or rational-legal authority is delegitimated by its own shortcomings. But charismatic authority is far more dependent on an ongoing display of the prowess and virtues of the leader. This why Weber considered charismatic leaders transitory historical figures and dedicated most of his analysis of charismatic authority to tracing the ways in which it will normally evolve into one of the other two types (Weber 1964: 363–386). When this evolution fails to occur in a charismatically led group, it will either soon cease to be or it will implode and become unstable. It is the latter path of development that often leads to violent behavior and confrontations. Fundamentally, the potential for violence in new religious movements stems, in part, from failing to cope with the more or less perpetual legitimation crisis experienced by charismatic leaders.

To sustain their legitimacy, charismatic leaders must strike a dynamic balance between asserting too much dominance and not asserting enough. To err in either way brings instability. It is too much dominance, however, that tends to bring violence. To achieve the optimum equilibrium, charismatic leaders must successfully manage four problems endemic to charismatic authority: (1) maintaining the leader's persona, (2) moderating the effects of the psychological identification of followers with the leader, (3) negotiating the routinization of charisma, and (4) achieving new successes. In dealing with these challenges, some leaders make choices that have the cumulative effect of fostering the social implosion of a group and hence violent behavior.

Maintaining the Leader's Image

Charismatic authority hinges on knowing the leader. Or at least it hinges on the pretense of a personal relationship between the leader and his or her followers. To this end, the leader must be seen and heard from with regularity. In fact, public and staged displays of the leader must be complemented by the continued exposure of some members, and new recruits in particular, to the personal presence of the leader. The charismatic aura must be continuously replenished with new, if highly programmatic, tales of the electrifying effects of private interviews with the leader. But this required exposure can be dangerous, for if too many people have too much access to the leader, his or her human frailties may begin to shine through the most polished image. Exposure may actually undermine the element of mystery and exaggeration essential to sustaining the tales of wonder, compassion, and extraordinary accomplishments used to establish the leader's charismatic credentials. To maintain this crucial element of mystery, many charismatic leaders deliberately practice a measure of segregation from their followers. Access to the leader is restricted to those who are especially prepared, especially loyal, or very much in need of guidance, while occasions of mass exposure are carefully managed to maximize their impact and minimize the chances of embarrassment. Too much exposure may delegitimate the leader and hence jeopardize the survival of the group. But too much isolation will also have deleterious effects on the stability of the group. To maintain their persona, and hence their charismatic authority, leaders must make decisions on a daily basis that maintain the appropriate balance between exposure and isolation. But the most loyal followers surrounding the leader, those with the strongest personal identification with the leader and investment in the leader's power, have a strong incentive to limit the exposure of the leader and to systematically suppress undesirable information about the leader. All assaults on the leader's identity or pronouncements are likely to be read as assaults on their own identity and interests (Wallis 1982: 37; Bass 1988: 55). With the sole possible exception of David Koresh, the leaders of the groups we are examining seem to have erred on the side of becoming too isolated.[1] The resultant tendency to shroud the leader in a protective enclave of absolutely devoted followers, and to separate the leader physically, or at least socially, from the mass of ordinary followers, can have several negative consequences.

On the one hand, charismatic leaders may find themselves surrounded by sycophants who are incapable of providing them with the negative feedback essential to making sound and realistic decisions for the future of the group. The resultant mismanagement of the organization is damaging in itself, but it may further bring the leader's charismatic authority into question, which can spur the leader to more extreme actions and demands to secure greater assurances of the loyalty of the followers. The need for impression management will persist or even intensify, but without the audience contact required to ensure the necessary teamwork that Goffman (1959) has demonstrated is a fundamental component of all successful social interactions. A degenerative cycle might be unwittingly initiated through the collapse of communication between leaders and their followers. The insulated condition of leaders may also prevent them from knowing that their authority is being flouted by subordinates with their own agendas, which will precipitate disruptive and destabilizing power struggles in the group, both before and after the divisions in the ranks eventually become apparent to the leader.

On the other hand, the rank and file of a movement can find themselves cut out of the processes of decision making altogether and quite ignorant of the extreme agendas that the inner circle of the leadership are pursuing with their unwitting support. This may place them in a collective position of jeopardy that is discovered only belatedly, when it is believed that the consequences cannot be escaped without an unacceptable loss of face or investment. The risk of this happening is increased by the reduction in normative dissonance (Mills 1982) that accompanies the escalating social implosion of the group as the inner circle becomes more defensive of the leader's integrity. The normal give-and-take of different opinions, norms, and values that moderates conventional social interactions is attenuated by the desire to achieve near-total commitment to the cause as embodied by the leader. Even constructive dissent becomes increasingly suspect and is habitually suppressed in and by the inner circle, establishing an organizational milieu in which obedience becomes disproportionately esteemed, if

---

[1] Do, the leader of Heaven's Gate, was in fact more physically isolated from his followers than previous media and academic reports had indicated (see Lalich 2000).

only as a means to advance through the ranks into the inner circle and gain its prestige and power.

In practice, of course, either of these consequences, or both simultaneously, may transpire in diverse ways. The isolation of Joseph Di Mambro may have contributed in both ways to the murders that accompanied the mass suicides of the Solar Temple. Clearly, some members from Quebec and elsewhere traveled to Switzerland without the slightest belief that their lives were at risk. They seem to have been caught in a struggle between Di Mambro and Luc Jouret, and between both leaders and a group of dissenters within the Temple. It also seems that many of even these more or less core members had a full grasp of the situation. But we lack adequate information to say what exactly happened. We can only make guesses based on the circumstantial evidence (Palmer 1996; Mayer 1999; Hall and Schuyler 2000). Most of the residents of Jonestown, however, thought they had little alternative to participating in revolutionary suicide, because they had been kept largely in the dark about such things as the deteriorating physical and mental health of Jim Jones, the relatively minor nature of the real threats posed to their community by ex-members and the government, and the millions of dollars the church had secreted away in foreign bank accounts (Chidester 1988; Maaga 1998; Layton 1998). Likewise, the followers of Shôkô Ashara seemed to have had little awareness of the murders perpetrated by the leaders of Aum Shinrikyô, let alone the wild schemes of mass destruction that they were preparing for and attempting. Consequently, many members continued to deny the culpability of the group long after the arrest of most of its leadership (Lifton 1999; Trinh and Hall 2000).

Moderating Identification with the Leader

If the devotion of the followers is based on something like the fusion of the followers' ego ideals with the image of the leader, then, as indicated earlier, all attacks on the leader are taken by the followers as attacks on themselves. Under these circumstances it is not surprising that, on the one hand, opponents and apostates are commonly demonized and the threat they pose is exaggerated, while on the other hand, the nature and depth of the psychological tie with the charismatic leader more or less ensure the fanaticism and intransigence of some apostates. Both processes work to inflame a group's interactions with outsiders, heightening the likelihood of violent confrontations. But insecure charismatic leaders can significantly aggravate the situation by choosing to exploit the tensions. They can use the tensions as a pretext for increasing the isolation of the group, or their own segregation, and they can use the tensions to rationalize an increase in their authority by encouraging even higher levels of psychological fusion with the leader. Regrettably, as Lindholm (1990), Lifton (1999), and Davis (2000) have each documented in detail, this is precisely what Jim Jones, Shôkô Asahara, and Marshall Herff Applewhite (Do, the leader of Heaven's Gate) did.

The demonization of the enemies of a group by its followers can lead to violent acts in defense of even the symbolic integrity of the leader and the group. The greater the fusion of the followers with the leader, the more extreme these defensive acts may become. One might think of the seemingly disproportionate hostility and fear directed at the Concerned Relatives by Jim Jones and his followers – a key factor in the disastrous move of the Peoples Temple to Guyana and their subsequent overreaction to the visit of Congressman Leo Ryan. Likewise, the even more systematic and potentially lethal violence of Aum Shinrikyô seems to have been set in motion many years prior to the subway attack by the unprecedented order to murder a follower who might have exposed the accidental death of another devotee during one of the group's ascetic practices. The violent fate of the organization was soon sealed by the even more audacious decision to kidnap and murder the attorney Sakamoto Tsutsumi, along with his wife and child, because he had begun to organize the first legal opposition to the group (Lifton 1999; Trinh and Hall 2000). Asahara used these criminal acts to ensure the future compliance of his inner circle, just as Jim Jones involved many members in illicit financial dealings and other fraudulent activities to secure their absolute loyalty. But as even the account of a hostile ex-member like Deborah Layton (1998) suggests, these coercive measures merely served to consolidate the deep identification of the followers with the leader that was already in place. Lifton (1999) repeatedly calls attention to the ideal of becoming clones of the master in Aum Shinrikyô. Followers spent hours, even days, locked in tiny cubicles endlessly watching videotapes of Asahara, and they wore electronic headsets contrived to tune them into his very brain waves. Likewise, members of Heaven's Gate seem to have sought to emulate Do in every way, suppressing all signs of their own "all too human" identity (Davis 2000).

This demand to fuse with the leader is conducive to violence in at least two other ways as well. First, it is likely that the submission of the followers to the charismatic leader is always accompanied by repressed feelings of resentment and aggression, for their peace of mind is purchased at the price of self-denial. If, as Freud asserted, the repressed always seeks to return to consciousness, then some measure of future rebellion against the leader is inevitable. The leader can avert that possibility "by channeling the accumulated hostility of the group outward, away from himself, and toward a despised other, who can be execrated and injured with impunity. In this way the leader allows the follower the gratification of deep aggressive desires that must ordinarily be kept sublimated and turned against the self" (Lindholm 1990: 55). The scapegoats invoked by the leaders, however, need not always be external to the group. So, second, the demand for greater psychological identification with the leader can be turned inward to locate and justify the expulsion of real dissidents or perhaps just expendable members who can be sacrificed to the aggressive impulses of the group. In any event, the rituals of symbolic self-transcendence, ascetic trials of self-mortification, confessional sessions, and perhaps even drug-induced episodes of altered states of consciousness that are instituted to promote and test the greater fusion with the leader will cause some followers to defect. These defections will further reduce the normative dissonance needed to moderate the behavior of these groups. As the groups become more homogeneous it will become harder to separate fact from paranoid fiction.

This whole cycle is sustained by the tendency of many apostates to demonize the charismatic leader and their group, perhaps as a defensive measure against the traumatic effects of the failure of the apostate's fusion with the leader (i.e., the apostate's vicarious ego ideal). An unusual need may exist to triumph over and destroy the false god in order to legitimate the act of apostasy itself and to deny the seeming failure of the follower's spiritual quest. Reverse scapegoating may occur to avert a new kind of self-loathing. Lindholm (1990: 55) hypothesizes that the revolt against the "parental tyrant" may also be accompanied by a new euphoria stemming from symbolic immersion in the seemingly egalitarian band of anticult activists. There can be no doubt that the tenacity and even at times the duplicity of the organized anticult movement, built on the atrocity tales of ex-members, has polluted the social environment in which all new religious movements must operate (e.g., Bromley and Richardson 1983; Shupe and Bromley 1994). The polarized atmosphere has certainly contributed to an unhealthy measure of paranoia on both sides of the struggle. The stubborn opposition of a few ex-members seems to have contributed significantly to the decision to commit murder or suicide in the case of the Peoples Temple, the Solar Temple, Aum Shinrikyô, and perhaps the Movement for the Restoration of the Ten Commandments of God (e.g., Reader 1996;

Layton 1998; Hall 2000; Sanders 2000). There is little doubt that the inflammatory rhetoric and advice of the anticult movement contributed to the brutal ending of the Branch Davidian siege in Waco (e.g., Lewis 1995; Tabor and Gallagher 1995).

Negotiating the Routinization of Charisma[2]

The very success of a charismatic leader's movement can pose problems for the leader. As the group survives and grows in size, it often becomes more bureaucratic, and charismatic leaders are inclined to resist this process of institutionalization. They seem to fear the "routinization" of their charismatic authority, to use Weber's well-known term. Growth impairs charismatic leaders' capacity to maintain the personal contact with followers from which their authority grew. Moreover they can no longer personally supervise all of the essential activities of the group. As in any established organization, authority must be delegated to others. In fact, it must become routinely associated with various designated positions, not particular persons. But this shift toward a more rational-legal mode of authority often is experienced by charismatic leaders as an unacceptable diminution of their own power. Indeed, as Johnson observes (1979: 317), with this shift "some members will not be as emotionally dependent on the leader as others and thus will have less reason to grant total loyalty to the leader."

"[L]arge groups inevitably are more heterogeneous than small ones, and the effects of this heterogeneity compound the [leaders'] problem of maintaining firm or absolute control over all [their] followers" (Johnson 1979: 317). Successful lieutenants, either individually or collectively, may begin explicitly or implicitly to usurp some of the prestige and power granted to the original charismatic leader as they conduct the daily business of the religious organization.

In these circumstances, charismatic leaders have employed a set of strategies to counteract the routinization of charisma. The actions taken are presented to the followers as ways of maintaining the purity, intensity, and quality of the vision and commitment of these group. But they frequently have unintended, or at least unanticipated, consequences that may eventually place the safety of the members in jeopardy. For these tactics tend to destabilize the movement, thereby increasing the dependency of the faithful on the symbolic presence and power of the charismatic leader just

---

[2] The following discussion of routinization draws on Dawson (1998: 142–148).

when the actual instrumental control of the leader is waning in the face of the organizational demands stemming from the group's success.

There are at least six such strategies that charismatic leaders use in different ways and combinations to preserve their authority:

(1) To keep followers off balance and focused on the words and wishes of the charismatic founder, the leader may shift doctrines and policies, sometimes rather suddenly and dramatically. This may come about through the announcement of new visions or revelations or, more simply, by claiming that the group is ready to experience a deeper level of understanding of the existing beliefs and practices. Shifts like these are intended to attract new members and tap new resources, but they also serve to push some of the old guard to the margins of the movement while elevating new people into the inner circle. The shifts have a leveling effect that reasserts the superiority and special place of the leader over all of his or her followers, while the new structures of training, administration, and reward that accompany the shifts fracture the patterns of influence and personal and professional alliances that have been established within the organization. The followers are kept busy and diverted from challenging the prerogatives of the charismatic leader. In the face of new knowledge or ways of doing things, all become equally dependent, once again, on the guiding insight and wisdom of the leader.

(2) Charismatic leaders may escalate the demands they place on members for personal service and sacrifice to the group. This is also what many of the shifts in doctrine, policy, and practice are about. The new views, procedures, and administrative structures are often preceded or accompanied by new rituals or other acts of commitment. Most notoriously, Jim Jones, for example, asked the members of Jonestown to undergo a series of "White Nights" in which they rehearsed their collective suicide. Members never knew whether the "poison" they drank during these rituals was real. In the face of the inevitable dissolution of loyalty that comes with time or organizational growth, charismatic leaders are challenged to devise ever more dramatic and overpowering rituals of commitment – the rituals that often play such a crucial role in generating and consolidation identification with the leader (Oakes 1997: 152–160).

(3) Charismatic leaders may play on a group's fear of persecution by inventing new and ever greater enemies and engaging in crisis-mongering. In the oldest political ploy known to humanity, the internal solidarity of the group is galvanized by the leader's call for unity in the face of a series of new threats and challenges. The people of Jonestown lived in terror of

the Central Intelligence Agency (CIA), waiting for the midnight raid of mercenaries that Jones said would kill their children (Chidester 1988; Layton 1998). Asahara ironically complained that the Americans were trying to use airplanes to spray his headquarters with the very sarin gas he was manufacturing to initiate the apocalypse.

(4) Dissent may be increasingly stifled through the careful control of information and the public use of ridicule and other means of peer pressure. Alternative sources of leadership arising in the group may be marginalized or simply ejected. Small, relatively inconsequential challenges to the authority of the leader are blown out of proportion and used to foment a sense of crisis, effect a shift in practices, discredit lieutenants, and justify the movement of people into and out of the inner circle. Jones used the privilege of leaving Jonestown to do the bidding of the Peoples Temple in the United States, Georgetown, Guyana, or elsewhere to control his lieutenants. Loyalty was ensured and delegated power removed by the periodic and unpredictable recall of members to the agricultural project (Layton 1998). At one point, Do (Marshall Applewhite) and Ti (Bonnie Nettles) simply sent those not adequately conforming to the plan off to establish a separate colony in Arizona, with every expectation that they would fail and defect from the group (Hall 2000).

(5) Similarly, many charismatic leaders seek to test the loyalty of followers, heighten the emotional dependency of followers, and generally disrupt potential sources of alternative authority, by undermining or physically separating couples or other close pairs within their groups. The bonds of romantic love or even good friendship must not be allowed to take precedence over the affective tie of each individual to the charismatic leader. Of course, religious orders in almost all cultures have long recognized the need to regulate and suppress sexual and other strong emotional attachments if higher spiritual ends are to be served. In our own culture, one need only think of the monastic orders of the Catholic Church. But in some instances, like the Peoples Temple, David Koresh at Waco, and to some extent the Children of God, the Solar Temple, Synanon, the Rajneesh movement, Heaven's Gate, and the Movement to Restore the Ten Commandments of God, the leaders' control of the sex lives of followers was more ad hoc and discriminatory in nature. Couples were separated and paired at the will of the leader to serve the superordinate interests of the group. In an extreme instance, David Koresh came to assert a monopoly on sexual access to all of the women in the Davidian compound. The commitment of the men to the apocalyptic worldview of the group was tested by the surrender of their

wives, lovers, and daughters (often at a quite young age), while the women involved were to be with Koresh out of a wish to fulfill his task, as the anointed messenger of God, to populate the world with his godly children, both spiritual and biological.

(6) Finally, when all else fails, and sometimes earlier, many charismatic leaders seek to consolidate their control and diminish countervailing influences by changing the location, and hence the operating environment, of their groups. Frequently these moves entail increasing the isolation of the group. Jim Jones moved the Peoples Temple from Indianapolis, to a rural and relatively secluded part of California, and then eventually to Jonestown, a settlement carved out of the jungle of Guyana, South America. Likewise, Moses David removed the Children of God, which began in southern California, from North America altogether for years. The Solar Temple, which began in Switzerland and France, sought to colonize Quebec, with the hope of eventually fully relocating there. The Rajneesh movement fled crowded southern India for an isolated ranch in the interior of the state of Oregon. Do and Ti kept Heaven's Gate on the road for decades, shifting their location and living conditions about every six months.

Achieving New Successes

Charismatic authority, as indicated, depends on an ongoing display of the prowess and virtues of the leader. This means that the leader must sustain at least the appearance of new successes, both concrete and spiritual. In new religious movements, success is most often concretely demonstrated through the recruitment of new members. But this success is complemented by claims of spiritual triumph as well. The two are often closely interrelated, since the spiritual claims are offered as an inducement to join the movement. Here I will focus on one particular set of these claims: the prophecies of the end of the world that figured so prominently in the contemporary tragedies we are considering.

For observers and members alike, charisma is most graphically present in the reaction of new converts to the leader. It is usually their accounts of their first few meetings with the leader that provide us with the most recognizable descriptions of the charismatic bond. This bond is likely to wane with time, and the leader is under considerable pressure to turn his or her attention to the cultivation of more new members. In some measure, this state of affairs may contribute to the extremely high rates of defection experienced by most new religious movements. On the one hand, this structurally induced turnover may work to destabilize the group, since there is insufficient continuity in the relationships among members and in various organizational positions. On the other hand, it may stabilize the group by regenerating the excitement of the charismatic relationship and perhaps preventing some of the struggles set off by the routinization of charisma. Paradoxically, it is the growth of the group that staves off the destabilizing effects of the leader's need to resist routinization, up to a point, while it is the growth of the group beyond a certain point that necessitates the routinization of charisma in the first place. The leader and the group are thus caught on the horns of a dilemma.

Extrapolating from Galanter's (1989: 98–116) systems analysis of new religious movements, it seems likely, however, that the real danger sets in when a group fails to recruit new members. If no new members are coming into the community, for whatever reason (including the movement of the group to an isolated location or the segregation of the leader), then the dynamic and the grounds for sustaining charismatic authority may change in undesirable ways. If the leader's charisma cannot be demonstrated by successes in the external world, or by his or her ability to appeal to outsiders, then charisma may have to be displayed through prowess in the control and manipulation of existing members. Their willingness to submit to ever more severe sacrifices and demands becomes the evidence of charisma. But within a relatively small and encapsulated group, there are only so many demands that can be made before matters escalate to the point of physical injury and life and death. This is clearly what happened to the Peoples Temple in Jonestown. It may also apply to Aum Shinrikyô, Heaven's Gate, and the Movement for the Restoration of the Ten Commandments of God (see, e.g., Lifton 1999; Davis 2000; Sanders 2000).

In each of the groups that ultimately descended into violence, prophecies of impending apocalyptic tribulation and cosmic revolution received increased attention as the groups turned inward and became increasingly alienated from their social environments. Such prophecies were used to raise the stakes, in terms of both the messianic status of the charismatic leader and the sacrifices and other proofs of loyalty demanded of followers. The prophecies became a focal point for displaying charismatic prowess. This pattern can be clearly detected in the last years of the Peoples Temple, the Solar Temple, Aum Shinrikyô, and Heaven's Gate (Chidester 1988; Hall 2000; Hall and Schuyler 2000; Trinh and Hall 2000).

Since many (though maybe not all) charismatic leaders emerge in times of cultural and social crisis, for which they offer radical or countercultural solutions, there is an impetus to sustain their authority by perpetuating the sense of crisis. In other words, there is an even broader reason than resisting routinization for crisis-mongering, and an ideological agenda that incorporates prophecies of impending doom facilitates doing so. But millions of people worldwide subscribe to apocalyptic beliefs, and studies of new religious groups that have experienced the failure of such prophecies (Dawson 1999; Stone 2000) reveal that most of them continue to pursue their material and spiritual objectives peacefully. There is nothing intrinsically dangerous, in other words, about making such prophecies. But the response of the leader to these failures plays a key role in determining whether a group will, on balance, suffer more from the seeming failure of the prophecy or benefit from the mobilizing effect of the prophecy (Dawson 1999). Leaders who develop sufficient rationalizations of the seeming failures, and manage to communicate these rationalizations in a prompt, pervasive, and persuasive way, can neutralize the negative consequences in most cases. Where groups have failed and disintegrated after a failed prophecy (which is rare), it is largely because the charismatic leaders failed to do their part in guiding the recovery. A delayed or feeble response may delegitimate the leaders and then the group itself. In the case of the Movement for the Restoration of the Ten Commandments, it is widely speculated that the mass killings of the membership were precipitated by rebellious actions on the part of the membership against the charismatic leaders after the failure of their apocalyptic prophecies for the year 2000 (e.g., Sanders 2000). Newspaper accounts say that the leaders somehow managed to kill 1,000 or more of their followers over a three-month period because they did not want to return the money that people had contributed to the movement. Certainly the forensic evidence suggests that the killings began shortly after the failed prophecy, but it is more likely that they were perpetrated to protect the legitimacy of the charismatic leadership. Either the killings were done because the leadership had failed to cope adequately with the prophetic failure, or they have resulted from ritualistic killings and suicides in bizarre fulfillment of the prophecy (as with the Solar Temple and Heaven's Gate). Either way, the resulting violence is instrumentally linked to the escalating dynamics of legitimating charismatic authority.[3]

[3] Research carried out by students of behavioral organization suggests that the successful adaptation of charismatic authority depends on "(1) the development of an administrative apparatus that puts the charismatic's program into practice, (2) the transfer of charisma to others in the organization through rites and ceremonies, (3) the incorporation of the

In any event, the evidence from the other cases suggests that these charismatic leaders were moved to make predictions that they could no longer manage successfully or had no recourse to brutally fulfilling. Each found himself driven to a point of no return by his own rhetoric and then chose to force the hand of destiny, effecting the ultimate act of charismatic legitimation. This is most abundantly apparent with Shôkô Ashara, as he repeatedly foreshortened the date set for the end of the world and shifted from preparing to be attacked with poisonous gases to unleashing those gases on others to precipitate a third world war (Lifton 1999; Trinh and Hall 2000). In a different but equally deadly way, Do seems to have grown tired of the struggle to sustain his group and somewhat arbitrarily seized on the rumors of a space ship trailing the Hale–Bopp comet to complete his followers' long course of training in how to rise to the "Evolutionary Level Beyond Human." Recruitment to Heaven's Gate had reached a standstill. A reduced core of mainly long-time devotees was prepared and waiting, and since 1993 the apocalyptic pronouncement had been in place: "The earth's present 'civilization' is about to be recycled – spaded under. Its inhabitants are refusing to evolve. The 'weeds' have taken over the garden and disturbed its usefulness beyond repair" (Hoffman and Burke 1997: 179, 196). Transit to the Next Level through the controlled death of their physical "vehicles" had been discussed for several years. Do may well have realized that great resourcefulness and energy would be required to sustain the mythology of the group much longer.

Overall, the dangerous potential of the dynamic of escalating legitimacy crises is aggravated by the more pronounced legitimation problems of charismatic authority in the contemporary world. Outside their own groups, the new leaders lack the conditions of broader social support that have traditionally existed for religious prophets. In modern societies they "are forced to struggle against the endemic structural marginalization of their efforts by a society that neither understands nor respects the special deference granted to charismatic religious leaders" (Dawson 1998: 141). Consequently, the expression of charismatic authority within the group may become exaggerated in compensation for the ridicule suffered at the hands of the media and other public authorities. In addition, from the psychoanalytic perspective, it might be argued that the very denigration of the

charismatic's message and mission into organizational traditions, and (4) the selection of a successor who resembles the charismatic founder, with sufficient esteem to achieve the charismatic's level of personal influence" (Trice and Beyer 1986, cited in Bass 1988: 59).

ecstatic experiences of merger associated with the charismatic relationship may guarantee "that in modern circumstances charisma will take radical forms when it does appear" (Lindholm 1990: 61). What is repressed often returns in a convulsive and antisocial manner.

Concluding Remarks

The retreat of charismatic leaders into isolation to preserve their personas, the increased demands for fusion with the leader, the tactics used to resist routinization, and the need to demonstrate new successes all work to draw groups into a dangerous cycle of deviance amplification. Wittingly and unwittingly, these actions lead to a progressive intensification and aggrandizement of the leader's power, along with the increased homogenization and dependency of their followers, thereby setting the conditions for charismatic leaders to indulge the "darker desires of their subconscious" (a phrase used by Wallis and Bruce 1986, cited in Robbins and Anthony, 1995: 247). The radicalization of the groups, in turn, heightens the negative response of the surrounding society to them, and the public hostility fans the fears, anxiety, and paranoia of the devotees – a fear that the charismatic leaders share and exploit to further bolster their authority. If a group subscribes to an apocalyptic worldview, this view helps to justify and perpetuate the vicious cycle of fear, resistance, homogenization, domination, and social isolation. Faced with a crisis, such groups are far more likely to adopt violent solutions.

In the end, though, it is important to reiterate that charismatic leadership is not intrinsically dangerous. The cycle of deviance amplification need not happen. Some highly charismatic new religious leaders, like Sun Myung Moon (Unification Church) and Daisaku Ikeda (Soka Gakkai), seem to have found ways to cope successfully with the problem of perpetually legitimating their authority. They have built organizations that blend elements of Weber's "pure" and "office" types of charisma (Galanter 1989; Hammond and Machacek 1999). We need to learn more about how these hybrid forms of charismatic leadership were created and operate.[4] But we

[4] Since the first news accounts it has become clear that about 780 people died, with about 400 of these dying, perhaps by murder, before the final death by fire that attracted the attention of the world. It also seems likely that the group's final apocalyptic prediction was set for December 31, 2000, and not 1999, as reported. Yet we know that the leaders of the group had made numerous previous prophecies, so the logic of my argument remains intact. What precisely happened in the first months of 2000 remains unknown at this point.

must also remember that Jim Jones, Joe DiMambro, and Do managed the demands of their charismatic authority quite well for some time before things began to go fatally wrong.

References

Bass, Bernard M. "Evolving Perspectives on Charismatic Leadership." In *Charismatic Leadership: The Elusive Factor in Organizational Effectiveness*, edited by Jay A. Conger and Rabindra N. Kanungo. San Francisco: Jossey-Bass, 1988: 40–77.

Bromley, David G., and James T. Richardson (eds.). *The Brainwashing/Deprogramming Controversy: Sociological, Psychological, Legal and Historical Perspectives.* Lewiston, NY: Edwin Mellen Press, 1983.

Chidester, David. *Salvation and Suicide: An Interpretation of Jim Jones, the Peoples Temple, and Jonestown.* Bloomington: Indiana University Press, 1988.

Conger, Jay A., and Rabindra N. Kanungo. "Conclusion: Patterns and Trends in Studying Charismatic Leadership." In *Charismatic Leadership: The Elusive Factor in Organizational Effectiveness*, edited by Jay A. Conger and Rabindra N. Kanungo. San Francisco: Jossey-Bass, 1988: 324–336.

Davis, Winston. "Heaven's Gate: A Study of Religious Obedience." *Nova Religio* 3 (2000): 241–267.

Dawson, Lorne L. "When Prophecy Fails and Faith Persists: A Theoretical Overview." *Nova Religio* 3 (1999): 60–82.

Comprehending Cults: The Sociology of New Religious Movements. Toronto and New York: Oxford University Press, 1998.

Downton, James V. *Rebel Leadership: Commitment and Charisma in the Revolutionary Process.* New York: Free Press, 1973.

Freud, Sigmund. *Group Psychology and the Analysis of the Ego.* Translated and edited by James Strachey. New York: W. W. Norton, 1959.

Galanter, Marc. *Cults: Faith, Healing and Coercion.* New York: Oxford University Press, 1989.

Gardner, William L., and Bruce J. Avolio. "The Charismatic Relationship: A Dramaturgical Perspective." *The Academy of Management Review* 23 (1998): 32–58.

Goffman, Erving. *The Presentation of Self in Everyday Life.* Garden City, NY: Doubleday, 1959.

Hall, John R. "Finding Heaven's Gate." In *Apocalypse Observed: Religious Movements and Violence in North America, Europe, and Japan*, edited by John R. Hall, with Philip Schuyler and Sylvaine Trinh. New York: Routledge, 2000: 149–182.

Hall, John R., and Philip Schuyler. "The Mystical Apocalypse of the Solar Temple." In *Apocalypse Observed: Religious Movements and Violence in North America, Europe, and Japan*, edited by John R. Hall, with Philip Schuyler and Sylvaine Trinh. New York: Routledge, 2000: 111–148.

Hammond, Phillip, and David Machacek. *Soka Gakkai in America: Accommodation and Conversion*. New York: Oxford University Press, 1999.

Hoffman, Bill, and Cathy Burke. *Heaven's Gate: Cult Suicides in San Diego*. New York: Harper Paperbacks, 1997.

Johnson, Doyle P. "Dilemmas of Charismatic Leadership: The Case of the Peoples Temple." *Sociological Analysis* 40 (1979): 315–323.

Kets de Vries, Manfred F. R. "Origins of Charisma: Ties That Bind the Leader and the Led." In *Charismatic Leadership: The Elusive Factor in Organizational Effectiveness*, edited by Jay A. Conger and Rubindra N. Kanungo. San Francisco: Jossey-Bass, 1988: 237–252.

Lalich, Janja. "Bounded Choice: The Fusion of Personal Freedom and Self-Renunciation in Two Transcendent Groups." Ph.D. dissertation. Santa Barbara, CA: Fielding Institute, 2000.

Layton, Deborah. *Seductive Poison: A Jonestown Survivor's Story of Life and Death in the Peoples Temple*. New York: Anchor Books, 1998.

Lewis, James R. "Self-Fulfilling Stereotypes, the Anti-Cult Movement, and the Waco Confrontation." *Armageddon in Waco: Critical Perspectives on the Branch Davidian Conflict*, edited by Stuart Wright. Chicago: University of Chicago Press, 1995: 95–110.

Lifton, Robert J. *Destroying the World to Save It: Aum Shinrikyô, Apocalyptic Violence, and the New Global Terrorism*. New York: Henry Holt, 1999.

Lindholm, Charles. *Charisma*. Oxford: Basil Blackwell, 1990.

Maaga, Mary M. *Hearing the Voices of Jonestown*. Syracuse, NY: Syracuse University Press, 1998.

Madsen, Douglas, and Peter Snow. *The Charismatic Bond: Political Behavior in Time of Crisis*. Cambridge, MA: Harvard University Press, 1991.

Mayer, Jean-François. "'Our Terrestrial Journey Is Coming to an End': The Last Voyage of the Solar Temple." *Nova Religio* 2 (1999): 172–196.

Mills, Edgar W., Jr. "Cult Extremism: The Reduction of Normative Dissonance." In *Violence and Religious Commitment*, edited by Ken Levi. University Park: Pennsylvania State University Press, 1982: 75–87.

Oakes, Len. *Prophetic Charisma: The Psychology of Revolutionary Religious Personalities*. Syracuse, NY: Syracuse University Press, 1997.

Palmer, Susan J. "Purity and Danger in the Solar Temple." *Journal of Contemporary Religion* 11 (1996): 303–318.

Reader, Ian. *A Poisonous Cocktail? Aum Shinrikyô's Path to Violence*. Copenhagen: Nordic Institute of Asian Studies Books, 1996.

Robbins, Thomas, and Dick Anthony. "Sects and Violence: Factors Enhancing the Volatility of Marginal Religious Movements." In *Armageddon in Waco*, edited by Stuart Wright. Chicago: University of Chicago Press, 1995: 236–259.

Sanders, Richard. "Credonia's Cult of Death." *The Mail and Guardian*, May 22, 2000.

Shupe, Anson D., Jr., and David G. Bromley. "The Modern Anti-Cult Movement, 1971–1991: A Twenty Year Retrospective." In *The Anti-Cult Movements in Cross-Cultural Perspective*, edited by Anson D. Shupe, Jr., and David G. Bromley. New York: Garland, 1994: 3–31.

Stone, Jon R. *Expecting Armageddon: Essential Readings in Failed Prophecy*. New York: Routledge, 2000.

Tabor, James, and Eugene Gallagher. *Why Waco?* Berkeley: University of California Press, 1995.

Trice, Harrison M., and Janice M. Beyer. "Charisma and Its Routinization in Two Social Movement Organizations." *Research in Organizational Behavior* 8 (1986): 113–164.

Trinh, Sylvaine, and John Hall. "The Violent Path of Aum Shinrikyô." In *Apocalypse Observed: Religious Movements and Violence in North America, Europe, and Japan*, edited by John R. Hall, with philip Schuyler and Sylvanie Trinh. New York: Routledge, 2000: 76–110.

Wallis, Roy. "The Social Construction of Charisma." *Social Compass* 29 (1982): 25–39.

Wallis, Roy, and Steve Bruce. "Sex, Violence and Religion: Antinomianism and Charisma." In *Sociological Theory, Religion and Collective Action*, edited by Roy Wallis and Steve Bruce. Belfast, Northern Ireland: Queen's University Press, 1986: 115–127.

Weber, Max. *The Theory of Social and Economic Organization*, translated by A. M. Henderson and Talcott Parsons. New York: Free Press, 1964.

Willner, Ruth A. *The Spellbinders: Charismatic Political Leadership*. New Haven, CT: Yale University Press, 1984.

6

PUBLIC AGENCY INVOLVEMENT IN GOVERNMENT–RELIGIOUS MOVEMENT CONFRONTATIONS

STUART A. WRIGHT

The problem of collective religious violence is poorly understood, in part, because it is relatively rare. In the decade before the dawn of the new millennium, a cluster of incidents involving apocalyptic new religious movements captured the attention of scholars, government authorities, and the public. Four prominent cases of collective religious violence in the 1990s can be singled out: the Branch Davidian standoff near Waco in 1993; the Solar Temple mass suicides in Switzerland and Canada in 1994, 1995, and 1997; the Aum Shinrikyô sarin gas attacks and homicides in Japan in 1995; and the Heaven's Gate mass suicides in California in 1997. The question of pinpointing a common set of variables to explain violence among the few cases on record remains a formidable challenge to researchers. Clearly, the greatest obstacle to developing such a theory or model is that the circumstances and conditions are varied, making comparisons and generalizations difficult. The point can be illustrated through a brief overview.

Four Cases of Religious Violence

The Branch Davidian incident began as a government raid that triggered a shootout between the agents of the Bureau of Alcohol, Tobacco, and Firearms (BATF) and sect members on February 28, 1993. Four federal agents and six Branch Davidians died in the gunfire. The failed raid led to a fifty-one-day standoff in which the Federal Bureau of Investigation's (FBI's) Hostage Rescue Team conducted negotiations and applied tactical pressures to force the Davidians to surrender. On April 19, 1993, the FBI launched a dangerous CS gas insertion attack to force members out of the barricaded structure. At about noon, the settlement caught fire and burned to the ground, killing seventy-four men, women, and children. This conflagration was repeatedly referred to by government officials and the media as "a mass suicide," but subsequent research and congressional investigations cast serious doubts on that claim (Reavis 1995; Tabor and Gallagher 1995; Wright 1995, 1999; *Investigation into the Activities of Federal Law Enforcement Agencies Toward the Branch Davidians* 1996: 4). Subsequently, in a string of embarrassing revelations for the government, it was learned that the FBI misled the attorney general, Congress, and the American public about the use of incendiary devices on the final day of the assault – after six years of denial – and also withheld pertinent documents and audiotapes authorizing approval of the military rounds. Some concerns were also raised about government gunfire into the complex suggested in an infrared video made by a surveillance camera during an overflight of the Branch Davidian compound on April 19. In the wake of the new evidence, the attorney general appointed an independent counsel, former Senator John Danforth, to investigate the charges, and Congress announced that it would hold a new round of hearings. The Justice Department also faced a $675 million wrongful death suit filed by the families of the Davidians killed during the siege and standoff. The government prevailed in the civil case, but disturbing questions about the procedure of the trial, particularly the exclusion of evidence, the judge's broad interpretation of the "discretionary function" exemption for federal officials, and the narrow scope of the interrogatories given to the jury, raised doubts about the verdict. The Office of Special Counsel (OSC), headed by Danforth, later issued an interim report clearing the government of starting the fatal fire or shooting at sect members trying to escape. It also documented a number of government misdeeds, including missing or concealed evidence, FBI misstatements to the attorney general and Congress, the failure of government prosecutors to turn over exculpatory evidence in the 1994 Davidian criminal trial, and withholding evidence of pyrotechnic devices by a government attorney in the civil trial, among other things. While the verdict in the civil case and the findings of the OSC report point toward mass suicide, the issue remains contested.

The Aum Shinrikyô case involved unprovoked attacks by the religious group on Japanese citizens in the release of deadly sarin gas in the Tokyo subway in March 1995. Twelve people died in the assault and over 5,000 others eventually received medical treatment, including 68 policemen and 48 firemen. Injuries were reported in twenty different subway stations. The nation and the world were befuddled by the developments surrounding this new religious movement. Nothing in the traditions of Buddhism, Shintoism, yoga, or other eastern philosophies could account for this emergent ideology of violence. Asahara Shôkô, the founder of the movement, initially planned to build communal Lotus villages across Japan where devotees were expected to follow a strict regimen involving yoga, asceticism, fasting, and spiritual testing. Apparently, Asahara began to invoke strong apocalyptic themes in the early 1990s. While he initially believed that the collective spiritual energies harnessed by his disciples would prevent the impending crisis, he abandoned this idea and came to believe that violence could serve as a catalyst to determine who would survive the day of the Last Judgement (see Hall with Schuyler and Trinh 2000). Unlike the Branch Davidian incident, there was no government provocation instigating a crisis. This case is unique in the sense that it entails a planned attack on the part of the religious group designed to disrupt the social order and initiate an apocalyptic war.

The other two cases have the best potential for comparison, but even here there are important differences. The Solar Temple murder/suicides and the Heaven's Gate mass suicides involved religious movements that sought to reach a higher plane of human spiritual evolution through death. The Transit to another star or spaceship trailing a comet symbolized the apocalyptic impulse to abandon the corrupt social order. However, the Solar Temple incident entails a more complex set of circumstances involving confrontations with law enforcement authorities, including the arrest of Luc Jouret, the charismatic leader, in a government sting operation. Jouret would claim that he was set up by a coalition of apostates, an anticult organization (Info-Secte), and government authorities. In the final Transit, letters were mailed to journalists asserting the belief that the group was the target of a conspiracy. Jouret and his disciples came to construe their travails as a consequence of persecution, and they resolved the crisis in a way that affirmed their mystical powers, the secret doctrine of soul travel.

No such conflict with authorities can be found in the case of Heaven's Gate. Marshall Applewhite and Bonnie Nettles, known alternatively as Bo and Peep, Do and Ti, or collectively as "The Two," led a small nomadic group of devotees who believed the prophecies of the Book of Revelation foretelling an endtime devastation on earth. Applewhite invoked Revelation 11:4–15: "The two witnesses are the two olive trees and the two lamps that stand before the Lord of the Earth." In the Bible, the Two would hold immense powers to stop the rain and turn rivers to blood in the Last Days. The message of The Two was that the elect or chosen would escape the wrath of God during the apocalypse by being transported by space ship to the Next Evolutionary Kingdom. In preparation for the transport, Do and Ti advocated an extreme program of asceticism and self-purification. In the early 1990s, they began to get clear signals that their "classroom" time was over. The group put out a satellite television broadcast series entitled "Beyond Human – The Last Call" and invited viewers to contact them. In November 1996, the group apparently got the signal it had been waiting for. An "unexplainable anomaly" was found near the Hale–Bopp comet in a photograph posted on the Internet. At Do's behest, the group packed for their voyage to meet the spaceship. Each member had a suitcase, a birth certificate, passport, or driver's license, and even money. They ingested pudding laced with vodka and phenobarbital and apparently had plastic bags placed over their heads, probably by the last few members to follow the procedure. Thirty-nine bodies were found by police a few days later, neatly laying in their beds and fully dressed.

As is evident here, the cases feature as many differences as similarities. On the one hand, the incidents took place in different cultures, drew from elements of different religious traditions, and gained members from different social strata. The Solar Temple was comprised of French, Swiss, and French Canadian citizens. Aum Shinrikyô garnered members exclusively from Japanese society. The Davidians were a mix of American-born citizens, Australians, British, and Canadians (Wright 1995: 379–381). Heaven's Gate members were all native-born U.S. citizens. The Solar Temple invoked neo-Templar and Rosicrucian religious traditions. Aum Shinrikyô can best be described as an eclectic Buddhist movement drawing on various Asian traditions such as yoga, Shinto, and Tibetan Buddhism (Mullins 1997: 315). The Branch Davidians were a schismatic sect of Seventh-Day Adventism. Marshall Applewhite, the Heaven's Gate prophet, was the son of a Presbyterian minister who synthesized elements of Christian millennialism, New Age mysticism, and UFO beliefs. The Solar Temple and Aum Shinrikyô were successful in drawing members from the professional class. The Davidians were largely working-class and low-income persons, including a sizable proportion of minorities. Heaven's Gate members were a diverse mix of people, though most hailed from middle-class backgrounds.

Polarization

One way to make sense of these cases is to conceptualize the propensity toward collective religious violence as a product of polarization. "Polarization" refers to the production of a state that exhibits opposite or contrasting tendencies relative to a body or system. For our purposes, the opposing pulls or contrasting tendencies along a continuum represent different sources of social control at the poles – charismatic and rational-legal authority. In a dispute or conflict involving an apocalyptic religious movement and representatives of the state, the contrasting claims of authority are accentuated. The potential eruption of disputes into heightened conflict is always structurally present when charismatic authority is challenged because it underscores the fundamental differences in constructed realities and the concomitant moral prerogative to exercise social control. "Charismatic domination," Weber (1968: 24) stated, "means a rejection of all ties to any external order in favor of the exclusive glorification of the genuine mentality of the prophet or hero. Hence its attitude is revolutionary and transvalues everything; it makes a sovereign break with all traditional or rational norms; it is epitomized in the saying, 'It is written, but I say unto you.'" Charisma, by definition, is not institutional. The holders of charisma must stand outside of the institutional structures. Authority inheres in the charismatic leader by virtue of inspiration and vision, not rules, regulations, or laws. The charismatic prophet is the messenger of God, whose authority is above all human institutions and offices. The threat to charismatic authority by the state therefore invites some level of confrontation and sets in motion the dynamics of polarization.

Polarization does not necessarily lead to violence or tragedy. Indeed, polarization may be diverted in a number of ways: through accommodative responses and concessions, through third-party intervention – mediation, arbitration, negotiation; or through other forms of dispute settlement. Where accommodation is absent or ineffective, polarization increases in direct proportion to the degree that opposing parties believe that the conditions for preserving their core identity and collective existence are being subverted and that these conditions are intolerable. In Chapter 2 of this volume, Bromley has described the process of increased polarization occurring at three levels of dispute – Latent Tension, Nascent Conflict, Intensified Conflict – and a final phase of Dramatic Denouement. Each level graduates upward (or outward) on a calibrated scale of threat culminating in Dramatic Denouement, in which one or both parties undertake a "project of final reckoning under the aegis of transcendent values (the state ultimately invokes civil religion claims) to reverse their power positions and to restore what they avow to be appropriate moral order." The task of researchers then is to explain how polarization proceeds unabated to the straining point of Dramatic Denouement.

One of the most promising efforts to explain collective religious violence has been the work of Hall and colleagues (Hall 1987, 1995; Hall and

Schuyler, 1997, 1998; Hall, Schuyler, and Trinh 2000). In an analysis of the Peoples Temple over a decade ago, Hall argued that the mass suicides were triggered in part by a relentless campaign of organized opponents, a group called the Concerned Relatives, who were successful in mobilizing support among journalists and some government officials to implicate Jim Jones in criminal activity. The fatal trip to the Peoples Temple's communal settlement in Guyana by Congressman Leo Ryan and his entourage in 1978 represented a critical peril to the survival of Jim Jones's religious movement. In the face of a government investigation that threatened to dismantle the group, Jones led his followers in a ritual of mass suicide.

In a subsequent work, Hall (1995) conducted a comparative analysis of Jonestown and Mount Carmel by examining the constructed narratives of the groups' antagonists. He found that in both cases, the tragic endings were fueled by adversaries through increased levels of pressure and agitation. In the case of the Branch Davidians, he concluded that the sect's adversaries attempted to exploit the theme of mass suicide, which inadvertently heightened tensions and helped propel the standoff leading to the very end the authorities sought to avoid. A group of apostates, led by the determined Marc Breault, teamed up with anticult organizations, a deprogrammer, and news reporters to construct an exaggerated menace in the form of the vilified cult leader, David Koresh. This inflated threat not only fueled the overreaction by the BATF in planning the paramilitary assault on Mt. Carmel, it continued to influence the framing of the situation in the minds of FBI agents during the standoff. According to Hall, "The cultural opponents of David Koresh reinvoked and reworked narratives about mass suicide in ways that shaped the escalating trajectory of conflict at Mt. Carmel" (1995: 206).

Hall and Schuyler (1997, 1998) developed this model further by extending the comparative analysis to the Solar Temple. In similar fashion to the previous cases, apostates emerged to force an alliance of cultural opponents in an escalating conflict. The researchers found that a key Solar Temple apostate, Rose-Marie Klaus, became a dogged opponent of the group following her husband's sexual partnership with another woman in the group. When Rose-Marie complained to the leadership, she learned that they approved of the relationship and attempted to couple her with another man. Ms. Klaus became disenchanted and contacted an anticult organization in Montreal, Info-Secte. Together they began mobilizing efforts to expose the group as dangerous and fraudulent. According to Hall and Schuyler, "the apostate career of Rose-Marie Klaus soon became connected to a different chain of events in Canada" (1998: 161). Mounting adverse publicity fueled a schism in the group and impelled the Temple's leader, Luc Jouret, to depart with a loyal following and form a new organization. His key ally, Jean-Pierre Vinet, helped Jouret establish himself on the lecture circuit as a management guru. Vinet and Jouret recruited a Canadian businessman named Herman Delorme to become president of the new organization, and in November 1992 Vinet asked Delorme to supply him with a pistol and silencer for protection. At about the same time, the Quebec police received as anonymous call threatening to assassinate the minister of public security, Claude Ryan. The caller claimed to represent a subversive organization called Q-37, a reference to the number of Quebeckers who belonged to the Solar Temple. Investigators saw a possible connection between Q-37's threats and Delorme's interest in buying guns. A sting operation resulted in the arrests of Delorme, Vinet, and Jouret. The sensational media coverage surrounding the event destroyed Jouret's credibility on the lecture circuit as news stories regaled readers about the "cult involved in illegal arms trafficking." In the face of cultural delegitimation and dwindling financial resources, the group retreated further into a mystical apocalypse as a way of salvaging their own construction of collective honor and legitimacy.

In all three cases, Hall and Schuyler (1998: 167) write, "a loosely institutionalized cultural opposition . . . was central to the production of circumstances in which mass suicide came to be regarded as a viable course of action by the principals of the group." Thus, the authors conclude that "the most extreme cases of collective religious violence do not emerge from an intrinsic property of the groups themselves" but rather as "conflicts *between* utopian religious movements, on the one hand, and on the other, ideological proponents of the social order, seeking to control 'cults' through loosely institutionalized, emergent oppositional alliances" (142). These alliances include (1) apostates and distraught relatives of members, (2) news reporters who frame cult stories as moral deviance, and (3) modern governments that have incorporated the religious interest in enforcing cultural legitimacy into a state interest in monopolizing political legitimacy.

This model is pertinent to an inquiry into the relation between religious violence and the state, the focus of this chapter. Without question, modern governments have taken an increased interest in new religious movements (NRMs) with apocalyptic beliefs in the wake of recent episodes of collective violence. It is a cruel irony that in some of the most extreme cases, the state fostered conditions leading to tragic outcomes by becoming aligned with the cultural opponents of NRMs. The three cases cited provide strong support for the model. But the model appears to be less predictive in two other high-profile cases of collective violence, Aum Shinrikyô and Heaven's Gate, as well as in the second and third clusters of the Solar Temple suicides.[1] In a forthcoming work by Hall, Schuyler, and Trin, the researchers attempt to develop a second independent variable to account for the anomalies: the cultural logic of "mystical apocalyptic death." This cultural logic may be formulated in two different ways. In the first formulation, the warring apocalyptic sect is engaged in a struggle against the forces of evil that becomes tantamount to the apocalypse enacted. Essentially, the perceived maelstrom of wickedness and calamity in society compels a warriorlike response from the sect to preserve the faith or defend the elect. In the second formulation, the mystical idea of transcendence through death invokes an apocalyptic motif of passage or flight from this world, one that achieves otherworldly grace through the ritualized practice of collective suicide.

Scholars of new religions may find the introduction of a second independent variable by Hall et al. less than satisfactory for several reasons. First, it appears that what the researchers really offer us is two distinct models, not a single integrated model or theory. There is nothing to tie together the two separate causes of collective religious violence; each operates autonomously. A second criticism is that the crucial insights provided by the oppositional alliance model may be overshadowed by or subsumed under the mystical apocalyptic death thesis, especially by hardline anticultists, who will likely argue that alliances of cultural opponents and the state are duly justified in order to prevent future incidents of collective religious violence. In turn, they will maintain the dubious contention that incidents such as Waco were tragic but necessary interventions by the state since the Davidians were determined to commit acts of violence anyway.

The second criticism may be difficult to avoid despite the best efforts of scholars. But with regard to the first point, I contend that a single inclusive model of collective religious violence may be forged if we reconfigure the problem in terms of polarization. The mystical apocalyptic death thesis

---

[1] Sixteen members of the Solar Temple committed suicide on the winter solstice of 1995 in a wooded area near the Swiss border, and five others died in a ritual suicide outside Quebec around the time of the spring equinox of 1997. In neither of these cases was there any confrontation with the state.

speaks to the fact that a religious movement may engineer its own path of disengagement and radicalization even when cultural opposition is minimal. The polarization model already allows for the possibility that a world-rejecting orientation initiated by the sect may lead to intensified cultural antagonism, malaise, and eventual destabilization. As Bromley has already noted, the rituals and actions of the apocalyptic movement can function to increase the holy struggle against the morally corrupt world. Contextualized in the situated meanings of these subcultures, these rituals and actions can be understood as holy rebellions in which the group attempts to seize the moral high ground, invoking divine authorization for their sacrosanct mission. To the extent that the self-imposed polarization proceeds unabated and reaches a point at which members come to believe that their core identity and collective existence *are being subverted* and that the circumstances are intolerable (darkness and wickedness abound), a project of final reckoning is launched.

The centrifugal force operating in the polarization model is the claim of subversion. Apocalyptic sects typically envisage a plan or plot of subversion carried out by forces of darkness. They come to believe that society is spiraling downward toward the ultimate end of self-destruction. Even in the absence of direct actions taken by the state against the sect, otherwise unrelated activities or policies may be assigned nefarious motives. Political leaders and civic authorities are thought to be mere pawns of Satan or the Antichrist, who is masterminding the devious ruination of humankind. The orchestration of these events is the result of a conspiratorial plot. The seditious scheme extends to the very borders of the elect community who know the "truth." The embattled sect represents only a remnant of God's chosen who will not forsake him. It is just a matter of time before the threatened group faces confrontation and possible extinction. Dramatic action is called for; true believers must be willing to fight and die for the faith, to be martyrs. Their salvation is predicated on the ultimate test of faith, the final battle of Armageddon.

We may conclude then that while the state can play a critical role in exacerbating the trajectory of conflict leading to collective religious violence, such episodes do not require actions by the state. On the other hand, it should be of considerable concern when cultural opponents are successful in recruiting government agents in campaigns to assail apocalyptic religious movements. With the state's monopoly on the legitimate use of force and its expansive power to regulate social life, minority religions are often at the mercy of the state's social control agents. An overwhelming show of force, or a threat of force, can induce acts of violence in apocalyptic groups who may see the state as playing out the prophetically scripted role of the Antichrist or some other symbolic oppressor. Since the focus of this chapter is the role of the state in religious collective violence, let me return to this aspect of the analysis.

Consistent with the polarization model, the ideological bridge connecting cultural opponents with the state, giving the two parties a common discourse and purpose, is also predicated on the claim of subversion. In evaluating cases of collective religious violence involving the state, Hall and Schuyler contend that NRM opponents were most successful when they framed the movement as a threat to the social order, emphasizing subversion themes. "If the opponents succeed in mobilizing agents of established social institutions (in our era, the mass media, politicians, and the state) to frame the movement as a threat to the established order, these agents may take actions intended to discredit the movement in the public eye, or subject it to actions and policies that undermine its capacity to exist as an autonomous organization" (Hall and Schuyler 1998: 143). Subversion themes, then, play to the receptivity of government officials to promote the cultural legitimacy of established institutions and to paint nontraditional challenges as a threat to the social order.

Bromley (1998) has suggested that NRMs tend to be labeled subversive organizations because they have low coincidence of interests with other organizations in their environment. Organizations labeled subversive are confronted with a broad coalition of opponents, face high levels of tension with mainstream society, and are accorded virtually no organizational or cultural legitimacy. As such, they have few allies. Consequently, claims against these organizations are easily marshaled, making them easy targets of social control. Moreover, dispute settlement processes may come to be controlled largely by oppositional coalitions. Because organizations defined as subversive are viewed as particularly dangerous, social control agencies are granted expanded powers. Indeed, if the situation can be defined as a crisis, then civil liberties protecting religious minorities can easily be trumped. When allegations or claims of threat arise, these organizations are less likely to be afforded deference. "Instead, the (suspect) organization is likely to be confronted with unilateral, pre-emptive, coercive control measures such as covert surveillance, planting of undercover agents, or even instigation of provocative incidents by agent provocateurs" (Bromley 1998: 24). Control of the dispute settlement apparatus by the oppositional coalition ensures powerful influence over the definition of alleged wrongdoings and information collected during investigation and prosecution of the stigmatized group.

From the perspective of cultural opponents, subversive organizations embody quintessential evil and are believed to pose a maximum degree of threat to the social order. Bromley (1998: 24) contends that a "countersubversion ideology" is constructed to justify expanded control over such groups, which follows a familiar pattern. First, subversive organizations are formed secret in order to orchestrate a conspiracy, which is seen as growing rapidly. Second, these organizations are based on principles and pursue goals that subvert the legitimate social order. Third, they are portrayed as having gained control over some segment of the conventional social order that serves as a base of operations. And fourth, the subversive organization possesses a unique power that is destructive to the integrity of normal individuals and social groups. This power is said to be capable of diminishing individual autonomy and collective loyalty while inhibiting the capacity for resistance. "Claimsmaking is thus cast in terms of manipulation, coercion, or even captivity at the hands of subversive agents. This countersubversion ideology becomes the working basis for the exercise of social control" (24).

The countersubversion theory clearly helps to explain how NRMs become targets of state control. However, what is most striking about confrontations between NRMs and the state is how *rarely* they culminate in collective religious violence. In what is still a preliminary effort, I have identified over 130 cases in the 1990s that qualified as confrontations between NRMs and the state (see Table 1).[2] The table presents a list of these confrontations, including the name of the group, the type of confrontation, the place of confrontation, and the year it took place. The data show that only three of the cases involving the state resulted in collective religious violence.[3] What is certain at this point is that there are a number of cases to be added to this list, none of which, to my knowledge, involve violence. So, the final number of cases ending in collective violence should amount to an even smaller fraction of state–sect confrontations. To illustrate my point, the German Enquiry Commission set up in 1996 to investigate so-called sects and psycho-cults named 800 dangerous groups in their initial report.

---

[2] "Dramatic confrontation" is defined operationally as government-imposed actions that threaten the cultural legitimacy of the religious movement.

[3] While the Solar Temple mass suicides/homicides occurred in three separate incidents over time, they are defined as a single case in this study.

Table 1. *Confrontations between NRMs and the State in the 1990s*

Group	Type of Confrontation	Place	Year
Ananda Marga	Listed as "dangerous" by gov't commission	Belgium	1997
Aum Shinrikyô[a]	Gov't raid, arrests	Japan	1995
Bahai	Defined as "enemies of the state"	Greece	1993
Bahai	Gov't raid, arrests	Iran	1998
Bahai	Listed as "dangerous" by gov't commission	France	1996
Bahai	Listed as "dangerous" by gov't commission	Germany	1997
Bahai	Listed as "dangerous" by gov't commission	Belgium	1997
Boston Church of Christ	Listed as "dangerous" by gov't commission	France	1996
Boston Church of Christ	Listed as "dangerous" by gov't commission	Belgium	1997
Brahma Kumaris	Defined as "enemies of the state"	Greece	1993
Brahma Kumaris	Listed as "dangerous" by gov't commission	France	1996
Branch Davidians[a]	Gov't siege; standoff	U.S.	1993
Calvary Christian Center	Listed as "dangerous" by gov't commission	France	1996
Calvary Christian Center	Listed as "dangerous" by gov't commission	Belgium	1997
Capital Worship Center	Listed as "dangerous" by gov't commission	Belgium	1997
Celestian Church of Christ	Listed as "dangerous" by gov't commission	France	1996
Celestian Church of Christ	Listed as "dangerous" by gov't commission	Belgium	1997
Center for Tibetan Studies	Defined as "enemies of the state"	Greece	1993
Charity's Daughters	Deportation	Greece	1993
Christadelphians	Defined as "enemies of the state"	Greece	1993
Christ Agape-Love Movement	Defined as "enemies of the state"	Greece	1993
Church of God Prophecy	Defined as "enemies of the state"	Greece	1993
Church Universal & Triumphant	Listed as "dangerous" by gov't commission	France	1996
Church Universal & Triumphant	Listed as "dangerous" by gov't commission	Belgium	1997
Concerned Christians	Gov't raid, deportation	Israel	1999
Concerned Christians	Deportation	Greece	1999
Deva-Light	Listed as "dangerous" by gov't commission	France	1996
Deva-Light	Listed as "dangerous" by gov't commission	Belgium	1997
Dynaris Institute	Listed as "dangerous" by gov't commission	Belgium	1997
Elijah Mohammed Foundation	Listed as "dangerous" by gov't commission	France	1996
EMIN Foundation	Listed as "dangerous" by gov't commission	Belgium	1997
The Family	Defined as "enemies of the state"	Greece	1993
The Family	Gov't raid, arrests, children held in custody	Spain	1990
The Family	Gov't raid, arrests, children held in custody	Australia	1992
The Family	Gov't raid, arrests, children held in custody	France	1993
The Family	Gov't raid, arrests, children held in custody	Argentina	1993
Falun Gong	Gov't ban, arrests, show trials, members sent to labor camps for reeducation	China	1999
Fellowship Friends Rennaissance	Listed as "dangerous" by gov't commission	France	1996
Fellowship Friends Rennaissance	Listed as "dangerous" by gov't commission	Belgium	1997
Friends of Edo	Listed as "dangerous" by gov't commission	France	1996

(continued)

Table 1. *(continued)*

Group	Type of Confrontation	Place	Year
Friends of Edo	Listed as "dangerous" by gov't commission	Belgium	1997
God's River Ministries	Listed as "dangerous" by gov't commission	France	1996
God's River Ministries	Listed as "dangerous" by gov't commission	Belgium	1997
Harmonious Life	Defined as "enemies of the state"	Greece	1993
Hasidic Jews	Listed as "dangerous" by gov't commission	France	1996
Ho-no-Hana Sampoygo	Gov't raids	Japan	1999
House of Prayer	Gov't raid, arrests, deportation	Israel	1999
Humana	Listed as "dangerous" by gov't commission	Belgium	1997
I AM (Vahali)	Listed as "dangerous" by gov't commission	France	1996
Insight Benelux	Listed as "dangerous" by gov't commission	Belgium	1997
Ishtar	Listed as "dangerous" by gov't commission	France	1996
Ishtar	Listed as "dangerous" by gov't commission	Belgium	1997
ISKCON	Defined as "enemies of the state"	Greece	1993
ISCKON	Listed as "dangerous" by gov't commission	France	1996
ISKCON	Listed as "dangerous" by gov't commission	Germany	1997
ISKCON	Listed as "dangerous" by gov't commission	Belgium	1997
Jain Association	Listed as "dangerous" by gov't commission	France	1996
Jain Association	Listed as "dangerous" by gov't commission	Belgium	1997
Jehovah's Witnesses	Removal of religious exemption from taxation	France	1995
Jehovah's Witnesses	Listed as "dangerous" by gov't commission	Germany	1997
Jehovah's Witnesses	Listed as "dangerous" by gov't commission	Belgium	1997
Jehovah's Witnesses	Arrests, imprisonment	Greece	1990
Jehovah's Witnesses	Arrests, imprisonment for proselytization	Greece	1993
Jiddu Krisna Murti	Listed as "dangerous" by gov't commission	Belgium	1997
Justus Freemen	Standoff	U.S.	1996
Kripalu Yoga	Listed as "dangerous" by gov't commission	Belgium	1997
Landmark Education	Listed as "dangerous" by gov't commission	France	1996
Landmark Education	Listed as "dangerous" by gov't commission	Belgium	1997
Mormons	Listed as "dangerous" by gov't commission	Germany	1997
Mormons	Listed as "dangerous" by gov't commission	France	1996
Mormons	Listed as "dangerous" by gov't commission	Belgium	1997
Mormons	Defined as "enemies of the state"	Greece	1993
New Acropolis	Defined as "enemies of the state"	Greece	1993
Omakeion	Defined as "enemies of the state"	Greece	1993
Open Christianity	Court-ordered shutdown of school; standoff	Russia	1999
Opus Dei	Listed as "dangerous" by gov't commission	France	1996
Pilgrim House Community	Arrests, deportation	Israel	1999
Quakers	Listed as "dangerous" by gov't commission	France	1996
Quakers	Listed as "dangerous" by gov't commission	Belgium	1997
Raelians	Listed as "dangerous" by gov't commission	France	1996
Raelians	Listed as "dangerous" by gov't commission	Belgium	1997
Radha Soami Satsang Beas	Defined as "enemies of the state"	Greece	1993
The Rose Croix d'Or	Listed as "dangerous" by gov't commission	France	1996

Table 1. *(continued)*

Group	Type of Confrontation	Place	Year
Sahaja Yoga	Listed as "dangerous" by gov't commission	France	1996
Sahaja Yoga	Listed as "dangerous" by gov't commission	Belgium	1997
Salvation Army	Gov't restrictions; leases withdrawn	Russia	1998
Sathya Sai Baba	Listed as "dangerous" by gov't commission	Belgium	1997
Saty Anandashram	Defined as "enemies of the state"	Greece	1993
Self-Realization Fellowship	Listed as "dangerous" by gov't commission	France	1996
Self-Realization Fellowship	Listed as "dangerous" by gov't commission	Belgium	1997
Servanta	Listed as "dangerous" by gov't commission	Belgium	1997
Seventh-Day Adventists	Defined as "enemies of the state"	Greece	1993
Seventh-Day Adventists	Gov't restrictions; defined as "dangerous"	France	1996
Seventh-Day Adventists	Gov't restrictions; defined as "dangerous"	Germany	1997
Seventh-Day Adventists	Gov't restrictions; defined as "dangerous"	Belgium	1997
Scientology	Gov't restrictions; defined as "dangerous"	France	1996
Scientology	Gov't restrictions; defined as "dangerous"	Belgium	1997
Scientology	Gov't raid	Belgium	1999
Scientology	Gov't restrictions; put under surveillance	Germany	1997
Scientology	Defined as "enemies of the state"	Greece	1993
Shri Ram Chandra Mission	Listed as "dangerous" by gov't commission	France	1996
Shri Ram Chandra Mission	Listed as "dangerous" by gov't commission	Belgium	1997
Siddha Shiva Yoga	Listed as "dangerous" by gov't commission	France	1996
Siddha Shiva Yoga	Listed as "dangerous" by gov't commission	Belgium	1997
Silva Mind Control	Defined as "enemies of the state"	Greece	1993
Soka Gakkai	Listed as "dangerous" by gov't commission	France	1996
Soka Gakkai	Listed as "dangerous" by gov't commission	Germany	1997
Soka Gakkai	Listed as "dangerous" by gov't commission	Belgium	1997
Solar Temple[a]	Arrests	Canada	1993
Solomon's Temple	Gov't raid, arrests, deportation	Israel	1999
Tai Chi	Listed as "dangerous" by gov't commission	France	1996
Tai Chi	Listed as "dangerous" by gov't commission	Belgium	1997
Tao Yoga	Listed as "dangerous" by gov't commission	France	1996
Tao Yoga	Listed as "dangerous" by gov't commission	Belgium	1997
Theosophy	Defined as "enemies of the state"	Greece	1993
Tradition Famille Propriete	Listed as "dangerous" by gov't commission	France	1996
Unification Church	Listed as "dangerous" by gov't commission	France	1996
Unification Church	Listed as "dangerous" by gov't commission	Germany	1997
Unification Church	Listed as "dangerous" by gov't commission	Belgium	1997
Unity Church	Defined as "enemies of the state"	Greece	1993
Wicca	Defined as "enemies of the state"	Greece	1993
Wicca	Listed as "dangerous" by gov't commission	France	1996
Wicca	Listed as "dangerous" by gov't commission	Germany	1997
Wicca	Listed as "dangerous" by gov't commission	Belgium	1997

(continued)

Table 1. *(continued)*

Group	Type of Confrontation	Place	Year
Worldwide Church of God	Listed as "dangerous" by gov't commission	France	1996
Worldwide Church of God	Listed as "dangerous" by gov't commission	Germany	1997
Worldwide Church of God	Listed as "dangerous" by gov't commission	Belgium	1997
World Fed. for Spiritual Healing	Listed as "dangerous" by gov't commission	France	1996
World Fed. for Spiritual Healing	Listed as "dangerous" by gov't commission	Belgium	1997
YWCA	Listed as "dangerous" by gov't commission	Belgium	1997
Zhong Gong	Offices closed down by gov't	China	1999
Zida Yoga	Listed as "dangerous" by gov't commission	Belgium	1997

[a] Involved or culminated in collective violence.

Minimizing Violence: The Role of Intermediate Groups

Given these data, we might ask why more violent confrontations don't erupt. In other words, perhaps researchers have been asking the wrong question. Turning the issue on its head, it may be argued that it is the overwhelming number, or pattern, of incidents that do not end violently that need to be explained. In this regard, efforts should focus on the development of moderating or mitigating factors in inhibiting violence, particularly the troubling pattern of state collaborations with cultural opponents. One line of inquiry that might prove fruitful is the extent to which NRMs have learned to forge alliances with *intermediate groups* – human rights organizations, civil liberties groups, ecumenical organizations, scholars, and others – to deflect overly aggressive state actions. For example, the influence of such groups exerted in the wake of some of the European parliamentary and other official reports generated after the Solar Temple incidents appears to have made a significant difference.

The early parliamentary reports – what Introvigne (1999) calls "Type I reports" – revealed the extent of alliances between anticult organizations and agents of the state, parroting claims of brainwashing and mind control, the destruction of free will, and inflated allegations of public threat. The oppositional coalitions, which were aided by key anticult leaders from the United States, were successful in controlling the composition of the commissions and the flow of information determining the tenor of the reports. However, the findings presented in the early reports evoked a wave of criticism from human rights groups, interfaith organizations, and European and U.S. scholars, as well as the U.S. State Department. The United Nations Human Rights Committee issued a censure of Germany, and U.S. State Department officials roundly condemned violations of religious rights in Europe. These protests and public sanctions apparently served to produce a more tempered approach in what Introvigne has called the "Type II reports." The general conclusions of the Type II reports were summarized by Introvigne (1999: 4) as follows:

1. Terms like "cult," "sect," and "religion" are extremely difficult to define, and it may not be the province of a secular state to make such an effort.
2. Although there is a concern that some NRMs may exert excessive psychological pressures on members, there is no agreement among scholars about the definition of brainwashing or mind control, and most scholars simply deny their very existence.
3. Militant ex-members are not the only reliable source of information about the groups they have left. Those who report positive experiences should also be heard.
4. Private anticult organizations may perform a legitimate function, but governments should not support them to the point of "cooperating in spreading prejudices."

The more tempered and scientifically supported conclusions of the Type II reports reflect the intervening influences of intermediate groups. The importance of the intermediate groups in defusing the sensationalistic subversion rhetoric of the earlier parliamentary reports should not be understated. It is entirely possible that, if left unchallenged, European governments might have adopted countersubversion narratives leading to more repressive measures deployed against a wide array of NRMs to combat the moral panic arising in the wake of the Solar Temple suicides/homicides. The heightened efforts of social control of apocalyptic religious movements would certainly have given legitimation to aggressive state actions such as police raids and sweeps to quell the seditious threats allegedly posed by so-called dangerous sects. In turn, the likelihood that the use of high-risk, deadly force would result in violent provocation of the targeted groups would also have increased, consistent with the model developed by Hall and colleagues.

Returning to the list of confrontations recorded in Table 1, the paucity of incidents ending in collective religious violence may be viewed as a consequence of the intervening influences of intermediate groups. This is clearly the case in the attempts by parliamentary commissions to blacklist NRMs in Belgium, France, and Germany, which were ultimately unsuccessful. The subversion frames failed to triumph, and therefore the potential escalation of violence arising from implementation of state-sponsored counterterrorism tactics of social control was avoided.

In this regard, we may hypothesize that intermediate groups serve two functions in reducing the risk of NRM violence. First, when intermediate groups counteract the control of information by cultural opponents, this will likely have the effect of *preempting* unwarranted, aggressive state actions that could lead to violence. Second, to the degree that NRMs enjoy institutional allies in disputes or conflicts, NRMs will likely exhibit more confidence in the ability of governments to settle them peacefully and justly, even after an aggressive state action has taken place. Hypothetically, even in the face of a government raid, if the NRM believes it has institutional allies that can become involved in the dispute settlement process, then the state's action is less likely to be met with a violent response. Essentially, group members are less likely to believe they might have to defend themselves in an armed confrontation or standoff with hostile authorities. The social order will appear less corrupt to marginalized movements when intermediate groups intercept and deflect prejudicial attitudes, reduce polarization of ideological camps, and promote tolerance of unconventional beliefs. On the other hand, the countersubversion ideology advocated by cultural opponents deepens the anxieties of targeted groups and only serves to exacerbate sectarian alienation and isolation. When cultural opponents are successful in forging alliances with state agents, the threat of state action becomes imminently more dangerous, fueling a self-fulfilling prophecy, as was evident in Waco.

A model illustrating an optimal risk of state–sect violence is shown in Figure 1. This model outlines the flow of information based on the countersubversion narrative flowing directly to state agents and the media, unabated by any input from intermediate groups. As the oppositional alliances are formed, the likelihood of paramilitary or tactical force being used is increased. The exaggerated claims made against the suspect groups are circulated by sympathetic media allies, which provides a public base of support for aggressive actions. The intermediate groups are circumvented in the framing and construction of the problem, precluding the opportunity to counter claimsmaking activities by cultural opponents. Intermediate groups may appear impotent to NRMs by virtue of their exclusion or ostensible silence. Where the lines of communication between NRMs

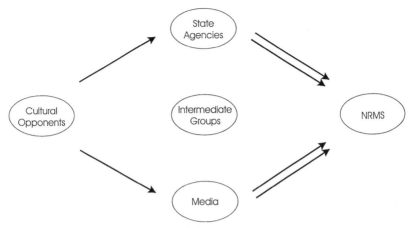

Figure 1. Optimal risk of state–sect violence.

and intermediate groups are weakest, antinomian tendencies of apocalyptic groups are probably highest and, hence, vulnerability to oppositional claims is greatest. While state agencies that exclude intermediate groups will risk the public appearance of "cooperating in spreading prejudices," often such images fail to seriously challenge official explanations or accounts by law enforcement agencies. If NRMs are sufficiently stigmatized, the public is not likely to believe the rantings of a "doomsday cult" over the police. NRM leaders may anticipate this lack of credibility ("no one will believe us") and opt for confrontation, martyrdom, or the "nobler death" of suicide (Droge and Tabor 1992) over captivity and persecution. This model is applicable to widely publicized cases of collective religious violence such as the Peoples Temple, the Branch Davidians, and the first wave of Solar Temple suicides/homicides.

In Figure 2, a model of minimal risk of state–sect violence is depicted. Here the flow of communication incorporates input by intermediate groups, giving authorities a more balanced view of NRMs, which serves to inhibit coalitions of cultural opponents and the subsequent development of a countersubversion ideology that fosters more aggressive state actions. At the same time, the flow of communication between NRMs and intermediate groups conveys the notion that religious pluralism and diversity are normative, reassuring the sect that they will get a fair hearing in the dispute settlement process. Institutionalized means of conflict resolution offer acceptable venues of redress. This model includes counterbalancing narratives and fact-finding. It is also more democratic, recognizing the pluralistic

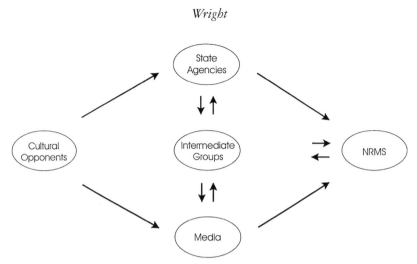

Figure 2. Minimal risk of state–sect violence.

nature of religious claims and the constitutional/human rights protections afforded minority religions. Ideological polarization is curbed, deviance amplification is constrained, and fearful overreaction of authorities is less likely to occur.

Conclusion

Most modern industrial nations are characterized by increasing cultural and structural pluralism. Most have constitutional safeguards that are designed to protect diverse religious beliefs and traditions, prohibiting discrimination while promoting tolerance and equal protection. There is no single authority or structure that can presume to embody the religious or spiritual life of pluralistic societies, though claims of orthodox privilege from established churches have been made. Many different religious movements, groups, and organizations coexist and pursue relatively autonomous courses. To the extent that many new religions have learned how to flourish in a climate of pluralism and tolerance by forging their own alliances with intermediate groups, oppositional forces have been restrained. Certainly there are a number of other examples, not discussed previously, that could be cited, including those involving The Family (Bainbridge 1997: 236–237; Richardson 1998, 1999), the Church Universal and Triumphant (Lewis and Melton 1994), and the Montana Freemen (Rosenfeld 1997).

Intermediate groups can play a significant role in avoiding or minimizing violence in sect–state confrontations. But a number of obstacles may prevent the effective utilization of such groups as resources. First, cultural opponents may promote their own "experts," leading authorities to adopt an inflated perception of threat. Authorities may not be aware of the extensive body of empirical and historical research on alternative religions or the community of scholars who study them. Second, law enforcement personnel may harbor their own biases. Nancy Ammerman, who was asked by the Justice Department to review the FBI's actions at Waco, found that some of the agents at Waco held deeply religious beliefs that "made it difficult for them to identify with someone [Koresh] whose faith was so different.... [T]hey could only see his group as heretical or perhaps as a 'cult' "(1995: 285). Finally, there is evidence to suggest that some federal agencies, or at least personnel within these agencies, may be disinclined to work with experts who have been critical of their actions in previous cases such as that of the Branch Davidians. This amounts to a gatekeeping function designed to protect an agency's public image and an attempt to control public perceptions of the agency's performance. It is important to keep these potential impediments in mind when considering the effectiveness of intermediate groups in curbing religious violence.

References

Ammerman, Nancy. "Waco, Federal Law Enforcement, and Scholars of Religion." In *Armageddon in Waco*, edited by Stuart A. Wright. Chicago: University of Chicago Press, 1995: 282–298.

Bainbridge, William Sims. *The Sociology of Religious Movements*. New York: Routledge, 1997.

Bromley, David G. "The Social Construction of Contested Exit Roles: Defectors, Whistleblowers and Apostates." In *The Politics of Religious Apostasy,* edited by David G. Bromley. Westport, CT: Praeger, 1998: 19–48.

Droge, Arthur J., and James D. Tabor. *A Noble Death: Suicide and Martyrdom Among Christians and Jews in Ancient Antiquity*. New York: HarperCollins, 1992.

Hall, John R. "Public Narratives and the Apocalyptic Sect: From Jonestown to Mt. Carmel." In *Armageddon in Waco: Critical Perspectives on the Branch Davidian Conflict*, edited by Stuart A. Wright. Chicago: University of Chicago Press, 1995: 205–235.

Gone From the Promised Land. New Brunswick, NJ: Transaction, 1987.

Hall, John R., and Philip Schuyler. "Apostasy, Apocalypse, and Religious Violence: An Explanatory Comparison of People's Temple, the Branch Davidians, and the Solar Temple." In *The Politics of Religious Apostasy*, edited by David G. Bromley. Westport, CT: Praeger, 1998: 141–170.

and Philip Schuyler. "The Mystical Apocalypse of the Solar Temple." In *Millennium, Messiahs, and Mayhem: Contemporary Apocalyptic Movements*, edited by Thomas Robbins and Susan J. Palmer. New York: Routledge, 1997: 285–312.

Hall, John R., with Philip Schuyler and Sylvaine Trinh (eds.). *Apocalypse Observed: Religious Movements, the Social Order, and Violence in North America, Europe and Japan*. New York: Routledge, 2000.

Introvigne, Massimo. "Misinformation, Religious Minorities and Religious Pluralism." Statement to the Organization for the Security and Cooperation in Europe (OSCE), Supplementary Meeting on Freedom of Religion, Vienna, March 22. 1999.

Investigation into the Activities of Federal Law Enforcement Agencies toward the Branch Davidians, Thirteenth Report by the Committee of Government Reform and Oversight Prepared in Conjunction with the Committee of the Judiciary, August 2, 1996. Washington, DC: U.S. Government Printing Office.

Lewis, James R., and J. Gordon Melton. *Church Universal and Triumphant in Scholarly Perspective*. Stanford, CA: Center for Academic Publishing, 1994.

Mullins, Mark R. "Aum Shinrikyô as an Apocalyptic Movement." In *Millennium, Messiahs, and Mayhem: Contemporary Apocalyptic Movements*, edited by Thomas Robbins and Susan J. Palmer. New York: Routledge, 1997: 313–324.

Reavis, Dick. *The Ashes of Waco: An Investigation*. Syracuse, NY: Syracuse University Press, 1995.

Richardson, James T. "Social Control of New Religions: From Brainwashing Claims to Child Sex Abuse Accusations." In *Children in New Religions*, edited by Susan J. Palmer. New Brunswick, NJ: Rutgers University. 1999:

"Apostates, Whistleblowers, Law, and Social Control." In *The Politics of Religious Apostasy*, edited by David G. Bromley. Westport, CT: Praeger, 1998: 171–189.

Rosenfeld, Jean E. "The Importance of the Analysis of Religion in Avoiding Violent Outcomes: The Justus Freemen Crisis." *Novo Religio* 1 (1997): 72–95.

Tabor, James D., and Eugene V. Gallagher. *Why Waco?: Cults and the Battle for Religious Freedom in America*. Berkeley: University of California Press, 1995.

Weber, Max. *Max Weber on Charisma and Institution Building*, edited by S. N. Eisenstadt. Chicago: University of Chicago Press, 1968.

Wright, Stuart A. "Anatomy of a Government Massacre: Abuses of Hostage-Barricade Protocols during the Waco Standoff." *Journal of Terrorism and Political Violence* 11 (1999): 39–68.

Armageddon in Waco: Critical Perspectives on the Branch Davidian Conflict. Chicago: University of Chicago Press, 1995.

7

WATCHING FOR VIOLENCE:
A COMPARATIVE ANALYSIS
OF THE ROLES OF FIVE TYPES
OF CULT-WATCHING GROUPS

EILEEN BARKER

Cults and violence are commonly bound inextricably together in the public mind. There have, after all, been some horrifying testimonies to their connection in the recent past: the murders and mass suicide of Jim Jones's Peoples Temple and the Solar Temple; the terrifying siege at Waco, which ended with the fire that killed the children trapped in the compound along with David Koresh and his followers; and, perhaps most ominous of all, the poisoning of innocent travellers on the Tokyo underground by members of Aum Shinrikyô.

Undoubtedly these tragedies would not have occurred had the movements not existed and carried out the actions that they did, but the actions did not take place in a vacuum. All of them, and even the Heaven's Gate suicides, were part of a "cult scene" that includes other members of the wider society – and among the key players in the "cult scene" are the cult-watching groups (CWGs). These are organisations and networks of people who, for personal or professional reasons, contribute to the complex of relationships between new religious movements (NRMs) and the rest of society.[1]

There are those who argue that, were it not for the existence of CWGs acting as ever-vigilant watchdogs, there would be far more violence than there has been. There are also those who argue that it is some of the CWGs themselves that have contributed to what violence there has been through their aggressive attacks on the movements, exacerbating rather than ameliorating the situation. Both of these positions have some truth – but truth is rarely simple. Although some reference will be made to violence occurring more or less directly between CWGs and NRMs, the primary aim of this chapter is to offer a more general comparative background to incidents

---

[1] For the sake of clarity, I shall use "group" to refer to one or another of the CWGs and "movement" to refer to cults, sects, or NRMs.

such as those mentioned earlier by pointing out some of the complexities of the "cult scene" and how, in a variety of situations, the activities of CWGs may or may not make a difference.

A number of points will be argued about the relationship between NRMs, CWGs, and violence. Firstly, it has to be recognised that violence can come from *either direction*, both to and from the NRMs or CWGs. Secondly, activities by CWGs can both *increase and decrease* the probability of a violent outcome. Thirdly, while some of the violence occurs *directly* between NRMs and CWGs, most of it is *indirect*, involving, as intervening variables, (1) *other actors* (such as the media, governments, law enforcers, vigilante groups, and the general public) and (2) aspects of the *general social environment* (such as the economy, the political situation, migration, and the self-perception of mainstream religions). Fourthly, *CWGs vary* enormously. It will be suggested (a) that it is helpful to understand their activities as stemming from the *interests and/or aims* of the group and (b) that their efficacy depends on the *resources* (such as funding and status) that they can command. Fifthly, *changes* occur in CWGs, NRMs, other key players, and society over time and across space. Sixthly, the same activities performed by the *same CWG can result in different outcomes on different occasions*; in one situation, the potential for violence can be increased by a CWG acting in almost the same way as it does when, in another situation, the potential is decreased.

Five Types of CWGs

There are numerous ways in which CWGs can be, and have been, distinguished from each other. Many of these distinctions are evaluative, even highly emotive, with members of one group assuming the worst about members of another. This is not a particularly helpful approach if we want to understand more about the dynamics of processes in which the groups are involved. Then it has been suggested that CWGs recently set up by governmental agencies should be distinguished from, say, those set up by parents; but the governmental groups have little in common with each other, and little follows merely from their origins (although, obviously enough, government-supported groups will have access to considerable resources). Others would distinguish between general CWGs and those that specialise in particular movements or types of movements; but, again, such divisions are not particularly illuminating.

Decades of research on the "cult scene" have led me to the conclusion that the most useful way of distinguishing between groups is to take as our key defining characteristic the *underlying question* to which each group is primarily devoted to giving an answer in its cult-watching activities. Other characteristics frequently follow from these questions. Thus, we can find governmental and nongovernmental groups subsumed under the rubric of one type of group, and other governmental and nongovernmental groups fitting more neatly into another type.

The types are not meant to represent reality but to function as conceptual tools, allowing comparisons to be made between the abstractions that serve as a kind of template. One will, therefore, find real groups and/or their individual members both overlapping different types and changing with the passage of time. The types can, nonetheless, help us to recognise (1) how differences between the groups' behaviour and influence are not necessarily idiosyncratic, but reveal systematic similarities and differences allied to their different interests; (2) where there are exchanges and influences between the groups; and, most relevant to our immediate concerns, (3) the effects that the different perspectives and related actions can have on promoting or defusing potential violence.

The types, which are illustrated schematically in Table 1, are cult-awareness groups (CAGs), countercult groups (CCGs), research-oriented groups (ROGs), human rights groups (HRGs), and cult-defender groups (CDGs). These labels are not altogether satisfactory, but they have been chosen partly in an attempt to avoid at least some of the derisory connotations and dismissive arguments that have come to be associated with categories such as "anticultist" and "cult apologist." My only defence for including the term "cult" in the type labels is that acronyms such as "NRMWG," "CNRMG," or "NRMAG" not only sound cumbersome, but would probably confuse and/or irritate more people than they pleased. I do, however, use the term "new religious movement" (NRM) in preference to "cult" when talking about the movements themselves rather than about their watchers.

To complicate matters slightly further, it needs to be recognised that, despite the overall category of CWGs, the extent to which members of the groups are actually engaged in watching NRMs varies enormously. Members of some groups have never met a member of an NRM face to face; others are former members, having been in one or other of the movements for periods ranging from a couple of days to twenty or more years; still others have come to know movements, and perhaps lived with them for varying periods, as part of their research. Those with no direct knowledge rely on secondary sources that they believe to be "trustworthy" – which can mean

Table 1. *Ideal Types of Cult-Watching Groups*

Ideal Type	CAGs	CCGs	ROGs	HRGs	CDGs
Main question underpinning existence	What (potential) harm is caused by "destructive cults"?	What are the heretical beliefs of NRMs?	What do NRMs do and believe? How do they relate to the rest of society?	How does society treat NRMs differently?	What is right and good about NRMs? How are they abused?
Main aims, interests, and/or purpose	Help victims; alert potential victims; control or ban dangerous cults	Explain where and how NRMs deviate from the truth	Increase understanding based on objective information	Protect human rights of religious minorities	Defending NRMs; exposing CAGs
Membership	Relatives; ex-members; exit-counsellors; mental-health professionals	Theologians; Apologists; believers of the faith community	Academics and other scholars and professionals	Human rights activists; professionals, esp. lawyers	Members and sympathisers of NRMs
Evaluation	Negative	Negative	Neutral	Neutral	Positive
Feared source of violence	Unidirectional – from destructive cults to members and nonmembers	Not primary concern (except when satanic or millennial)	NRMs and/or society; concerned with interaction and comparison	Any abuse of human rights	Unidirectional – from society in general or particular groups
Ignored or rejected for NRM image	Good, normal, and/or acceptable behaviour	"Correct" and/or shared beliefs	Truth of beliefs and nonempirical judgements	Beliefs, actions irrelevant to discrimination	Bad acts of NRMs; social tolerance

Sources of information for cult-watching activity	Ex-members; relatives; media; own counsellors; negative information from scholars	NRM literature; testimonies of ex-members	NRMs; ex-members; family; society; group dynamics; rest of society	Legislation; treatment of and/or violence to NRMs	NRMs; CWGs; media; society
Direct knowledge of NRMs	Anxious parents and former members of NRMs	Reading the literature; own previous belief	Observation, questionnaire, interview, literature	Limited acquaintance	Membership, Acquaintance
Methodological approach	Generalising from distressing individual cases	Hermeneutic comparison of Scriptures	Empirical testing with comparison	Collecting data related to human rights abuses	Collecting data; generalising
Funding (all groups use some volunteers)	Membership dues; government; trusts; fees for counselling and expert witnessing	Internal to believers; churches; selling literature	University research funds; government; churches; police; trusts;	Larger bodies; non-government organizations; churches	NRMs (directly or indirectly); membership fees
Credibility to non-CWGs	Mixed – most used by media	Low outside faith community	High among noncommitted	Mixed; high if larger group	Low
Influence	Strong	Weak	Varies	Varies	Weak
Indirect contribution to violence	Lowers as watchdog; heightens through polarisation	Rarely affects situation in modern secular democracies	Lowers it by providing accurate information and direct contact	Lowers it as watchdog of civil rights violations	Negligible effect, though, can heighten through polarisation and exposing CAGs

Abbreviations: CAG, cult-awareness group; CCG, countercult group; ROG, research-oriented group; HRG, human rights group; CDG, cult-defender group.

ferreting out information that will fit and reinforce their preconceptions of the movements.

Members of CWGs usually agree on some basic facts about a movement (such as when, where, and by whom it was founded), but all of us both include and exclude particular aspects of actions, beliefs, organisations, and processes in our descriptions of phenomena. This selection is not merely arbitrary, but shaped partly by our interests – where we are "coming from" – which means that those who share a common agenda are likely to share similar images of the movements (Barker 1995). As part of the battle to get their own positions heard, the different CWGs also construct images of themselves and of the other groups, each trying to promote its own perspective in as positive a light as possible whilst, to a greater or lesser extent, denigrating those of the other types.

Cult-Awareness Groups

The fundamental question underlying the activity of CAGs is "In what ways do or might the movements harm individuals and/or society?" The predominant concern is to warn others of dangers and to control the activities of the movements.

CAGs have frequently originated with the organisation of those who have suffered personally as distressed relatives or former members of movements. They may also include deprogrammers, exit counsellors, and thought re-form consultants (many of whom are ex-members); and, sometimes, private detectives, lawyers, medical health practitioners, and clinical psychologists who bring their professional skills to helping those who seek their assistance. Some CAGs have been initiated by governments (as in France) or are predominantly supported by the national church (as in Russia).

Members of CAGs perceive themselves as caring and experienced in the suffering that the movements inflict upon families, and concerned about the dangers threatening society at large – as evidenced by the violence, criminal activities, and other antisocial behaviour in which cults have indulged. Given the question they are addressing, it is not surprising that CAGs paint a picture of the movements that highlights what they see as the bad characteristics while ignoring anything that could be seen as praiseworthy or even ordinary. The analogy has been made with asking a divorce lawyer what marriage is like. Members of CAGs associate with those who have suffered (especially parents and former members) and encourage them to define their experiences in terms that stress the role of the NRM and minimise the responsibility of the "victim." Particularly impressive witnesses for CAGs are the apostates who testify to the horrors they underwent while in an NRM; they (like the divorcee) were *there* – unlike academic researchers, who, the argument goes, see only what the movement's hierarchy wants them to see.

There is a sense in which stories of violence (the self-immolation of members of Ananda Marga or the murder of Sharon Tate by the Manson Family) are welcomed by CAGs. They prove the point, and repeated reference is made to movements as "destructive" and/or "doomsday cults," with frequent mentions of the violence, murder, and/or mass suicide associated with Jonestown, Waco, Aum Shinrikyô, the Solar Temple, and/or the Movement for the Restoration of the Ten Commandments of God – even when the movement that is being talked about is a peace-loving community that has never harmed anyone.

CAGs want not only to warn people of the dangers of cults, but also to try to ensure that their behaviour is controlled – even, in some cases, outlawed altogether. To this end they hold meetings, produce literature, and lobby governments, other organisations, and individuals who could support their cause. They also make extensive use of the Internet. Several members of CAGs offer themselves as expert witnesses in court cases, testifying in particular about the mind control techniques that they claim, with more or less sophistication, are used by the movements.

Countercult Groups

For CCGs the important question is not what NRMs *do*, but what they *believe* and how these beliefs differ from what they, the countercultists, hold to be true beliefs (Introvigne 1995). CCGs' descriptions of NRMs thus concentrate on "wrong" beliefs, rather than on those beliefs that they have in common, and frequently rely on an interpretation of their Holy Scripture to demonstrate the error of a movement's theology.

Members of CCGs are likely to include clergy, theologians, some former members who have converted to the new faith, and others who are committed to the theological position shared by that particular group. Countercultists often have a missionary zeal and not infrequently present themselves as saviours of lost souls; they may, however, be denigrated as religious fanatics and/or bigots by their opponents. A more common problem they have to face is ignorance of their existence or just being ignored by those who do not share their faith.

ROGs ask the questions "What are the movements like?" and "How can we understand and explain their beliefs and actions, and the ways in which they interact with the rest of society?" While ROGs include the cult-awareness question about the harm that NRMs might cause, they are equally interested in investigating situations in which harm is not perpetrated and in finding more "ordinary" information about the movements: their beliefs, practices, organisation, and the processes that occur both internally and as a result of their direct and indirect relationships with nonmembers. This means that (as in this volume) they are concerned with tracing the roles (if any) played by nonmembers in the exacerbation or amelioration of situations that might result in violence. ROGs are also concerned to point out changes that occur with the passage of time – that, for example, children raised in ISKCON are now protected from violence and other kinds of abuse as carefully as almost any children in the West – and possibly considerably more so than many.

Furthermore, ROGs try to contextualise information through comparison with other religions and/or those who share socioeconomic and various demographic characteristics with members of the movement concerned. They might compare the rate of violence in an NRM with the rate of violence among, say, Roman Catholics or Methodists, possibly concluding that members of the new religion exhibited a lower rate of violence than their peers in an older religion. The research-oriented scholar would then investigate what factor(s) could account for the different rates. In other words, while violence certainly occurs in some NRMs, comparisons can show that this does not necessarily mean that violence is typical of NRMs and atypical of other religions or, indeed, of ordinary citizens.

ROGs are less likely than CAGs to accept theories of mental manipulation as being the overriding reason for an individual's joining a movement and/or his or her behaviour while a member. Scholars will, nonetheless, examine the influence that a movement has on potential converts and their members, and will study different patterns of authority and dependence, systematically taking into account several more factors than other CWGs are wont to do. Interestingly enough, such research methods can result in ROGs becoming aware of real or potential problems that are overlooked

---

[2] At this point, I ought to declare an interest. In 1988, with the support of the British Home Office and mainstream churches, I was responsible for founding INFORM, an ROG now based at the London School of Economics (Barker 1995).

by the more generalising condemnation that can arise from a CAG's approach.

ROGs consist primarily of scholars (particularly of religious studies and the social sciences) but may include members of mainstream religions, relatives of members of movements, and former members who want the public to be alerted to both real and potential problems, while also having a desire to promote as balanced and objective a picture of the new religions as possible. There may also be a network of specialists such as lawyers, doctors, professionally trained counsellors, and therapists upon whose services the ROG can call or to whom it can refer those who come to it for expert assistance. Like the CAGs, ROGs rely heavily on former members, both for information and for offering support to others who have left a movement. ROGs are, however, aware that some former members will have had (both in the movement and, perhaps, after leaving it) experiences that may not be the same as other former members' experiences and may thus portray the movement in different ways – just as some divorcees manage to maintain a relatively happy relationship with their ex-spouse, while others grow increasingly bitter after the split (Lewis 1986).

ROGs perceive themselves as seekers of objective information in order to provide the most reliable basis for action. Their methods include participant observation, interviews, and questionnaires, but the fact that, qua social scientists, they have no special expertise that allows them (1) to evaluate nonempirical theological beliefs or (2) to make moral judgements frequently results in their detractors claiming ROGs do not care about (a) "The Truth" (a complaint of some countercultists) or (b) the suffering of individuals (an accusation frequently raised by members of CAGs, who sometimes label ROGs as cult defenders when they refuse to condemn all NRMs as destructive cults. The cult defenders themselves are likely to complain that ROGs are members of CAGs because they refuse to offer unequivocal support for the movements).

ROGs differ from each other along the proactive dimension. Some, such as Research Network on New Religions (RENNER), meet for conferences that are not open to the general public, exchange scholarly papers resulting from their research, and publish their findings in academic journals or books. Others, such as Information Network Focus on Religious Movements (INFORM), make information readily available to anyone who asks for it; like CAGs, they produce leaflets and popular books, organise public seminars, give talks at schools, universities, church groups, youth clubs and various other places, and appear on both radio and television. Some also give evidence in court – either for or against a movement. Members of ROGs have also found themselves increasingly called upon by government departments and law enforcement agencies around the world, not only to give factual data about the movements, but also to help such people understand more about the interactive processes that could lead to unintended and undesired consequences – including violence.

Human Rights Groups

HRGs are more concerned with asking how society treats the movements than with what the movements themselves do; one might, therefore, argue that they should be labelled "watching-out-for-cults groups." Like ROGs, HRGs are neutral in their evaluation of the movements in that they consider the rights of NRMs to be on a par with those of any other organisations, irrespective of beliefs and actions that, while they may contravene social mores, do not harm others or contravene the criminal law.

HRGs consist, not surprisingly, of people who believe strongly in human rights issues and frequently include persons with legal training; but, unlike CAGs, which believe that the movements take away the rights of their members and their members' relatives, HRGs tend to concentrate on preserving the rights of the movements. Some HRGs include members of ROGs, CDGs, and/or NRMs among their number; some human rights activists know relatively little about the movements.

Cult-Defender Groups

CDGs ask questions about how NRMs have been mistreated and/or misrepresented. They present themselves as fighters for the truth about the NRMs, indignantly preserving the freedom of religion and standing up for an unpopular cause, frequently, they claim, against "secular humanists." In some ways like a mirror image of CAGs, CDGs focus on positive aspects of the movements, ignoring or explaining away any dubious actions and what they dismiss as anticultists' "atrocity tales." They are particularly vocal in their condemnation of deprogramming and exit counselling. They may also claim that violent situations are the fault of CAGs, the government, law enforcement agencies, the media, or some other body or individuals, rather than the NRMs themselves.

CDGs may consist of sympathisers, members of an NRM, or of people belonging to a more traditional (or no) religion who are of an ideologically liberal disposition and have become disturbed by what they perceive as unfair treatment of the movements. They are also quite likely to include members of NRMs, who have, indeed, initiated some CDGs (such as the Scientologists' Alliance for the Preservation of Religious Liberty [APRL]) and/or provided resources for their activities. It has also been the case that some academics, worried about the negative representation of the NRMs, have worked closely with some NRMs in order to present the other side of the picture. This can raise problems about whether a group such as Association of World Academics for Religious Education (AWARE), which has published some interesting studies of NRMs that had invited the academics and paid them to study their movement, is an ROG or a CDG. According to my definitions of my types, it wobbles between the two. It is a CDG insofar as only positive accounts of the NRM are selected at the cost of more negative aspects; and it is an ROG insofar as its members construct a balanced image of the NRM, investigating its beliefs and actions, whether these are good or harmful. A study of the Church Universal and Triumphant (Lewis and Melton 1994) has been criticised by some scholars on account of the role that the movement played in the data collection. Some of the chapters were impeccable insofar as their scholarly approach was concerned; others appeared to be more affected by the movement's perspective than research-oriented methodology would demand.

But the difficulty in distinguishing one type from another is not necessarily due to potential overlaps. In the 1970s, there appeared an apparently extreme CAG called POWER (People's Organized Workshop on Ersatz Religions), which advocated brutal deprogrammings in a quite widely circulated manual. Many readers were shocked by its violence-promoting contents but scholars familiar with the NRMs did not have to reach far into the manual before becoming convinced that it was a ruse instigated by one of the movements themselves. More recently, the "new CAN" (Cult Awareness Network) joined the ranks of CDGs after the "old CAN," which was unambiguously anticultist, was declared bankrupt as the result of a court case involving a forcible deprogramming. Its name and telephone number were taken over by a consortium led by Scientologists, which now provides a cult-defender service for those who contact it, possibly under the illusion that they are dealing with the old CAN.

CDGs that include members of several NRMs tend to have a rather short and not very productive life. There are, of course, disagreements to be found within all CWGs, but the problem is particularly acute in CDGs when NRMs that have agreed to co-operate to further a common cause find themselves being expected to defend movements whose beliefs and practices are in sharp opposition to their own.

Direct Violence

Relationships between CWGs and NRMs, while they have included some fierce litigation, unpleasant threats, and irritating inconveniences, have seldom resorted to direct violence. When there has been violence, it has usually involved sections of the cult-awareness movement. The lawyer Sakamoto Tsutsumi, who, with his family, was murdered by Aum Shinrikyô, was making enquiries on behalf of an incipient CAG; and one might (although it is rather stretching the definition) call the population of Antelope, Oregon, which was subjected to salmonella poisoning, members of an CAG.

Most members of CAGs eschew the path of violence for themselves, but some do feel that a "just war" may be necessary in certain circumstances. And there are a few who are undoubtedly belligerent. There have been incidents in which members of CAGs have directly attacked members of one or another of the movements, but direct violence has been more frequently carried out by vigilante groups. There were, for example, a series of attacks on minority religions in Armenia in the mid-1990s by a group of paramilitaries; and violent assaults resulting in broken limbs have been carried out by angry relatives who might belong to a CAG but are not necessarily acting as representatives of their group.

The most obvious example of systematic violence by CAGs has been forcible deprogrammings, which have relied heavily on the "brainwashing" metaphor to explain "recruitment" to the movements. Parents who turned to a CAG for help, or received a telephone call in which the caller reported having heard that they had a "child" (who might be over thirty) in a dangerous cult, could be advised that, if they (the parents) really loved their child and wanted to see him or her again, a deprogramming could be arranged (at what might be a cost of tens of thousands of dollars).

Although the deprogrammings have become less violent over time, some have undoubtedly been terrifying, and at least one suicide occurred shortly after a young woman went through the ordeal. Not uncharacteristically, the media blamed the movement from which the woman was forcibly "rescued" for the tragedy.

Numerous testimonies by those who were subjected to deprogramming describe how they were threatened with a gun, beaten, denied sleep and food, and/or sexually assaulted (Kilbourne and Richardson 1982; Barker 1989). But one does not have to rely on the victims for stories of violence: Ted Patrick, one of the most notorious deprogrammers used by CAGs (who has spent several terms in prison for his exploits), openly boasts about some of the violence he employed (Patrick 1976); in November 1987, Cyril Vosper, a committee member of Family Action Information and Rescue (FAIR), the British CAG, was convicted in Munich of "causing bodily harm" in the course of one of his many deprogramming attempts; and a number of similar convictions are on record for prominent members of CAGs elsewhere.

Deprogramming continues in Japan, where, thanks to the activities of local CAGs, around 200 Unificationists may be forcibly abducted for deprogramming in a single year. But by the late 1990s, "exit counselling" and "thought reform consultancy" (neither of which employs forcible abduction) had all but replaced deprogramming in the West. Nonetheless, the practice of deprogramming has contributed to worsening relations between NRMs and CAGs and has provided the NRMs with some good atrocity tales.

Indirect Violence

As suggested earlier, violence rarely takes place in a vacuum. There has nearly always been a buildup of antagonisms, resentment, hostility, and/or hatred that can involve a number of contributory rather than direct causes for the eventual outbreak; the scene has been set before the catastrophe occurs and the proverbial straw finally breaks the camel's back. The rest of this chapter adopts a more dynamic approach, exploring the more *indirect* ways in which CWGs make a difference in the cult scene by using and/or being used as a resource by other key actors and the wider society.

Given that few cult watchers *want* to see outbreaks of violence, our problem is to understand some of the unintended consequences of cult watching. This is not an easy task. To begin with, there are methodological problems. Almost none of the well-known cases of violence involving NRMs in the West was predicted in advance by *any* CWG, and numerous predictions by the media and CAGs of impending mass suicides or violence have *not* been fulfilled. Indeed, the overwhelming majority of NRMs have shown little or no sign of directing any violent behaviour towards either themselves or anyone else. Violence has been the exception rather than the rule, and generalisations from these exceptions, especially when they are made without systematic comparison with the violence that takes place within the older religions and in other areas of society, should be treated with the utmost caution.

In addition, as other authors in this volume illustrate, those cases of violence that have occurred have differed from each other in several important respects, making it difficult to use these cases by themselves to test theories of what leads to (or away from) violence. Next, although we can construct a story that purports to explain some of the factors leading up to violence, it is impossible to prove a negative by claiming that, had it *not* been for the role of a CWG (or another group), there *would have been* violence. We can, however, point to a number of cases in which the defusing of a volatile situation would clearly seem to have been facilitated by mediation between a movement and nonmembers who had been informed by reliable information and understanding. Examples might include the bloodless conclusion of the siege involving the Covenant, the Sword, and the Arm of the Lord (Noble 1998).

Another problem is the sheer complexity of the cult scene. To obtain a full picture, one has to take into account several other key players including the mass media; the general public; mainstream religions; and officials such as law enforcement agencies, politicians, lawyers, and others in a position to act on behalf of society. Any or all of these can influence and be influenced by each other, with the CWG being but a link in a complicated interactive chain. Exploring such interconnections can help us to understand better the considerable disparity in the extent to which the CWGs succeed in making a difference.

On the "supply side," the strength and effectiveness of a CWG's contribution will depend not merely on what the CWG has to say (be this positive, negative, or neutral; accurate, inaccurate, or biased), but also on the extent to which and by whom it is heard, which, in turn, will depend on the group's ability to secure such resources as funding and status, and, thus, access to and credibility with other players.

On the "demand side," the various target groups in the wider society will be more or less open to accept the different CWGs' depictions of the NRMs. We cannot, however, consider the various other players in isolation; they themselves will have more or less power and/or inclination to influence the cult scene, depending on a number of factors related to the structure and culture of the wider society – not insofar as these are part of the cult scene but insofar as they comprise the stage upon which the cult scene is enacted. The setting of this wider society may be a village, a nation, or the entire globe, and it may include properties related to the economy, immigration, and the religious and/or political situation.

One way to elaborate the significance of a comparative perspective is to start from the observation that countercultists, insofar as they are concerned (by definition) with the question of theological error, have not been very successful in making a difference beyond their own faith circles in most of contemporary western society. Complaints about theological error have limited appeal, partly because in a pluralistic society not everyone shares one faith, partly because of the relative secularisation that has occurred at the societal level, and partly because of de jure or de facto separation of church and state. While a parish newspaper might print an article on the heresy of nontrinitarian beliefs, the rest of the world will not rush to read it or turn on a programme discussing the niceties of interpretation of some (to them) obscure verse in Holy Scripture.

But this has not always been the case. Until fairly recently, theological arguments carried far more weight (Jenkins 2000). Witches and heretics such as the Cathars have been burned at the stake; the Inquisition was a CCG par excellence, convinced that the violence in which it indulged was in accordance with the will of God. Conversely, today we can find some Islamic countries with little demand for CCGs because their interpretation of the shari'ah (Muslim code of religious law) provides sufficient criteria for distinguishing the faithful from infidels, and laws for dealing with the infidel are already in place. A countercult group in Afghanistan would appear to be surplus to requirement. It might thus be hypothesised that *both* the more secular and democratically pluralistic *and* the more monolithically religious a state, the less demand there is for CCGs.

If we turn to postcommunist societies, however, we can find CCGs playing a significant role. Mainstream religions, having suffered under an atheistic state, frequently promote countercult sentiments in attempts to reclaim their flock; but their arguments stress nationalism and identity rather than engaging in theological debate (Barker 1997) – although Jehovah's Witnesses' beliefs have been declared false in a Russian court. For political reasons, the state is likely to support the church in its attacks on what it considers to be foreign or destructive cults, with the media eagerly publishing stories supplied by local and foreign CCGs about the movements' alien and heretical (that is, treacherous) beliefs.[3] In such circumstances, local officials have felt no compunction to prevent vigilante groups and, on occasion, even priests from

---

[3] It might be added, however, that indigenous NRMs can equally well be attacked for providing an alternative to the national religion.

violently attacking Krishna devotees, Unificationists, and members of other NRMs.

But, while it is important to recognise the role of social demand, it also has to be recognised that the salience of what a group has to supply can itself attract attention in the contemporary West. In the 1980s, nasty stories of satanic violence (including the rape and slaughter of virgins and the ritual impregnation of "brood mares" to produce infants for human sacrifices) were widely publicised, first in the United States and, then elsewhere around the world. All too frequently, however, the violence turned out to be a creation of a few evangelical CCGs, a particular type of therapist or law enforcer, and/or the media. Despite intensive investigations, little was found to substantiate the gory claims that were being made. There is, however, evidence that the very fact that the media were circulating such stories gave some paedophiles and murderers ideas about how to gain an added frisson (and perhaps a defence they hoped would provide First Amendment protection). Furthermore, some young people, wishing to experiment and/or shock, have been stimulated by lurid accounts in the media to pursue satanic rituals that have occasionally resulted in violence (Richardson, Best, and Bromley 1991).

In short, while CCGs are not normally a powerful force outside their own constituencies in the present-day United States, comparative analyses indicate that there have been, and still can be, situations in which they can contribute significantly to promoting violence. They, like the other CWGs, are more readily heard in some times and places than in others.

Of course, some ears are clearly more influential than others. To have the ear of officials, especially members of the government, is likely to promote a cause more successfully than the agreement, however enthusiastic, of the "man (or woman) in the street."

There is, nonetheless, a very real sense in which the standpoint of the general population is of considerable importance to CWGs. Relatively few people have firsthand experience of the movements and, however much CWGs organise conferences, produce literature, or talk to people, they are unable to make direct contact with more than a very small percentage of the general population. For the vast majority of people, their knowledge comes through the mass media, and several studies have shown that the conventional wisdom that has been picked up through the media (including the Internet) consists far more of negative evaluation than of factual information (Beckford 1999).

Although CDGs would like to reverse this situation, and although some have had access to considerable resources such as money for lawyers or the publishing of literature, their credibility in the wider society has not been high, and what little effect they have achieved has been more a result of their exposing (and antagonising) others than of getting their own message across. Indeed, CDGs tend to be treated with as much suspicion as the movements whose interests they try to promote, a "good story" about a "good cult" being regarded as almost a contradiction in terms and not something likely to attract the media.

On the other hand, the better-known HRGs, such as Amnesty International and the Organization for Security and Co-operation in Europe (OSCE), enjoy considerably higher status. They have included reports of violations of the human rights of NRMs in literature with a limited but relatively influential distribution; but, not altogether surprisingly, their defence of NRMs has far less appeal in most quarters than their cries for help for starving children in North Korea, flood victims in Bangladesh, or AIDS sufferers in sub-Saharan Africa. HRGs that focus more specifically on minority religions (such as the International Academy for Freedom of Religion and Belief) have less widespread status, but have made some difference by holding conferences, publishing material, and visiting officials around the world.

It is probable that HRGs' protests and presence have reduced some of the more extreme violations of the rights of NRMs at the legal and/or governmental level, especially when the society is a signatory of international declarations and its rhetoric, if not always its practice, proclaims that human rights should be extended to all, whatever their beliefs. It is, however, always possible for human rights protests to be counterproductive, especially if they are interpreted as interference in another state's internal policies. U.S. pressure has evoked somewhat tart responses not only in Russia but also in Germany and France.

Generally speaking, the CWGs most likely to make a difference to potentially violent situations in the contemporary West are CAGs and ROGs. Both can play a significant role as watchdogs. If no one were keeping a watchful eye on new alternative movements, a few of these might believe that they could get away with anything. Knowing that they are being watched, and that a violation of laws (or even social niceties) can result in restrictive responses, they might be more circumspect in their behaviour. Violence may well be prevented if people are alerted with information that will help them to recognise and assess the movements, and officials can intervene to curtail the more violent proclivities of the movements.

It should, however, be recognised that there will be occasions when aggressive watchdogging is counterproductive because either the NRM thrives on confrontation and/or society reacts to information about the NRM in an exacerbating rather than a preventive manner. Such exacerbation can, paradoxically enough, be the unintended consequence of the very concern that CAGs have to prevent violence.

The relative balance of influence that CAGs and ROGs exert on other key players varies from country to country and is constantly changing. In Britain, although a number of CAGs exist and succeed in obtaining considerable coverage in the media, they have not been as successful as ROGs in obtaining resources or credence from the government, law enforcement agencies, or the mainstream churches. Here, as in most parts of Scandinavia and the Netherlands, there is a relatively long tradition of religious tolerance and relatively little fear of NRMs causing major problems for the status quo. The churches may not be doing well, but they are unlikely to blame the new religions; and politicians, although they may declare that they do not like the movements, would be unlikely to gain many votes by passing laws that violate their countries' (sometimes violently gained) liberal democracies.

In France and Belgium, however (and, to a lesser extent, in Austria and Germany), CAGs have had considerable success in persuading the government to set up commissions to report on cults and government-funded groups to fight the cults. The reports included the names of cults or sects supplied almost exclusively by CAGs, and although officials claim, quite correctly, that these are not official lists, they are taken as such by the public and have resulted in discrimination and violence directed towards the named movements (a short time after the Unification Church featured in one report, a bomb was thrown into its Paris centre).

There are various theories as to why such societies have been so open to CAG influence: that, for instance, it is an expression of widely held antireligious sentiments or that there are few, if any, organised ROGs to counter the wilder claims made by the CAGs. Such explanations could also feed into an understanding of the attitudes of postcommunist countries, but one should add variables such as economic and political unrest, the precarious position of traditional religion, and increasing expressions of nationalism combined with fear, distrust, and resentment of foreigners. And, of course, when an NRM performs an apparently inexplicable atrocity, there is a universal desire to prevent the recurrence of such a tragedy. The

CAGs were listened to with far greater attention after over 900 followers of Jim Jones died in Guyana; French-speaking countries were severely jolted by the Solar Temple deaths; the whole world was horrified when Aum Shinrikyô released sarin gas in the Tokyo underground. In the wake of such bizarre violence, it is hardly surprising that the CAGs' question "How do we control the harm perpetrated by NRMs?" was given added salience and urgency.

Given the media's interest in attracting and keeping a wide audience of readers, listeners, and viewers, and the assumption that most people have a voyeuristic curiosity in the uncomplicated, the sensational, the novel, and the violent, CAGs usually have the edge on other CWGs when it comes to disseminating their image of NRMs. A circular symbiotic relationship develops, with CAGs reproducing the media's stories in their literature and, indeed, recycling them to the media, as well as supplying them to government officials and others. In general, CAGs can reap the benefit of unqualified "good stories" and appeals for sympathy in cases of very real tragedy; they are, moreover, likely to attract the support of *individuals* with power, status, and/or financial resources who have a personal or professional interest in cults.

On the other hand, ROGs can claim credibility and respectability through their recognised qualifications; it is their *professional* expertise, with methodologically laid down standards for assessing competing truth claims, that is responsible for whatever status and access to resources they acquire. Put another way, CAGs have the advantage of constructing an attention-attracting human story, while ROGs have the advantage of using more reliable methods to construct a possibly less arresting story (Barker 1995).

Curiously enough, it is possible that the more extreme members of CAGs help ROGs to gain access to both the movements and other key players just because CAG depictions of the NRMs can be so generalised and negative. Firstly, the NRMs are more likely to give ROGs access that they deny the media and CAGs in the hope that the researchers will at least be fair. Secondly, after continually hearing the litany of movements as "brainwashing-exploitive-potentially-violent-cults-under-the-control-of-a-ruthless-pathologically-unstable-leadership-whose-real-purpose-is-not-religious-or-spiritual-but-financial-gain-sexual-perversion-and/or-political-and-personal-power," governmental officials, law enforcers, and others have come to reject the extreme CAGs' caricature as predictable and as less reliable and useful than the more detailed and objective information that ROGs can provide. Both official organisations and relatives of converts to NRMs have also concluded in a number of countries that not only can

ROGs provide information free of the potentially vested interests of church and state, but they can also generally be trusted not to fan the flames in a delicate situation. And although they are renowned for cumbersome qualifications rather than snappy sound bites, ROGs are being increasingly used for comment on news and current affairs programmes when a cult story comes up, with at least some of the media trying to offer the public an "objective middle position" – usually between that of a member of a CAG, on the one hand, and a member of a movement, on the other. Of course, a middle position is not necessarily the correct position, and there can be many middles between two extremes. The world is too messy to be able to assume that an average gives the truth.

Constructing the "Other"

To repeat, ROGs are aware of, and concerned about, the possibility of violence. One of the potentially dangerous characteristics of many new religions offering an alternative to the status quo is that they make a sharp distinction between "us" and "them." Their vision of nonbelievers as "other" is reinforced by describing the latter as "agents of The Enemy," members of "the System," or "Babylon," or merely those who are not among the elect, and by encouraging their members to distance themselves from former associates (Luke 14:26). This makes the movements difficult to study and potentially dangerous when neither leaders nor followers are subjected to questioning from alternative perspectives or outside control.

It has, indeed, frequently been observed that recruiting people to carry out violent acts is made much easier when the person on whom the violence is being perpetrated has been defined as other, abnormal, and/or not fully human. When there is a clear label, we know more easily who is on our side and who is the enemy – rather like the uniforms worn in a war or even the shirts worn in a football game and the scarves worn by the fans. Left merely to our own devices, we might mistake one of them for one of us. Such processes of distancing can be found at the root of racial (or football) violence and have frequently been an integral part of the mindsets that encourage people of one nation to kill the people of another without compunction. Derogatory labels such as "Hun," "yid," "nigger," "Jap" – or "cultist" – identify and dehumanise the other. The Nazi state had a terrifying lack of difficulty in convincing those who assisted in its eugenics programmes that the "patients" were less than truly human and ought to be eliminated for the good of humanity (*id est*, the Aryan race).

The power that an authority figure can wield is, moreover, not restricted to Joseph Mengele's coworkers at Auschwitz. Ordinary people, under no great pressure, have administered potentially lethal electric shocks when asked to do so by someone wearing a white coat (Milgram 1974); ordinary people can go along with the majority, doubting the evidence of their own eyes when all their peers appear to be seeing something different (Asch 1959). It is normal for people to kill others when their country calls; indeed, it is the Jehovah's Witnesses who are considered abnormal when they refuse to take up arms against others – and it is for this reason that they have been killed and subjected to all manner of violence.

This construction of otherness, found in some NRMs and in a not insignificant proportion of the general population, can also spring from a CAG's concern with harm emanating from NRMs. Through the media, CAGs have not only supplied good stories, they have also provided the concepts and the grammar with which the general public (including officials) can frame their understanding of NRMs. Nouns such as "cult" and "pseudo-religion"; verbs such as "brainwash," "manipulate," and "exploit"; adjectives such as "bizarre," "fanatic," and "violent"; and use of the passive voice for "victims" who *have been* duped and *had to be* rescued effectively diminish the likelihood that members of NRMs could have made choices and/or be capable of leaving (although, in fact, most do of their own free will). Cultists become reduced to another species, incapable of the normal reasoning and morality of real people, and, thus, not to be treated as if they were like us.

If it is part of the conventional wisdom that cults are dangerous, then law enforcers, politicians, and others (including vigilante groups) will be "given permission" to attack NRMs verbally, legally, or physically (or to turn a blind eye when others attack them) without drawing as much wrath upon themselves (or losing as many votes) as might have been the case were they to attack older, more respected religions in a similar fashion, even when these religions may well be just as, if not more, harmful. It is far safer (less likely to result in negative repercussions for the attacker) if the objects of an attack are generally considered to be "getting no more than they deserve." There may be general agreement that "something ought to be done" about the danger in our midst, and that drastic measures may be called for in what has come to be perceived as a drastic situation. Such rhetoric can be seen as fanning the violence that has been meted out to NRMs in parts of Europe and the former Soviet Union – and, indeed, in the United States of America.

Deviance Amplification and Diminution

It has been suggested that both CAGs and an NRM itself may construct images that define the NRM as fundamentally atypical of the rest of society. It has also been suggested that research shows that this is unlikely to be true; NRMs tend to be far more normal than either they or their opponents would have us believe. But what is also suggested by the study of instances in which there has been a violent outcome is that frequently both sides have, to a greater or lesser extent, been engaged in dehumanising and mud-slinging activities across the divide, resulting in behaviours that in turn lead to a process termed "deviancy amplification," with each pointing to the bad behaviour of the other to justify worse behaviour on its own part – which is, in turn, taken as a justification for further inflammatory actions by the other side, resulting in an escalating spiral of deviation from normal behaviour.

Thus, the dissemination of what an NRM perceives as negative, inaccurate, and/or biased depictions of itself can goad the movement and nonmembers alike into accentuating antagonisms as each sees the other behaving increasingly badly. Deprogrammings, confrontational television programmes, costly court cases, or the Scientologists' acquiring the records of the old CAN have not endeared either side to the other. Others then become involved in the battle, consciously or unconsciously adopting an increasingly anti-or pro-cult perspective. Eventually violence may erupt, which, with hindsight, might have been avoided had not only the NRM but also the other key players behaved differently.

The events that occurred in Waco in 1993 are frequently referred to as an example of such a situation, with cult-awareness sentiments expressed by an apostate, social workers, and the media encouraging law enforcement officers to accept a CAG-inspired perspective of the Branch Davidians as a dangerous cult. An interesting twist can be observed at the time of writing (February 2001), when another confrontation that could easily spiral into further violence concerns Falun Gong and the Chinese government. The latter, having accused the former of multiple murders and suicides, as well as threatening the stability of the state, banned the movement in 1999 (Ji Shi 1999). The twist lies in the fact that, in this confrontation, the western media seem to be taking the side of the NRM rather than that of their opponents, the Chinese government, and are suggesting that to date the violence has been administered almost entirely by government officials. But, at the beginning of 2001, Falun Gong's founder, Li Hongzhi, announced that members facing persecution could rightfully go beyond the movement's principal virtue of forbearance: "The way the evil is currently performing shows that they [government forces] are already utterly inhuman and completely without righteous thoughts" (www.clearwisdom.net). Not long after ward, some people claiming to be Falun Gong practitioners set fire to themselves in Tiananmen Square – and a new CAG of ex-members was formed in Yunnan Province in the hope of doing "something to assist the Party and the government to root out all cult organizations" (*People's Daily*, January 17, 2001). It would seem that the scene could be well and truly set for further violence.

But it is not impossible for an upward spiral of deviance amplification to be countered by a downward spiral of deviance diminution or, perhaps more frequently, for a social response to NRMs to encourage accommodation and peaceful coexistence rather than bitter antagonisms.

By not concentrating exclusively on its negative aspects, an ROG perspective can construct a more normal (and understandable) picture of a movement and thus lower the temperature. Scholars have also noted that although *new* NRMs may initially emphasise what distinguishes them from the wider society, with the arrival of their second generation they are likely to undergo several changes, including a tendency to stress how similar they are to other religions and the rest of society (Barker and Mayer 1995). If they are encouraged or merely allowed to become more normal, then their investment in the society becomes increasingly salient and (ceteris paribus) violence is less likely to erupt. Such changes tend to be recognised and publicised by ROGs more than by CAGs, which prefer to perpetuate stories about the movements' earlier, more defiant beliefs and practices.

Furthermore, the very fact that scholars have often spoken to and, more importantly, listened to NRMs can in itself diminish the divisive them—us attitudes that movements might have created and members of CAGs reinforced (Barker 1999). ROGs have sometimes been able to conduct or facilitate mediation, presenting alternative lines of action to the movements, which may decide that, although not on their side, ROGs are not on the other side either. Moreover, by studying an NRM's beliefs, scholars can learn to "speak the language" and thus "translate" to others (who may include law enforcement negotiators in volatile situations) the ways in which members of an NRM are thinking and what their behaviour is likely to be under certain circumstances. In the United States and a number of other countries, law enforcement agencies that must deal with violent situations, particularly in the wake of Waco and Aum Shinrikyô, and in anticipation of millennial violence, have now established relationships with scholars associated with ROGs. An increased understanding of what are considered by the NRM to be matters of ultimate concern can both increase the possibility of anticipating the unintended consequences of certain actions, on the one hand, and enabling greater communication, on the other (Wessinger 2000).

Concluding Remarks

Let me repeat that the types I have used are no more than constructs that are more or less useful for understanding the complicated processes of social interaction. Individual cult watchers straddle and move between the types, and the groups themselves change significantly in response to other players and their own experiences. Some CAGs have become far more professionalised in recent years, and some of their members have started co-operating with some members of ROGs and even some NRMs that have expressed a desire to amend erstwhile harmful practices. But while either groups or movements become willing to break down boundaries, there is always the possibility of the more fervent members breaking away to form a "purer" schismatic group or movement. And, of course, entirely new movements and groups are continually appearing on the scene.

Stress has been laid on methodological difficulties and the intricacy of the social context, in which CWGs comprise only some of the threads of the complicated tapestry that is being woven at any particular time and place. The general thrust of this chapter has, however, been that, although one cannot predict that violence is inherently more likely or less likely due to the involvement of one type of group rather than another, CWGs can play, have played, and will doubtless continue to play a significant, though usually indirect, role in the cult scene.

It has been suggested that *insofar* as a CWG is primarily concerned about the danger that NRMs pose for individuals and society, the more likely the group is to point to whatever negative attributes it can while ignoring the good and normal. *Insofar* as it labels all NRMs as destructive cults, without specifying particular practices of particular movements; *insofar* as it dehumanises, and defines as other, movements in which members are reputedly brainwashed by psychotic and unstable leaders; and *insofar* as it can draw on the stories of worried, anxious relatives and, even more forcefully, disillusioned and angry apostates, it is likely to attract the attention of the media. *Insofar* as the media accept and reinforce the image of all NRMs as *intrinsically and typically* sinister, bizarre, and a dangerous threat, such an image will become accepted as part of the conventional, taken-for-granted wisdom of the general population. *Insofar* as it is generally accepted and agreed that members of NRMs are less than normal human beings, people, including those in positions of authority, will be given permission to treat them as not deserving of the respect due to normal citizens and will even be applauded for attacking them verbally, legally, or/and physically. This can (but often does not) lead to encouraging the movement to react in an increasingly negative fashion, which can fan the flames of escalating antagonism on both sides – and eventually result in the kind of violent outcome we witnessed at Waco.

On the other hand, what is presented as abnormal from a cult-awareness perspective might be seen as far more normal from a research-oriented perspective. Of course, potential dangers of NRMs should not be ignored because they occur elsewhere, but if we wish to understand processes that could lead to the perpetration of violence, we would be foolish not to recognise that we might understand these processes more easily if we acknowledge that they are not peculiar to NRMs and that there is much to be learned from wider studies. It is also true that selective and generalising images that sensationalise and dehumanise NRMs can obscure more than they enlighten us about beliefs, practices, and processes involving NRMs.

Insofar as a group is asking what a movement is like, and is using a methodology that provides as balanced and objective a picture as possible, it is likely that it will be made easier to alert people (potential converts and those in authority) to actual and potential dangers and to reassure them when the members of the movement are presenting no special threat to anyone. In fact, given the limited number of NRMs that have been involved in violent behaviour, our question "Why is violence associated with cults?" might become "Why is there so little violence?"

Be that as it may, violence has occurred more often than any CWG would like, and none but the foolhardy would expect there not to be more violent incidents in the future. We might, however, become more aware of the ways in which situations can be exacerbated or defused. Our present state of knowledge is limited, but we have had the opportunity to learn something and we have the opportunity to learn more, both from the well-publicised incidents that have occurred in the United States and elsewhere and from the behaviour of ordinary citizens.

We have learned that if we wish to increase our understanding of the cult scene sufficiently to reduce the prospect of future violence, cult watching is necessary. We have also learned that watching the cult watchers is necessary.

References

Asch, Solomon. "Effects of Group Pressure upon the Modification and Distortion of Judgements." In *Readings in Social Psychology* (3rd edition), edited by Eleanor E. Maccoby, Theodore Newcomb, and Eugene Hartley London: Methuen, 1959: 174–183.

Barker, Eileen. "Taking Two to Tango." In *Sociology and Religions*, edited by Liliane Voyé and Jaak Billiet. Leuven: Leuven University Press, 1999: 204–226.

"But Who's Going to Win? National and Minority Religions in Post-Communist Society." In *New Religions in Central and Eastern Europe*, edited by Irena Borowik. Kraków: Nomos, 1997: 7–44.

"The Scientific Study of Religion? You Must Be Joking!" *Journal for the Scientific Study of Religion* 34 (1995): 287–310.

New Religious Movements: A Practical Introduction. London: Her Majesty's Stationery Office, 1989.

Barker, Eileen, and Jean-François Mayer, eds. "Twenty Years On." *Social Compass* 42 (1995): 147–279.

Beckford, James. "The Mass Media and New Religious Movements." In *New Religious Movements*, edited by Bryan Wilson and Jamie Cresswell. London: Routledge, 1999: 103–119.

Introvigne, Massimo "The Secular Anti-Cult and the Religious Counter-Cult Movement." In *New Religions and the New Europe*, edited by Robert Towler. Aarhus: Aarhus University Press, 1995: 32–54.

Jenkins, Philip. *Mystics and Messiahs: Cults and New Religions in American History*. New York: Oxford University Press, 2000.

Ji Shi. *Li Hongzhi and His "Falun Gong": Deceiving the Public and Ruining Lives*. Beijing: New Star, 1999.

Kilbourne, Brock, and James Richardson. "Cults versus Families: A Case of Misattribution of Cause?" *Marriage and Family Review* 4 (1982): 81–101.

Lewis, James. "Restructuring the 'Cult' Experience." *Sociological Analysis* 47 (1986): 151–159.

Lewis, James, and J. Gordon Melton. *The Church Universal and Triumphant in Scholarly Perspective*. Stanford, CA: Center for Academic Publication, 1994.

Milgram, Stanley. *Obedience to Authority*. New York: Harper and Row, 1974.

Noble, Kerry. *Tabernacle of Hate*. Prescott, Ontario: Voyageur, 1998.

Patrick, Ted. *Let Our Children Go*. New York: Ballantine, 1976.

Richardson, James, Joel Best, and David Bromley (eds.). *The Satanism Scare*. Hawthorne, NY: Aldine de Gruyter, 1991.

Wessinger, Catherine. *How the Millennium Comes Violently*. Chappaqua, NY: Seven Bridges Press, 2000.

8

MASS SUICIDE AND THE BRANCH DAVIDIANS

JOHN R. HALL

Long before the U.S. Bureau of Alcohol, Tobacco, and Firearms (BATF) set out on their ill-fated raid against the Branch Davidians' Mount Carmel compound on February 28, 1993, long before the April 19, 1993, conflagration that engulfed the compound, causing the death of some seventy-four Branch Davidians and ending their standoff with the Federal Bureau of Investigation (FBI), David Koresh's apocalyptic sect was becoming "another Jonestown." So said former Branch Davidians more than a year before the sect's shootout with BATF sharpshooters (Breault and King 1993: 11–12). I believe that the apostates were prophetic: Waco became a new Jonestown in the minds of the public. But was the former members' prophecy in part self-fulfilling? To probe this question, I examine here how cultural opponents of David Koresh reinvoked and reworked the central public meaning of Jonestown – mass suicide – in ways that shaped the conflict at Mount Carmel.

There is deep irony in the early prophetic warnings by former members against Mount Carmel as another Jonestown – a "cult." The people who put the most effort into labeling countercultural religious groups as "cults" typically are not passive bystanders or critics after the fact. They are active opponents. In the case of Jonestown, the movement *against* the Peoples Temple contributed to the dynamic of accelerating conflict that ended in the murders and mass suicide (Hall 1987). If, as I believe, Mount Carmel must be understood as another Jonestown, then we must ask whether anticult labeling played into the conflict.

The Peoples Temple and the Branch Davidians both approximated the "apocalyptic sect" as an ideal type. In such sects the "end of the world" is taken as a central tenet. Thus, we can theorize that on the basis of their internal organization and ideology alone, they are structurally more likely than other religious movements, to become involved in conflicts with an established social order (Hall, Schuyler, and Trinh 2000). But much depends on any given sect's response to its construction of the Apocalypse as collective life unfolds. At one extreme, a group may retreat to an otherworldly heaven-on-earth, disconnected from the evil society in its last days. Alternatively, it may seek out the battle of Armageddon – that last and decisive struggle between the forces of good and manifest evil (Hall 1978). Thus, no conclusions can be drawn in advance about the trajectory of an apocalyptic sect. For groups that have not stabilized a heaven-on-earth, the play of events is especially contingent on the interaction of the group with the wider social world. Because neither Jim Jones nor David Koresh established a stable heaven-on-earth, we cannot understand either the Branch Davidians or the Peoples Temple as a group with its own autonomous fate. Instead, we need to recognize that, like the tragedy at Jonestown, the conflagration at Mount Carmel was the product of religious conflict between a militant sect and opponents who, wittingly or unwittingly, helped fulfill the sect's emergent apocalyptic vision.

The apocalyptic visions of Jim Jones and David Koresh were quite different, of course. Jones blended Pentecostal and liberal Christianity with political sympathies toward the world-historical communist movement, and he consolidated a politically engaged movement built on the apocalyptic premise that the Peoples Temple would offer an ark of refuge in the face of a prophesied U.S. drift toward race and class warfare. Koresh (whose birth name was Vernon Howell) was only twenty years old when he joined the Branch Davidians in 1979, and he did not forge a new apocalyptic vision; he appropriated a longstanding one. The Seventh-Day Adventists, from whence the Branch Davidian sect had emerged, was founded in the nineteenth century on a prophecy about the end of the world. From this messianic beginning, Adventists tried during the twentieth century to attain a legitimate denominational status within U.S. religion by suppressing their most florid apocalyptic visions, but in doing so they opened themselves to critiques by Adventist splinter sects that would reclaim the "true faith." The apocalyptic rhetoric of David Koresh is little different from the rhetoric of other such groups opposed to the Advent establishment, groups whose rhetoric is equally filled with references to the Seven Seals, plagues (AIDS), visions of glory, enemies of the faith, apostates, and the day of testing that is "just before us."

Despite their differences, however, Jones's Temple and Koresh's Branch Davidians had much in common. Both Jones and Koresh took up the project of founding expansionary religious movements. Like early Mormon polygamists, both Jones and Koresh fathered children with multiple sexual partners, in Koresh's case, some of them under the legal age of sexual consent. Koresh also seems to have established a military "men's house" separated from the women (Weber 1978: 357). Communally organized gender patterns of polygamy and the men's house can be used to create a militant proto-ethnic religious movement, bound together by the prophet's patrimonialist cadre of followers and hereditary succession of prophecy. Following such a protoethnic formula, Jones and Koresh each established what amounted to a "state within a state" – Jonestown, close to Guyana's border with Venezuela; and Mount Carmel, a tiny principality on a back Texas road. Through interaction with real (and, in Jones's case, sometimes imagined) opponents, both Jones and Koresh prepared for militant armed struggle. For his part, Koresh consolidated his sectarian leadership through a violent confrontation in 1987 with the competing claimant to the Mount Carmel legacy, George Roden. In the face of increasing external opposition, Koresh, like Jones, steeled his followers to "metanoia" – revolutionary rebirth – in which the meanings of life – and death – became bound up with unfolding events.

Such parallels show that the Peoples Temple and the Branch Davidians shared a structural propensity toward conflict with outside opponents and authorities, but they do not account for the tragedies. In the case of Mount Carmel, how the standoff between the Davidians and the FBI was precipitated by the BATF raid has been the subject of minute analysis. The U.S. Treasury Department report defended as legal and legitimate the BATF pursuit of Koresh for weapons violations (1993: 120), and it strongly denied that the BATF acted against Koresh because of his deviant religious beliefs (1993: 121). However, the latter claim is open to question, since Mount Carmel was cast as a "cult" in the affidavit in support of applications for search and arrest warrants at Mount Carmel (U.S. District Court 1993). Indeed, the U.S. Treasury review is self-refuting on the supposed irrelevance of Koresh's religion, since it evidences the threat that Koresh posed by reference to his apocalyptic theology. These incongruities suggest the need to understand how cultural rather than official lenses shaped the vision of BATF in the conflict.

Because cultural narratives about "cults" are distinctive in comparison to the rhetoric of law enforcement, it is possible to trace the interplay between cultural constructions and legal ones. One cultural signification – mass suicide – is central in some ultimate sense to understanding both Jonestown and Mount Carmel. After Jonestown, "mass suicide" became a term of general cultural currency, a touchstone for describing the stark danger posed by cults. The existence of diverse documents makes it possible to trace in detail the emergence of mass suicide as a cultural meaning about Mount Carmel well *before* the BATF raid that led to the FBI standoff. Shifts in the significance of mass suicide can be traced by examining the "intrinsic narratives" that were offered by various social actors as events unfolded (Sewell 1992; Hall and Neitz 1993: 11; Hall 1999: chap. 3). As I will demonstrate, cultural opponents used a scenario that anticipated mass suicide as a basis for raising the alarm against the Branch Davidians. In turn, state social control agencies – especially the BATF – were strongly influenced by this scenario, and in ways that decisively affected the course of events at Mount Carmel.

The Narrative of Apocalyptic Militancy

The central narratives of Waco are, of course, those of David Koresh and his committed followers. Unfortunately, they are also the narratives about which we know the least, and most of what we know is filtered through their protagonists, both former group members and governmental authorities. Yet available information suggests a pattern that parallels the emergence of the mass suicide motif at Jonestown. Jim Jones specifically appropriated Huey Newton's Black Panther Party analysis. Living for the cause could also mean dying for the cause. Mediated by the Peoples Temple's struggles with its opponents, revolutionary suicide ultimately became mass suicide. But this outcome was not foreordained (Hall 1987: 135–136).

The Branch Davidians did not invoke the Black Panthers. If Koresh's political sentiments ran in any direction, it was to the antistate populism of right-wing Christian survivalist movements. But Koresh's and his followers' attachments to apocalyptic theology were, if anything, stronger than those of the Peoples Temple. From its origins in the 1920s, the Branch Davidian movement was centered on the classic Seventh-Day Adventist questions about how exactly to interpret the Book of Revelations's clues about the last days. Koresh did not have to create an apocalyptic theology from the ground up; he did not even have to shift it from a pacifistic to a militant dispensation, for Adventist discourse already had well-developed themes of militancy, sacrifices made by the faithful, and their subjection to trials from the outside – in short, the strongest motifs drawn from a long tradition of Christian martyrdom (Hall 1987: 296–298).

Yet there is considerable evidence that Koresh was an existentialist, not a predestinationist: He anticipated the apocalypse, but its form was open-ended. During the long standoff with the FBI, Koresh kept waiting for "signs" that would reveal the godly course of action. Before the BATF raid, he acted with civility and a degree of compliance toward governmental officials, including a sheriff and a deputy who served an arrest warrant over the Roden shootout in 1987. After the BATF raid, the prosecuting district attorney involved in the 1987 arrest, Vic Feazell, recounted, "We treated them like human beings, rather than storm-trooping the place. The were extremely polite people" (*Houston Chronicle*, March 2, 1993).

To note the existential civility of the Branch Davidians is not to deny that Koresh was willing to resort to violence. However, neither is it evident that Koresh was preparing to attack, and it is at least plausible, as even the Treasury Department review acknowledges, that he "might simply have been preparing to defend himself against an apocalyptic onslaught" (U.S. Treasury Department 1993: 127). In the final analysis, these considerations about what directions the apocalyptic struggle *might* have taken are moot, for tensions heightened considerably early in 1992, and Koresh came upon direct signs that he could interpret by way of ancient biblical prophecies about the last days.

The Narrative of Mass Suicide in the Opponents' Cries for Help

Given the long standoff before the final FBI assault and the subsequent fire, it is clear that David Koresh had no single apocalyptic scenario in mind before the BATF raid. Although there was a generalized apocalyptic narrative within Mount Carmel before the raid, the first specific invocation of mass suicide came from outside the Branch Davidians, from former sect members who had become opponents. What was this narrative, and how and where did it become more widely diffused? There were complex pathways, but as with Jonestown (Hall 1987: chaps. 9, 10), relatively small and converging clusters of opponents, informed by the discourse of the anticult movement, raised the alarm with the media and multiple governmental agencies.

Certain details about how the discourse of mass suicide emerged, and then spread from the private into the public and governmental domains, have not yet (and may never) become public knowledge. But the major channels are clear. Mostly they trace from Marc Breault, a Roman Catholic from Hawaii, who joined the Branch Davidians in 1986. Breault left after becoming increasingly dismayed about Koresh's practice of engaging in sexual relationships and siring children with young teenage girls whom the leader initiated into the "House of David." As Breault recounted, he became disgusted by witnessing thirteen-year-old Aisha Gyarfas pass by his desk after spending the night with David Koresh sometime in July 1989. On August 5, 1989, Breault heard what he called Koresh's "New Light" doctrine justifying the sexual economy of the Branch Davidians, a doctrine connected to the role Koresh assumed as the "sinful messiah" (Tabor and Arnold, in Koresh 1995: 206). In September, Breault flew to Australia and took up the role of "cultbuster," working tirelessly to bring Koresh down. Gradually Breault consolidated a band of Australian apostates, and they began to engage in a clandestine struggle, seeking to avoid what they feared were Koresh's stakeouts by meeting in the middle of the night (Breault and King 1993: 151, 213).

By small steps, a story about possible violent retribution for their opposition emerged among the gathering apostates as they worked to help other people break away from the Branch Davidians and raised the alarm to governmental agencies. Two families were central to their efforts – the Bunds and the Jewells. Koresh had banished David and Debbie Bunds. They later claimed that they received a threatening phone call after Breault got in touch with them, and they decided to move from Waco to California. There they linked up with David Bunds's sister, Robyn, a Koresh "wife" who broke with Koresh over a period of months beginning in the summer of 1990. In Breault's description of Robyn's defection, he suggests a theme that went beyond vengeance against enemies – child sacrifice. Robyn Bunds had given birth to a child that remained with the Branch Davidians, and she became distraught about her son: "I've heard that he's talking about sacrificing children! My God, what if he tries to kill Wisdom?" (Lindecker 1993: 145–146; *Washington Post*, April 25, 1993). As Breault explains, "We were worried that Koresh might be thinking about human sacrifices. We didn't know for sure, but Koresh was unstable enough to make even our darkest nightmares seem possible" (Breault and King 1993: 220). This sort of "atrocity tale" became repeated, elaborated, and amplified over time. Similarly, Breault became concerned about his own life: "Koresh wanted to lure me back to Mount Carmel and kill me" (Breault and King 1993: 226, 233). To date, we have no way of tracing such stories back from Breault's accounts. Taken together, they weave a vision of sadistic violence and unrestrained retribution. But for the most part, the narratives do not claim to be about actual events: they are about rumors, nightmares, and anticipated agendas.

Nightmares were not cause for governmental intervention, but other matters were. In March 1990, the defectors hired an Australian private investigator, Geoffrey Hossack, to help them in their struggle against Koresh. The following August, Breault called his band of defectors to a meeting in Australia and offered a "Bible study on human sacrifices." He told the assembled persons a story that he said he had been told by Koresh's close associate, Steve Schneider: "God was going to demand that Koresh do with his son Cyrus what Abraham of old was commanded to do with Isaac." (According to the book of Genesis, God instructed Abraham to stop short of sacrificing his son only at the last moment.) Breault's wording here is intriguing: He did not say that God actually made any such demand of Koresh, and although he asserted that he was in possession of damaging tape recordings of Koresh's preaching, he did not quote Koresh directly on the matter. Yet the story of child sacrifice, in various versions, became a key element in Breault's account of the dangers at Mount Carmel. Borrowing a page from the tactics of so-called cults themselves (Hall 1987), Breault used the story at the Australia meeting to "shock" his audience and "weeded out those [he] couldn't trust." Those whom Breault could trust drew up affidavits about statutory rape, immigration violations, food and water deprivation, and concerns about child sacrifices. Hossack flew to the United States with the barrage of affidavits, and in September 1990 he met with officers from the LaVerne, California, police department and, in Waco, with an investigator from the Texas Department of Public Safety, Lt. Gene Barber of the McClennan County Sheriff's Department, the McClennan County district attorney, and the assistant U.S. attorney. Hossack also talked with the Internal Revenue Service and the Immigration and Naturalization Service. Soon after these meetings, the FBI and the assistant U.S. district attorney, Bill Johnston, determined that no federal violations had occurred, and closed their case (U.S. Treasury Department 1993: D3).

Like the opponents of the Peoples Temple (Hall 1987: 228–235), Breault and his allies became frustrated at the lack of official response, and they pursued other avenues, namely, the media and their own court actions. In late 1991 and early 1992, they worked through two connected efforts – a television exposé and a custody struggle (Breault and King 1993: 256). In October 1991 Breault attracted the interest of the Australian Channel Nine program *A Current Affair*. The Australian television crew undertook what they believed to be a dangerous mission – exposing Koresh "as a cruel, maniacal, child-molesting, pistol-packing religious zealot who brainwashed his devotees." When they visited Mount Carmel in

January 1992, they already had been warned by "former cult members" that Mount Carmel might become "another Jonestown" (Breault and King 1993: 256–257).

The Australian television program did not yield much in the way of direct results. But the other initiative, the custody struggle, was critical to consolidating the movement against Koresh in the United States. The effort began in June 1991, well before the television program planning. Marc Breault had returned to the United States from Australia, having decided to target Kiri Jewell, the daughter of Branch Davidian member Sherri Jewel and her former husband, David, a disk jockey who had never been a Davidian. Breault was concerned that the preteenager was "destined" for the House of David. Unlike Breault's many woefully unsophisticated legal initiatives, the custody struggle over Kiri Jewell involved a specific grievance on the part of someone with legal standing. Once David Jewell learned from Breault in the fall of 1991 about the fate that awaited Kiri in the House of David, he promptly engaged an attorney and worked to obtain a Michigan court order for temporary custody when her mother sent the child to Michigan for the Christmas holidays.

Breault and the staff of *A Current Affair* had planned the January 1992 visit by the Australian TV crew partly to distract Koresh's attention from Kiri Jewell. As these events unfolded, the opponents received information that reinforced their vision of cultic destruction, and they, in turn, used the information to further spread alarm. In a January 1, 1992, letter to Breault, David Bunds reported that his sister had told him what his mother, Jeannine Bunds, had said sometime the previous summer. In this thirdhand account, Koresh was said to be telling people that his goals would be accomplished in half a year. "My mother also got the impression of mass suicide or homicide, she was not really sure."

The custody battle was the focal point. Koresh sent Steve Schneider to help Sherri Jewell in the February court case, and Breault and his allies decided to contact the Schneider family. On February 22, 1992, during preparations for the Jewell custody case, Sue Schneider, Steve's older sister, gave Breault chilling news:

> She said that Steve had called them to say goodbye. He said that he would probably have to do something which would cause him to die, but that he would be resurrected shortly thereafter and fulfill Isaiah 13 and Joel 2. . . . He sounded suicidal. The something which would cause him to die was termed "the end." This was not something

limited entirely to Steve himself, but concerned the whole group. (Breault and King 1993: 268)

Breault could not sleep one night, "thinking of my best friend blowing his brains out, or taking cyanide [part of the Jonestown mass suicide potion], or getting shot in a gun-fight with the authorities" (Breault and King 1993: 276; U.S. Treasury Department 1993: 28; cf. Hall 1987: xii).

Things actually went much better. On February 28, 1992, before the court case was concluded, David Jewell and Sherri Jewell reached an agreement for joint custody of Kiri. The custody case was over. However, like the apostates and relatives who opposed Jim Jones, David Jewell, Marc Breault, and others embraced a vision that transcended individual interests in the custody of children. They collectively worked to stop someone they regarded as morally abhorrent. When David Jewell learned of "two thirteen-year-old friends [of Kiri] also targeted to become brides in the House of David, he telephoned the Texas Department of Human Services" (Breault and King 1993: 279; Linedecker 1993: 144 [quote]; *Washington Post*, April 25, 1993; Waco *Tribune-Herald*, March 1, 1993: 9A). On the basis of a complaint on February 26, 1992, from "outside the state of Texas," as the affidavit supporting a search warrant put it, Joyce Sparks, of the Texas Child Protective Services (CPS), visited Mount Carmel with two sheriff's deputies the next day. Subsequently, Koresh came to see Joyce Sparks at the Waco CPS office in early March, and Sparks visited the compound two more times, on April 6 and 30, 1992. Davidian children and adults denied any abuse, and examinations of children produced no evidence of current or previous injuries. Over the objections of Sparks, the nine-week investigation was closed. Sparks then became a key informant for other government agencies, talking with the FBI in May 1992, maintaining contact by telephone with Koresh through June 1992, and providing the BATF with floor plans of the Mount Carmel compound in early December 1992 (U.S. Treasury Department 1993: D3–4; ABC *Primetime*, January 13, 1994).

Soon after the custody court case, in March 1992, Breault, David Jewell, and their allies began to spread the word that the Branch Davidians might commit mass suicide. All the substantive evidence that Breault and King offer on this key question comes from second- and thirdhand statements of Jeannine Bunds and Sue Schneider (Linedecker 1993: 152–153). The cited evidence is ambiguous at best, but like Peoples Temple dissidents (Hall 1987: 234), Koresh's opponents embellished their accounts in order to magnify the dangers of the organization that they sought to expose. In

March 1992, both Jewell and Breault wrote quite specific letters to David Jewell's congressman in Michigan, Fred Upton, about the possibility that the Branch Davidians would end their lives during Passover. In Breault's words, "the cult leader, one Vernon Wayne Howell [David Koresh], is planning a mass suicide somewhere around April 18th of this year. . . . Every day brings us closer to another Jonestown" (Breault and King 1993: 290–291). The letter quickly found its way to the FBI, which opened an investigation of Koresh for "involuntary servitude." In May 1992 they interviewed Joyce Sparks of the Texas CPS. But in June the FBI closed the investigation, apparently for lack of evidence (U.S. Treasury Department 1993: D4).

The account of mass suicide also began to percolate through other governmental and media channels. But on the question of whether there was ever any plan for mass suicide in April 1992, we have no direct evidence. Although Koresh's opponents spread the story widely, the event failed to materialize. The only public account of the reason is a cryptic statement, "The suicide plan was called off," in the *Washington Post* a year later (April 25, 1993: 1). Breault's book with Martin King is silent on why the suicide prediction was not fulfilled. The first record of David Koresh making any statement on the subject was his response to a Waco *Tribune-Herald* reporter at the time. Koresh asked why, if the stories were true, the Branch Davidians would be improving the facilities at Mount Carmel: "I've got the water-well man coming in. I mean, two weeks in a row we're supposed to be committing suicide. I wish they'd get their story straight" (quoted in Bailey and Darden 1993: 152).

My own view is that the opponents of David Koresh engaged in a long-standing fundamentalist practice – citing "proof texts" – to build a particular theological interpretation out of the deeply apocalyptic discourse that Koresh shared with other renegade Adventist sects. However, it is also evident that Koresh would have perceived increasing external signs of opposition during the first half of 1992. In January, he was the target of the Australian TV story informed by his opponents' claims against him. Throughout January and February, there was the custody struggle over Kiri Jewell. At the end of February, Mount Carmel was visited by Joyce Sparks of the Texas CPS. During the same days in early March when Koresh met in Waco with Sparks, a SWAT (Strategic Weapons and Tactics) law enforcement team undertook practice exercises near the "Mag Bag," a building some miles from Mount Carmel owned by the Branch Davidians. It was in these circumstances, beginning on February 1, 1992, and accelerating on and after March 9, 1992, that Koresh made his great leap forward toward a siege mentality. He began arming his followers at Mount Carmel with assault rifles and other paramilitary equipment, and he called upon some forty Branch Davidians to come to Mount Carmel from California and England (U.S. Treasury Department 1993: B168ff., D3–4). The timing in relation to the custody dispute and the subsequent Texas CPS investigation suggests a not unreasonable inference: Koresh likely believed that authorities might try to remove Branch Davidian children forcibly from the compound (as has happened at other religious communities both before and since), and he may have decided to resist by force any such possible move. No CPS raid ever occurred. However, the efforts of Koresh's opponents did lead to a distinctively heightened siege posture at Mount Carmel.

Mass Suicide as a Narrative of Strategic Law Enforcement

To this point, I have shown how the cultural opponents of David Koresh gleaned a narrative of mass suicide from Koresh's preachings and the hearsay accounts of defectors, and concretized and spread that narrative to governmental agencies and politicians at the state, federal, and local levels and to the media. The question to be addressed, in turn, is how narratives about mass suicide became infused into the scenarios that authorities constructed in relation to the Branch Davidians. To be sure, much other information came into the hands of officials, but by sticking to the question of mass suicide, it is possible to trace the influence of a central cultural motif and a potentially decisive causal factor.

The BATF investigation was initiated in May 1992 after a United Parcel Service driver discovered empty grenades in a package delivered to the Branch Davidians and reported his discovery to the McClennan County Sheriff's Department, which passed the information to the BATF Austin office. Agent Davy Aguilera was assigned to investigate, and he met on June 4, 1992, with Waco Assistant U.S. Attorney Bill Johnston and with Gene Barber of the sheriff's office – both of whom had been at the 1990 meeting with the Breault faction's private investigator, Geoffrey Hossack. To be sure, the BATF had its own interest in demonstrating its effectiveness as a law enforcement agency in relation to an armed "cult." But the BATF investigation became deeply immersed in webs of discourse that had been spun by Koresh's opponents (U.S. Treasury Department 1993: D4, 121, 125).

On July 23, 1992, agent Aguilera sent a report to BATF headquarters listing shipments to the Mag Bag and requesting an analysis of whether the Davidians were "possibly converting or manufacturing Title II weapons."

In October 1992, Aguilera was told to begin preparing an affidavit for search and arrest warrants (he also was authorized to set up an undercover house near the Mount Carmel compound). On November 2, 1992, BATF headquarters reported that there was not sufficient evidence based on the firearms listed in the July 23 report to justify a search warrant (U.S. Treasury Department 1993: B190, 193–194, D5). It was only – and immediately – after the disappointing news about lack of probable cause for a warrant that the BATF began to contact former members and relatives of Branch Davidians directly.

The contacts were extremely sensitive, because the BATF did not want to compromise their secret investigation; for this reason, it would seem, they limited themselves to interviewing committed opponents of Koresh. The contacts were substantial. On November 3, Davy Aguilera flew to California and met both with LaVerne police and with Isabel and Guillermor Andrade, who had two daughters living at Mount Carmel, one of whom, they said, had given birth to a child fathered by Koresh. Aguilera arranged for the Andrades to fly to Waco to visit their daughters on November 5 through 7, and then he "debriefed" them. In addition, on the basis of sexual allegations made by the defectors, the BATF contacted Joyce Sparks, the Texas CPS caseworker, who reported that she had never been able to confirm any abuse because of staged tours, but she had seen a target range and heard a child talk about (and herself saw) "long guns." She also quoted Koresh as having told her, "My time is coming. When I reveal myself as the messenger and my time comes, what happens will make the riots in L.A. pale in comparison." From LaVerne police, Aguilera learned about Marc Breault and the Bunds family on December 12. Jeannine Bunds told Aguilera about a "hit list" that she said Koresh once mentioned to her, and David Bunds recounted a conversation in which his father, Donald, had said that he was armed and prepared to die for Koresh. When Aguilera telephoned Breault on December 15, he reinforced these accounts (Breault and King 1993: 294–301; U.S. Treasury Department 1993: 27–30, 211, B24, D5–7).

The BATF operatives drew no clear line between the gathering of evidence to establish probable cause for the search warrant and obtaining intelligence for tactical planning (which began even while agents continued to gather information for probable cause). Moreover, the BATF tended to treat opponents' accounts as facts without considering whether the former members had "individual biases, or if they had an ax to grind," as two outside reviewers later pointed out (U.S. Treasury Department 1993: B19, 129–130). Thus, both the warrant and the BATF's tactical plan for responding to Koresh used information supplied by Koresh's opponents.

Tactical planners adopted the view that the BATF had to take action to deal with the Mount Carmel case. They did so partly because Koresh's documented 1987 attack on George Roden had established his propensity toward violence and partly because of reports to the BATF about "alleged threats against former cult members." The BATF "simply did not want to risk the added possibility that cult members would turn their weapons against members of the community," although they did not specify what evidence led them to this concern.

With the decision to take action made, at various points the BATF envisioned three alternative scenarios: (1) attempting to serve warrants peaceably and, if they met resistance, laying siege against Mount Carmel with negotiations for surrender, (2) staging a "dynamic entry," in which agents would storm the compound and secure it for the search and any arrests, and (3) luring Koresh away from the compound in order to facilitate an execution of the search warrant. Planners tended to discount the third option, partly because Joyce Sparks (incorrectly) told the BATF that Koresh rarely, if ever, left Mount Carmel. Moreover, at this juncture, the BATF did not have an arrest warrant, and it is possible that they downplayed this option because they did not believe that they had probable cause to detain Koresh. The BATF's initial plan, laid out at a meeting in Houston on December 18, 1992, was to pursue the serve-and-siege option. But a December 24 briefing at BATF headquarters in Washington, D.C., led to demands for slowing down tactical operations planning and requests for further development of probable cause. At the request of tactical planners, Davy Aguilera subsequently made arrangements to interview Marc Breault, the Bunds, and the Andrades in California from January 7 to 9, 1993, working jointly with William Buford, a BATF agent who was a member of the Special Response Team (SRT) that would be conducting any tactical operation at Mount Carmel (U.S. Treasury Department 1993: B47, 44, D7–8, 43). Breault also helped the BATF locate a man named David Block, who had spent several months at Mount Carmel, and on January 25, 1993, Aguilera and Buford interviewed Block (Breault and King 1993: 303–309; U.S. Treasury Department 1993: 38, 53, 151, D7–8).

The BATF agents' interviews with former Davidians and other opponents of Koresh contributed to the tactical thinking of the BATF concerning how to approach enforcement of weapons laws at Mount Carmel. Aguilera and Buford asked Breault what Koresh would do if he were issued a summons. Breault told them that Koresh would not answer a firearms summons, but he thought Koresh would respond to a Texas CPS summons because he "feels he has beaten that rap." What would Koresh do if authorities surrounded the compound: would he let the women and children go free? "No way," Breault replied, "He would use them as hostages." The U.S. Treasury Department report also indicated a deeper concern that surfaced: "Several former cult members, most forcefully Breault, noted the distinct possibility that Koresh might respond to a siege by leading his followers in a mass suicide; Breault expressed a particular fear for the children at the Compound" (Breault and King 1993: 305–306; U.S. Treasury Department 1993: 46 [quote], 53).

The BATF agents knew that David Block had been "deprogrammed" by an anticult operative. Professional intelligence procedures would have suggested that the validity of both his and other opponents' accounts should remain an open question. Instead, the BATF inserted tropes from the narratives of opponents into the scenario that they began to work up about the situation that they faced at Mount Carmel. David Block claimed that Koresh controlled the distribution of weapons. It may be that this account was out of date, but it aligned closely with Breault's anticult portrayal of Koresh as a despot who possessed "absolute control" over his followers. Overinterpreting information of questionable accuracy, the BATF made serious strategic errors in developing its final tactical plan for action. More generally, the opponents' narratives about Koresh's stance of forcible resistance to authority and the threat of mass suicide shaped the development of the tactical plan.

The BATF largely discounted the possibility that Koresh would submit willingly to a peacefully served warrant, so serving a warrant became strongly linked to the siege option. In late December 1992, the tactical planners saw logistical difficulties in a siege because of the open terrain around the compound and the possibility of injuries, but as late as January 21, 1993, they were still developing the siege option. However, "the concept of surrounding the compound and announcing their intention to enforce a warrant was discarded by BATF agents" at tactical meetings in Houston from January 27 to 29. Having come to regard the "lure-away" option as unlikely to materialize, and having rejected the siege option, the tactical planners overinterpreted the (probably inaccurate) information provided by David Block that Koresh controlled the weapons. Given the timing of the BATF shift in strategy relative to the times of interviews with opponents, it is likely that bad analysis of intelligence from David Block tipped the balance toward "increasing optimism" about the strategy of dynamic entry. If the assault could be carried out quickly under conditions in which Koresh's followers could not get to the weapons, the element of surprise would minimize the threat of mass suicide. On February 26, two days before the raid, BATF Director Stephen Higgins explained to Treasury Department officials – who wanted to call off the raid – that a siege would probably not work and that the use of scores of heavily armed agents to execute the warrant by force was necessary "because BATF feared that Koresh and his followers might destroy evidence or commit mass suicide if given the opportunity." No doubt sensing that a dynamic entry raid was a risky undertaking, BATF strategists continued during February 1993 to make efforts to lure Koresh out away from the compound, but without result (U.S. Treasury Department 1993: 53, B126 [quote], 142–145, B49, 65, 179, D9, 11–12; also Bailey and Darden 1993: 157–158; Breault and King 1993: 303–309).

The final scenario for the BATF raid was dynamic. "Ideally, if all went according to the script, all SRT teams would be able to 'exit the transportation vehicles in eight seconds, get into position and make entry at the front door in approximately 33 seconds.'" This rapid execution of the raid was deemed essential to the BATF's ability to keep men [*sic*] separated from the weapons supposed to be under Koresh's control (U.S. Treasury Department 1993: 64, B128).

Paradoxically, the accounts of mass suicide that shaped this scenario of dynamic entry may also have contributed to the failure of the BATF coordinators and commanders to call the raid off when they learned, on the day of the raid, that the element of surprise had been lost. The strategy of dynamic entry invested a great deal in the narrative of surprise. According to BATF reviewers, any dynamic raid gathers "momentum" from participants' bravado and will to succeed, and from the specters of failure, loss of tactical advantage, judgment by higher officials, and bad public relations. At Mount Carmel these pressures were exacerbated because there was an "absence of any meaningful contingency planning for the raid" (U.S. Treasury Department 1993: 175).

Why was there no fallback strategy? It must be recognized that a latent narrative of mass suicide would resurface if the scenario of dynamic entry were abandoned. Any scenario of failed surprise would be a scenario of siege. There is no way to pinpoint the exact magnitude of this influence on command decisions during execution of the attempted raid. But certain evidence is suggestive. The BATF had developed and justified the scenario of dynamic entry by a contorted process that eliminated an alternative scenario – serving a warrant and falling back to a siege position if resistance was encountered – because the alternative scenario of siege might lead to mass suicide. On the day of the raid, to lose the element of surprise in effect would reopen the scenario of siege, and by extension, mass suicide. The lack of contingency planning, articulated in latent ways with the narrative of mass suicide, amplified the momentum of the raid. Ironically, taking mass suicide seriously had the effect of avoiding it within tactical planning by designing a scenario in which it would not be an issue.

In turn, the repressed narrative of mass suicide may have directly influenced the actions of BATF commanders on the day of the raid – Sunday, February 28, 1993. That morning, Robert Rodriguez, the BATF undercover agent who was visiting the compound, heard Koresh announce, "Neither the ATF nor the National Guard will ever get me. They got me once and they'll never get me again." "They are coming for me but they can't kill me." Rodriguez knew that he had been "burned" (i.e., that his "cover" had been lost), and he knew that Koresh was making specific reference to the raid that had been planned for an hour later. Rodriguez left the compound, returned to the undercover house across the road, and reported on his conversation with Koresh. On hearing the news, one BATF "forward observer" at the undercover house was so convinced that the raid would be called off that he started to pack up his gear. But the response of the raid commanders at the command post some miles away was exactly the opposite. BATF agent Chuck Sarabyn, who took the call from Rodriguez, learned that the element of surprise had been lost. In turn, he asked Rodriguez whether he had seen any weapons, a call to arms, or preparations. Rodriguez replied that when he had left the compound, people had been praying. After confirming with another agent, who was watching the compound, that there was no sign of activity, Sarabyn offered the opinion that the raid could still go forward if the agents moved quickly. He briefly conferred with other raid commanders. They broke from their huddle and moved to various tasks, using language like "Let's go," "Get ready to go, they know we're coming," "We better do this ASAP," and "They know ATF and the National Guard are coming. We're going to hit them now." Despite the effort to "hurry up," the agents conducting the raid did not arrive at the compound until forty minutes after the first report from Rodriguez (U.S. Treasury Department 1993: 89 [quotation], 91 [quotation], 166–167 [quotation], 195 [quotations], 197, B43).

The Treasury Department review argues that the decision to hurry up "made no sense": either Koresh was not going to prepare for the raid, in which case accelerating the schedule was unnecessary, or he was going to prepare, in which case – given the time required for the logistics of getting the raid underway – acceleration was useless (U.S. Treasury Department

1993: 171–172). In short, hurrying up does not salvage lost surprise. Was there then some other available meaningful definition of the situation? One alternative motive that offers at least some rationale for hurrying up is concerned with "prevention of an imminent event." If something is about to happen, quick action may prevent it. But what was about to happen? The imminent event cannot be lost surprise because at the time of hurrying up, lost surprise was an event of the past, not the future. However, a clear concern that shaped the development of tactical strategies in the months before the raid was that Koresh and his followers might commit mass suicide. With the loss of surprise, might the raid commanders ask whether such an action was imminent? The three BATF raid commanders had all been present at the meetings in Houston from January 27 to 29 at which concerns about mass suicide were discussed. With this concern already established in all their minds, once the element of surprise was lost, it would have been reasonable for the raid commanders to consider the possibility of mass suicide. At the compound were deeply apocalyptic religious people, reading the Bible after having been informed that the authorities were coming after them. In his conversation with Robert Rodriguez, Koresh referred to the "Kingdom of God," and stated, "the time has come" (U.S. Treasury Department 1993: 89). Whether the raid commanders received this information from Rodriguez and explicitly interpreted it within the framework of mass suicide, I have no way of knowing. But the motive structure for accelerating the raid makes a good deal more sense within such a framework than it does within the context of lost surprise. On this analysis, BATF raid commanders discounted the importance of lost surprise because accepting it would have required canceling the raid, and canceling the raid would have precipitated a siege. Because of the specter of mass suicide, a siege was not a fallback option; it was an imminent event to be avoided.

Conclusion

The BATF raid on February 28, 1993, was a monumental failure. At the end of the ensuing standoff between the FBI and the Branch Davidians, the April 19, 1993, FBI's teargas assault on the compound and the ensuing fire (whatever its cause) fulfilled only one stated objective – that of suppressing an armed group. The children, who were ostensibly to be saved from abuse, died instead. Was this the mass suicide that Marc Breault and the other opponents had predicted? U.S. governmental interpretations of events led to conclusions that cast doubt on their defense of their actions.

Facing persistent public controversy, the government worked hard to lay to doubt any questions concerning whether their own actions at Mount Carmel constituted a legitimate exercise of governmental authority. In two investigations (Scruggs, Zipperstein, Lyon, Gonzalez, Cousins, and Beverly 1993; Danforth 2000) and in the wrongful-death suit brought by Branch Davidian survivors and relatives (U.S. District Court 2000), the government officially sustained its position that it did not hold any responsibility for the April 19 fire and, hence, for the deaths.

But theirs is a narrow analysis. It seems incontrovertible that the fire that did occur would not have happened in the absence of the FBI assault. Even if the FBI assault was not the sole cause of the fire, the assault was an antecedent condition causally necessary for any explanation of the subsequent fire, the deaths that ensued, and the obliteration of Mount Carmel. If the Branch Davidians started the fire on purpose, as the government's evidence indicates, the Davidians' act certainly could be understood as an act of mass suicide. Because such an act would snatch victory away from their opponents at the cost of their own lives, it would directly parallel the deaths of over 900 people in the 1978 mass suicide and murder at Jonestown. In both cases, the actions emerged in the process of extended and pitched conflict with opponents. At Jonestown, the threat to the destruction of the community was more emblematic than immediate, but at Mount Carmel on April 19, the FBI was engaged in the rapid and systematic physical destruction of the Branch Davidians' home. The mass suicide at Mount Carmel – if that was what occurred – lacked the ritualistic and collective character of the mass suicide at Jonestown. In the face of the continuing assaults, people at Mount Carmel died in different parts of the building, some from the fire, others from gunshot wounds, either self-inflicted or "mercy killings" at the hands of others.

The play of narratives about mass suicide in the FBI standoff with the Branch Davidians up to April 19 is a subject in its own right (for a comparative analysis, see Wagner-Pacific 2000). However, even a cursory examination suggests that the FBI viewed mass suicide as an inherent and static predisposition of a sect rather than as a possible response to a dynamic and shifting situation. After the conflagration, the FBI justified the tactical view they had taken in planning the assault – that mass suicide would not be a likely outcome – by citing David Koresh's future-oriented statements *in the absence of the assault*, such as his interest in auctioning his book rights (*New York Times*, April, 22 1993: A1, 13). This static view of predisposition is based on a tendency that governmental authorities share with the anticult movement, a tendency to see the dynamics of "cults" as internal to such groups, rather than examining external social interaction in conflict between a sectarian group and opponents and authorities themselves.

Unfortunately, both authorities and opponents (and sometimes the media) have compelling vested interests in depicting the dynamics of "cults" as internal rather than external, and they are thus systematically biased toward misunderstanding the very social processes in which they assert the legitimacy of their interests. Despite the clear significance of their actions, cultural opponents have never seriously weighed their own roles in the negative outcomes of pitched conflicts with alternative religious movements. This avoidance of critical review does not align well with the legitimacy routinely extended by some governmental authorities and the media to operatives of the anticult movement. The modus operandi of anticult groups is to target "cults" with increasing pressure on a number of fronts (Zilliox and Kahaner n.d.). At both Jonestown and Mount Carmel, the cultural opponents succeeded in bringing authorities and the media to their side. In turn, the opponents could point to the tragic outcomes to validate their initial alarm.

I believe that Koresh's opponents must have pursued their mission according to the dictates of their consciences, and I cannot believe that any opponent of alternative religions would want to precipitate violence in order to prove a point. Nevertheless, in effect, the anticult movement benefits from "cult" tragedy. It is worth noting that in cases where the anticult movement did not play an active role in precipitating conflict, governmental authorities were sometimes able to bring a standoff to a peaceful resolution (as they did in the 1985 siege against the Arkansas communal settlement of armed white supremacists who called themselves the Covenant, the Sword, and the Arm of the Lord). On the other hand, there have been truly devastating and disastrous results in two cases where the anticult movement played a strong role – Jonestown and Mount Carmel. My own assessment based on these facts is this: insofar as participants in the anticult movement fail to acknowledge that their strategies can lead to the escalation of apocalyptic conflict, both the media and governmental authorities should treat the movement as lacking in portfolio in matters concerning deviant religious sects.

The First Amendment to the U.S. Constitution legally proscribes the state from taking sides in matters of religion. Defenders of state action will no doubt emphasize the obligation of the state to enforce its laws. They already claim (for example, in the Treasury Department review) that this was the objective at Mount Carmel. But such a defense of state action is flawed. It would be one thing if cultural opponents and governmental authorities acted independently of one another, even if they shared an affinity of goals due to different interests. But the emergence of narratives about mass suicide shows something quite different. The degree to which certain governmental authorities consciously took up the cause of the cultural opponents remains an open question. Whatever the answer to that question, the connection of governmental action to cultural opposition runs much deeper. Mount Carmel does not just bear comparison to Jonestown as a similar but independent event. Instead, there was a *genetic* bridge between Jonestown and Mount Carmel. Specifically, the opponents of Koresh took tropes about mass suicide derived from the apocalypse at Jonestown, reworked them, and inserted them into accounts that they offered about the Branch Davidians. In turn, the opponents' reports about mass suicide directly structured the development of tactical scenarios for the BATF raid, and they may well have figured in the motive structures of BATF commanders on the day of the raid. In these direct yet presumably un-self-conscious ways, BATF operations became subordinated to the narratives of cultural opposition.

Meanings in the realm of public life are formed in part by the stories that people tell and the ways that other people hear these stories. On the basis of the stories that they hear, along with their own personal and cultural structures of meaning, and in relation to their own readings of their resources and situation, people make new meanings in both their accounts of past events and their scenarios of projected actions (cf. Sewell 1992: 16–17). As is demonstrated by examining the conflict that developed between the Branch Davidians, their cultural opponents, and the state, personal narratives of salvation from the evil of a cult can shape cultural cries for help, and in turn become elements of official state discourse – with disastrous consequences.

References

Bailey, Brad, and Bob Darden. *Mad Man in Waco: The Complete Story of the Davidian Cult, David Koresh, and the Waco Massacre.* Waco, TX: WRS Publishing, 1993.

Breault, Marc, and Martin King. *Inside the Cult: A Member's Chilling, Exclusive Account of Madness and Depravity in David Koresh's Compound.* New York: Penguin Signet, 1993.

Danforth, John C. *Interim Report to the {U.S.} Deputy Attorney General concerning the 1993 Confrontation at the Mount Carmel Complex, Waco Texas.* Pursuant to order 2256–99 of the Attorney General. July 21, 2000. Internet address: www.osc-waco.org.

Hall, John R. *Cultures of Inquiry: From Epistemology to Discourse in Sociohistorical Research.* New York: Cambridge University Press, 1999.

Gone From the Promised Land: Jonestown in American Cultural History.* New Brunswick, NJ: Transaction, 1987.

The Ways Out: Utopian Communal Groups in an Age of Babylon. Boston: Routledge & Kegan Paul, 1978.

Hall, John R., and Mary Jo Neitz. *Culture: Sociological Perspectives.* Englewood Cliffs, NJ: Prentice-Hall, 1993.

Hall, John R., with Philip D. Schuyler and Sylvaine Trinh. *Apocalypse Observed: Religious Movements, the Social Order, and Violence in North America, Europe, and Japan.* New York: Routledge, 2000.

Koresh, David. "The Seven Seals of the Book of Revelation," with an "editorial preface" by J. Phillip Arnold and James D. Tabor and "A commentary on the Koresh manuscript" by James D. Tabor and J. Phillip Arnold. In James D. Tabor and J. Phillip Arnold, *Why Waco?* Berkeley: University of California Press, 1995: 187–211.

Linedecker, Clifford L. *Massacre at Waco, Texas: The Shocking True Story of Cult Leader David Koresh and the Branch Davidians.* New York: St. Martin's Press, 1993.

Scruggs, Richard, Steven Zipperstein, Robert Lyon, Victor Gonzalez, Herbert Cousins, and Roderick Beverly. *Report to the Deputy Attorney General on the Events at Waco, Texas, February 28 to April 19, 1993.* Redacted version. Washington, DC: U.S. Department of Justice, 1993.

Sewell, William H., Jr. "A Theory of Structure: Duality, Agency, and Transformation." *American Journal of Sociology* 98 (1992): 1–29.

U.S. Department of the Treasury. *Report of the Department of the Treasury on the Bureau of alcohol, Tobacco, and Firearms Investigation of Vernon Wayne Howell, Also Known as David Koresh.* Washington, DC: U.S. Government Printing Office, 1993.

U.S. District Court. "Special Interrogatories" [to jury] Civil No. W-96-CA-139, *Isable G. Andrade et al.* v. *United States of America.* Western District of Texas, Waco, Texas, 2000.

"Application and Affidavit for Search Warrant," W93–15M, and "Warrant for Arrest, Case #W93–17M, *U.S.A. v. Vernon Wayne Howell, AKA David Koresh.*" Western District of Texas, Waco, Texas, filed February 26, 1993.

Wagner-Pacific, Robin. *Theorizing the Standoff: Contingency in Action.* New York: Cambridge University Press, 2000.

Weber, Max. *Economy and Society*, edited by Guenther Roth and Claus Wittich. Berkeley: University of California Press, 1978.

Wood, James E., Jr. "The Branch Davidian Standoff: An American Tragedy." *Journal of Church and State* 35 (1993): 1–9.

Zilliox, Larry, Jr., and Larry Kahaner. "How to Investigate Destructive Cults and Underground Groups." n.d: 138 (photocopy).

9

OCCULT MASTERS AND THE TEMPLE OF DOOM: THE FIERY END OF THE SOLAR TEMPLE

MASSIMO INTROVIGNE AND JEAN-FRANÇOIS MAYER

On October 5, 1994, the Swiss police found the bodies of forty-eight members of the Order of the Solar Temple (OTS) on a farm in Cheiry and in three chalets in Granges-sur-Salvan. This tragic incident changed the entire picture of cult controversies in Western Europe, much more than events at Jonestown did in 1978 in the United States (Shupe, Bromley, and Breschel 1989). Its impact was reinforced by two subsequent OTS suicides, as well as by the Aum Shinrikyô case in Japan. Although active from the early 1970s, the European anticult movement had received minimal public support. After 1994, parliamentary commissions were appointed to investigate the danger of cults, and they produced, particularly throughout French-speaking Europe, official reports that essentially mirrored the views of the anticult movement. Although later reports were somewhat more moderate (Introvigne 1999a; Richardson and Introvigne 1999), documents produced in France (Assemblée Nationale 1996, 1999), Belgium (Chambre des Représentants de Belgique 1997), and the Canton of Geneva (Audit sur les dérives sectaires 1997) maintained a strict anticult position. It is significant that in addition to Quebec, the largest numbers of victims in the 1994 OTS tragedy were located in France (where an official "Mission to Fight Cults" was established in 1998), Belgium, and the Canton of Geneva.

In this chapter we discuss how a violent relationship between the OTS and the social order developed. As preliminary steps, we first briefly summarize the history of the OTS and then examine how different socially constructed narratives compete in accounting for what really happened to the OTS members. On these bases, we offer in the third section our own interpretation of the possible causes and dynamics that led to the tragedy. The fourth section offers some confirmation of this interpretation by presenting comparative observations of some similar cases.

A Short History of the OTS

The history of the OTS has been recounted in detail elsewhere (Introvigne 1995b, 1999b; Hall and Schuyler 1997; Mayer 1998, 1999a,b), and we therefore confine ourselves here to a brief summary. A number of new religious movements draw heavily on the western esoteric tradition and claim a (usually mythical) continuity with real or imaginary institutions dating back to the Middle Ages. One important group of movements claims a connection to the Rosicrucians (a mythical brotherhood of supposedly remote antiquity). The largest contemporary Rosicrucian movement is AMORC (the Ancient and Mystical Order Rosae Crucis), headquartered in San Jose, California, and founded by the American Harvey Spencer Lewis (1883–1939). Another group of movements claims an equally mythical connection with the medieval Knights Templar, a Catholic religious order suppressed in 1312. A few of these groups are connected, in turn, to the so-called Arginy movement, an esoteric renewal movement started by French author Jacques Breyer (1922–1996) following a mystical experience he claimed to have shared with two companions in 1952 in the ruins of Castle Arginy in France. The key figure in the OTS tragedy, Joseph Di Mambro (1924–1994), joined AMORC in 1956, left it around 1970, and apparently became associated with the Arginy movement in the 1960s. Having moved to Switzerland, he established himself as a full-time teacher of occult philosophy and organized the Golden Way Foundation in 1978. In 1982, Luc Jouret (1947–1994) joined the Golden Way Foundation. Jouret was a successful Belgian homeopathic doctor and a former member of various esoteric groups. Di Mambro was never a particularly engaging speaker, and in Jouret he gained an effective spokesman who was soon to become well known in the French-speaking cultic milieu. Jouret became active on behalf of Di Mambro's organization through the Amenta Club (later renamed Archedia) and a variety of other ventures. Di Mambro also used Jouret to gain control of one of the largest neo-Templar orders, the Renewed Order of the Temple (ORT). This order had been founded and incorporated in 1970 by Raymond Bernard (b. 1923), who at that time was the leader of AMORC in the French-speaking world. In 1971, Bernard designated Julien Origas (1920–1983) as the new president of the ORT. Although by his own account Origas initially was only a "straw man" for Bernard (Caillet 1997: 56), at the end of 1972 the American leadership of AMORC persuaded Bernard to abandon the neo-Templar venture and Origas continued on his own. Origas was in touch with Di Mambro from the time when they were both members of AMORC and regarded himself as part of Breyer's Arginy movement.

On March 21, 1981, the ORT, the Sovereign Order of the Solar Temple (another neo-Templar organization established in 1966 as part of the Arginy movement), and the Golden Way Foundation met together in Geneva in a ceremony later regarded by Di Mambro as a founding event for the OTS. Di Mambro, however, did not control the ORT in 1981. He managed to introduce Jouret to Origas, and evidence exists that before his death in 1983, Origas designated the Belgian doctor as his successor. This claim was contested, however, by the Origas family, and the majority of the old ORT members have continued to maintain a separate ORT with several hundred members that has no relation whatsoever with Di Mambro, Jouret, and their group. Because of the disputes on the legal rights to the name ORT, Di Mambro and Jouret decided in 1984 to incorporate a new neo-Templar organization called ORT-Solar Tradition, later renamed the International Order of Chivalry-Solar Tradition and finally the Order of the Solar Temple.

In 1984, the OTS attempted to expand into North America. Because all of its leaders spoke French, the order attracted fewer than twenty members in the United States even with the publication of a book in English (Delaforge 1987). More than eighty joined in Quebec, however, where Jouret became a popular speaker; and a commune was established in Sainte-Anne-de-la-Pérade. At its peak in 1989 the OTS had about 500 members internationally.

In 1991, the OTS started attracting the attention of anticult organizations, initially in Martinique, where it had a small branch. In addition, there was an investigation by the Canadian police in 1993 following an attempt by the OTS to buy illegal semiautomatic guns with silencers. Two members were arrested but were quickly released in Quebec; they (and Jouret) were later fined. Discreet (and inconclusive) financial investigations were also carried out in France and Australia following suspicious money transfers by Di Mambro. The first known internal text relating to the "Transit," together with the Canadian investigation, both date from February 1993. By this time, the OTS also was experiencing serious internal problems. In Canada there was a division within the organization, referred to as a "schism" at the time by the OTS lawyer, following open criticism of Jouret, who had moved to Quebec as a local leader. To call the incident a schism was an exaggeration, however, since both of the resulting branches still acknowledged Di Mambro's final authority. Di Mambro's leadership was seriously challenged in Europe, however, as members discovered that visible manifestations of "Masters of the Temple" actually were electronic and other tricks arranged by Di Mambro himself. Further, the leader was suffering from health problems. Finally, his "cosmic child" Emmanuelle (1982–1994), allegedly the fruit of a mystical act of intercourse between Di Mambro's mistress, Dominique Bellaton (1958–1994), and a discarnate Master, was growing restless and experiencing increasing problems in accepting her designated role.

When, in connection with the pending police investigations, Di Mambro's wife, Jocelyne (1949–1994), was denied renewal of her French passport in 1994, the OTS leadership stated in an internal document that their order was "the hottest [police] file on the planet, the most important of the decade if not of the century." The OTS leaders concluded that "the game is afoot, and the concentration of hate against us will supply the energy needed for our departure." Messages from discarnate entities channeled by both Di Mambro and Camille Pilet (1926–1994), a prominent Swiss businessman who had joined the OTS around 1987, also confirmed the need for a Transit. The Swiss police investigation revealed that a large number of the members who had congregated in Cheiry in October 1994 (unlike those in Salvan) were probably not planning to commit suicide. They expected the Transit to another planet to take place in a supernatural way, perhaps through the arrival of a space ship. Only a core group of members was aware of all the details of the planned suicide; Di Mambro's opponents, who were regarded as traitors, were lured innocently to their deaths. There was a similar sequence of events in Canada, where the Dutoit family, who knew about the electronic tricks Di Mambro employed and was regarded as untrustworthy, was executed in Morin Heights, Quebec, by two Swiss members, who then committed suicide three days before the Swiss tragedy. On October 5, the Swiss police found twenty-three bodies in Cheiry and twenty-five in Salvan at farms destroyed by incendiary devices. Most victims in Cheiry had been killed by pistol shots after they had ingested a soporific substance, and plastic bags had been placed over their heads. Those in Salvan were poisoned, although some died (while already agonizing) in the subsequent fire. The Swiss police investigation and the documents sent by the OTS to the press, former members, and scholars (the so-called Testament) agreed on the fact that there were different victim categories in the Swiss incidents. Traitors were executed, most of them in Cheiry. Core members and the leadership committed suicide, mostly in Salvan. There was also a third category, of weaker members, who may have accepted the idea of suicide but needed some "help" in accomplishing it. Children who shared the faith of their parents were obviously not in a position to make a decision and were simply murdered.

A second tragedy occurred in 1995. On December 23, sixteen members of the OTS including three children, were found dead in the mountains of Vercors near Grenoble, France. French authorities are still investigating the incident at the time of this writing. Finally, on the night of March 21, 1997, another five members of the OTS committed suicide in Saint-Casimir, Quebec. In this episode the teenage children of those committing suicide were asked whether they wanted to join in the suicide and decided they would rather not. The final tragedy in Saint-Casimir suggests that, although only a handful of former OTS members remain loyal to OTS ideology, it is possible that some of them will continue to believe that a Transit is ultimately their only logical option.

Conflicting Narratives of the Tragedy

The tragedy of the OTS was highly unusual, with its most dramatic elements taking place in Switzerland, a country not normally associated with scenarios of doom. Members did not match the typical stereotype of cultists. Most were middle-aged, upper-middle-class, solid Swiss and Canadian citizens. Some were well-respected figures in the business community. Camille Pilet was recently retired as director and international sales manager of a Swiss multinational watch corporation and was in the process of launching his own brand of designer watches. Patrick Vuarnet (1968–1995), who mailed the Testament after the first tragedy and died in the second in France, was the son of the president of an international fashion company and former Olympic ski champion Jean Vuarnet. Robert Falardeau (1947–1994) was the chief of a (minor) department at the Ministry of Finances of Quebec. Joyce-Lyne Grand'Maison (1950–1994) was a former contributing editor of the financial section of the daily *Journal de Québec*. Robert Ostiguy (1940–1994) was mayor of Richelieu, Quebec.

Not surprisingly, reconstruction of the tragedy soon became the feeding ground for competing narratives oriented to both exegesis and hermeneutics. While exegesis evaluates the degree of analogy between narratives and reality, hermeneutics deals with their interpretation. From the point of view of exegesis, primary narratives of the OTS tragedy are found in the police reports, some of them quite simple and others more elaborate. These reports were more interested in ascertaining what happened rather than why. Actors other than law enforcement agencies (the media, the anticult movement, and scholars) entered the hermeneutic field, however, and proposed what we may summarize as five different narratives.

Immediately after the 1994 events, a large section of the French-speaking media immediately applied to the tragedy the anticult stereotype. Swiss sociologist Roland Campiche (1995: 32–35) analyzed the main op-ed sections of six leading Swiss French-language daily newspapers in the week after the first OTS tragedy and found a number of common elements. All newspapers called the OTS a "cult" (*secte*, a somewhat derogatory word in French that bears many of the same connotations as the English word "cult") rather than the softer word that translates into English as "sect"). Members were labeled as "weak," "marginal," "naive," "sheeplike," and even "gullible fools (*doux dingues*)." OTS doctrine was dismissed as the "manipulative ideas of a guru" (believed in the immediate aftermath of the tragedy to be Luc Jouret), "fanaticism" or "delirium." The main thrust of the newspaper articles centered on the "danger of the cults" and the lack of an appropriate response to it. Within two weeks, however, the media realized that most of the victims were middle-aged and quite well off. The anticult movement, taking over from the media, introduced the usual arguments about brainwashing and mind control, claiming that the wealthy and the powerful are not immune to the power of brainwashing gurus. A psychiatrist in private practice in France, Jean-Marie Abgrall, emerged as the main spokesman for a crude brainwashing interpretation of OTS activities and was actually appointed as a court expert in the French case (Abgrall 1999).

The Belgian parliamentary report (1997) also applied to the OTS a classical brainwashing interpretation. The Belgian report repeatedly quotes Lifton's (1989: 419–437) eight psychological themes of thought reform or ideological totalism. Lifton's themes are then described as being typically represented both in the OTS and in other "dangerous cults" engaged in mind control. There are a number of problems inherent in this reconstruction, however. First, Lifton (1987: 211) cautioned not to "use the word brainwashing because it has no precise meaning and has been associated with much confusion." Second, as Anthony (1996) has shown, brainwashing arguments (built around the idea that conversions to cults are involuntary and caused by powerful extrinsic techniques) and totalitarian influence arguments à la Lifton are not identical. The latter, unlike the former, "are built around the core idea that conversions to totalistic ideologies result primarily from predisposing motives, i.e. a genuine inner interest in such ideologies" (Anthony 1996: 125); they also require the conversion to take place in a particular milieu. Third, a study of the OTS would not entirely satisfy the first of Lifton's (1989: 420) eight themes: "milieu control," or separation of the individual from the outside world. (1987: 212). A number of OTS members either did not live communally or lived communally only for a comparatively short time. Some of them, including fanatical proponents of the Transit such as Pilet, had extremely successful business or social lives outside the OTS. They were literally businesspersons by day and servants of the occult Masters by night. They had to be exposed to a variety of other relationships and information within the context of free societies (such as Switzerland or Quebec) as opposed to the situation in Communist China studied by Lifton. In order to counter these objections, those who want to interpret the OTS tragedy on the basis of the anticult paradigm need to claim that milieu control can be achieved by means of psychological manipulation only and that such manipulation is equally effective for all sorts of different individuals. In doing so, they move away from Lifton's totalitarian influence argument toward the usual anticult brainwashing argument, which magnifies the differences between the two. It is unfortunate that in the post-OTS European cult wars, Lifton's works have been so often quoted in support of a crude brainwashing rhetoric. Some of his themes might otherwise have been very useful in interpreting the OTS. In his 1999 study of Aum Shinrikyô, Lifton still uses the word "cults" to designate totalistic and manipulative religious movements. However, having clarified that not all cults are inclined to violence, he introduces a subcategory of "world-destroying cults" whose key feature is "an ideology of killing" that includes a theological justification of murder (Lifton 1999: 202–213). He thereby further distances himself from the anticult interpretation by admitting that not all cults are inherently dangerous and that ideology and doctrine play a key role. Ignoring ideology in favor of a stereotype of cult is precisely the fatal flaw of the anticult interpretation of the OTS. It fails to explain why a cult such as the OTS ended up in tragedy, while other cults that apparently were no less totalistic than the OTS did not.

A second narrative, adopted by some media sources independently of any brainwashing argument, suggested that the OTS was not 'really' a religious movement but a front for something else such as a huge money-laundering enterprise, right-wing terrorist plans, organized crime, or illegal big business. A conspiracy narrative was gradually unfolding. It is now recognized that the exaggerated figures quoted for OTS bank holdings originated in a misreading of a telefax. One of the authors of this chapter (Introvigne 1995a,b) unwittingly contributed to the conspiracy myth by mentioning the fact that some neo-Templar movements, predecessors of the

OTS (but not the OTS itself), had a history of connections with the French Service d'Action Civique (SAC), a private right-wing organization with ties to the Gaullist party that was halfway between a private secret service and a parallel police unit. Since the French interior minister, Charles Pasqua, had maintained a connection with the SAC, the fact that Di Mambro ordered Vuarnet to send his and his wife's passports to Pasqua after the first tragedy may have implied an allusion to those old stories. This interpretation gained credibility because Di Mambro had already been part of the neo-Templar milieu when the SAC connections were widely discussed in the 1970s. This information resulted in widespread reports that the OTS was connected to the secret services and organized crime. When neither scholars nor the Swiss police were able to confirm the conspiracy narrative, both parties were simply represented as being part of the conspiracy (Marhic 1995, 1996; Bédat, Bouleau, and Nicolas 1996). The fact remains, however, that no evidence of a conspiracy has emerged.

A third narrative with a more social-psychological character comes primarily from scholars, who in their initial comments often adopted a kind of neo-Weberian interpretation in an effort to determine what sort of charisma could rightfully be attributed to OTS leaders. They were initially confused by the assumption that Luc Jouret was the primary leader. This impression might at first have been supported by their reading of the only pretragedy scholarly study of the OTS, by one of the authors of this chapter (Mayer 1993), in which Jouret figured prominently. It became clear subsequently that the main character was indeed Di Mambro, whom Jouret regarded as his leader. There were occasional disagreements between them, however, that apparently persisted to the end. Some of the versions of the Testament were supplemented by a short note that probably was written by Di Mambro's wife between the first incident in Cheiry and the second in Salvan. The note cited "the barbarian, incompetent and aberrant behavior of Dr. Luc Jouret" as having transformed into "a real carnage" what should have been "a Transit performed with Honor, Peace and Light." Once Di Mambro was discovered to be the real leader, social-psychological interpretations focused on him. When information alleged that Di Mambro was compelled to wear diapers and that he had seen his authority threatened by internal dissent, it was concluded that he had felt threatened by loss of charisma. Rather than see his charisma evaporate, it was argued, Di Mambro chose to use what charisma he still had to lead the OTS to its ultimate annihilation. In killing both others and themselves, loyal OTS members in October 1994 were acting out the paranoid delusions of one man. Although this interpretation, advanced by Susan Palmer (1996) and others, has its merits, it still leaves some questions unanswered. After the second and third tragedies of 1995 and 1997, it became even more apparent that Di Mambro's manipulative behavior could not have been the only explanation for the OTS process of self-destruction. Di Mambro's own problems might explain why he issued certain kinds of orders in 1994. But why did the OTS members comply? Why did some of them continue to execute Di Mambro's orders in 1995 and 1997, when he had been dead and buried for more than a year? These are key questions that the third narrative somewhat fails to answer.

Addressing precisely these questions, a fourth narrative slowly emerged, reflecting on the social-psychological situation not only of the leaders but also of the group as a whole. It was described as a "fragile" millennial group, ready to be ignited by an external incident (Hall and Schuyler 1997, 1998; Wessinger 2000). The external catalyst was, in this case, represented by the police investigation that interacted with various internal dynamics. This is a promising road, one that we will try to follow in the third part of the chapter. We will, however, also include elements from a fifth narrative that focuses on the essence of the OTS ideology. The authors of this chapter have noted in previous writings that Di Mambro's peculiar ideology was far from irrelevant to the events that transpired and that it played a crucial role in the OTS's ultimately fiery end (Introvigne 1995a,b, 1999c; Mayer 1998, 1999a,b). Others have mentioned the risks associated with a peculiar syncretistic brand of New Age belief, noting that syncretism may create an "explosive cocktail" (Campiche 1995: 9). The question remains, however, as to which syncretistic cocktails have the potential to "explode" while most others remain comparatively benign.

Why the Tragedy?

We argue that four factors may explain the OTS tragedy: predisposing apocalyptic ideology, perception of external opposition, internal dissent and apostasy, and crumbling charismatic authority of the leader. While each of these factors alone would probably not have been sufficient to cause the tragedy, it was ultimately their combination that led to the 1994 episode. The OTS was not unlike many other occult or New Age groups and began as a peaceful community. It is true that Di Mambro had been sentenced to a six-month suspended jail sentence in France in 1972 for breach of trust and for writing bad checks, but he had never been accused of physical violence. The same can be said of his followers: Only one of them had a police record, and this was due to drug use before he came in touch with the OTS. The group was certainly not a criminal community. It did, however, end up killing several people, including a three-month-old baby, who was repeatedly stabbed. What is more, the criminal actions were premeditated and carefully prepared. The strong apocalyptic component of the message created a climate in which the idea of the Transit could develop. In the 1980s, however, the OTS understood the Apocalypse not as the end of the world but as the end of a cycle. In a seminar that Jouret held in Lausanne, Switzerland, in October 1987, which one of the present authors attended, he explained that the Apocalypse should not be understood just as a description of external events; those events, in fact, reflect internal transformations. Humankind is now at the end of a 6,000-year-long Kali-Yuga, or Dark Age, he said. It is about to enter into a new world, one that will be era thanks to experience gathered by humankind in the course of those 6,000 years. Significantly, the title of the seminar was "Apocalypse: Which Future for the New Man?" Apocalypse, as the OTS understood it, definitely included cataclysmic events and disasters, but it was a prelude to a better world: "Positive forces are also at work" that can "stave off global disaster, or at least ensure that there will be enough survivors to carry the species toward the evolutionary blueprint intended for mankind" (Delaforge 1987: 132–133).

Strange as it may seem in retrospect, the message of the OTS was fundamentally one of survival and not of death. Money was gathered in order to establish so-called survival centers, and properties were investigated or bought for this purpose in Quebec and Australia as late as the early 1990s. The Canadian police investigation concluded that the guns bought illegally in 1993 were intended for the self-defense of people gathered in survival centers in the event of apocalyptic contingencies. A handbook for emergency help and advice in case of disasters such as a nuclear war was published by the group in 1986. The expectation of the advent of a New Age was counterbalanced by a very strong environmental concern within the OTS leadership. The topic of ecological disasters has been incorporated into a number of apocalyptic currents since apocalyptic traditions are "continually being revised and made relevant in response to changing circumstances" (Wojcik 1997: 173). Jouret's public lectures frequently stated that the Earth (seen as a living organism) was on the verge of an ecological disaster.

Apocalyptic beliefs created the background for the unfolding of the OTS drama but did not directly cause it. In order to get to the root of the events, we should perhaps begin by considering what the documents that the OTS sent to the media can teach us since they may reveal more than was intended by their authors at the time. The first document, "Transit for the Future," explains that "positive and creative forces" have been rejected; as a consequence, "we withdraw from this world where our voices can no more be heard" before the imminent destruction of the present kingdom. "Some will call this a suicide or an act of cowardice in the face of difficulties [. . .] THEY ARE WRONG" (emphasis in the original). The second text, "The Rosy+Cross," opens by explaining the perceived mission of the Rosy-Cross throughout the ages, and it goes on to state that the Elder Brothers of the Rosy-Cross had to interrupt their mission "prematurely" because of a lack of understanding, blackmail, police pressure, and slander. The third document, "Last Message," chronicles human failure despite the efforts of initiates to prevent it. They were greeted only with "mendacious calumnies and treason," as well as orchestrated scandal (an obvious allusion to the OTS's own problems in 1993). Traitors will be punished: "We are truly administrators of justice, sent by a Higher Order." There is no other way than to leave before "the terrible trials of the Apocalypse," but the Transit is "by no means a suicide in the human meaning of the word." Finally, the fourth text, "To the Lovers of Justice," presents an eight-page denunciation of the trials to which the OTS was subjected in Canada in 1993, explaining that as a result of them the group was compelled "to prematurely leave this earth" and accusing the justice system, police, media, and government agencies of "a collective murder."

The perception of an opposition does not necessarily match reality; actually, the group had met with relatively little opposition, except in Martinique in late 1992 and in Canada in 1993. In a few cases, police agencies had been intrigued not by the OTS, but by Di Mambro himself, who traveled extensively and seemed to have a good deal of money to spend without any known source of income. The investigations were inconclusive, however, and the original suspicions of money laundering were discarded. However, the manifestations of opposition were interpreted by the group as proof that it was the victim of a major conspiracy. This was at the same time a self-serving interpretation, "proving" that the tiny OTS and its message were considered to constitute a major threat to the established powers. The standards by which insiders perceive the meaning and extent of opposition can be very different from those applied by outsiders. Was the Transit, then, the direct consequence of the 1993 police investigation? If so, this would be a real irony, because the investigation was the result of a mistaken identification of OTS members as suspected terrorists. Former members subsequently revealed, however, that the idea of a Transit had been promoted earlier within the group, although it may have been understood by some to be nothing more than a geographical relocation. In addition, the wiretapping conducted in February 1993 shows that Jouret was already expressing an eagerness to leave this Earth, and that a few trusted OTS members had already begun firearms training. Finally, the fact that in 1993 there was an attempt to buy not just guns, but guns with silencers, is significant. It was a gun with a silencer that was used to inflict the fatal wounds on most of the victims gathered in Cheiry in October 1994. The Canadian police may even be right in thinking that, without knowing it, their intervention resulted in the postponement of the originally planned Transit. Even if they do not figure prominently in the documents left behind for public consumption by the OTS, we should perhaps look more closely at the so-called traitors, who were briefly mentioned a few times. After all, Di Mambro's followers could have tried to kill the Canadian journalist denounced by name in the "To the Lovers of Justice" document. However, only critical members or former members were victims of Di Mambro's wrath.

Beginning around 1990, some people close to the core group (including Di Mambro's own son, Elie, found dead in Salvan) left the movement, and this deeply shocked Di Mambro. During the following years, more people left and internal dissent grew. This constituted a serious threat in Di Mambro's mind. None of the former members had spoken publicly about the OTS, however, except for one in Canada who had not reached a very high level and had only limited knowledge of what was going on. But the risk that a former trusted participant in the inner circle might reveal everything he or she knew was obviously a nightmare scenario for Di Mambro. Police investigations after 1994 revealed that he agreed to repay sums of money to at least three people and that one of them was still blackmailing him. A draft agreement was prepared in early 1994 in order to meet the financial expectations of this former member. It states that in order to get the money, the member would have to surrender all documents relating to Di Mambro and Pilet still in his possession and to certify that he had destroyed all other relevant documents. He also had to promise to avoid any situation that would lead to a "national or international scandal." Just before leaving this world, Di Mambro still found the time to send a letter to the attorney general of the Geneva Canton denouncing the blackmail of which he believed he was a victim. Another former member, whose companion had also received some money when leaving the community, told the investigators: "We have never spoken to anybody about the community, which must have set Di Mambro's mind at rest and maybe has saved our lives." Several critics inside the group were killed at the time of the Transit, and Di Mambro apparently tried unsuccessfully to attract other people he wanted to eliminate. Di Mambro did not want to leave dissidents behind who might throw an unfavorable light on his life's work.

In order to understand the dynamics leading to violence in the OTS case, it is necessary to distinguish between Di Mambro and his followers. Di Mambro had to face not just internal dissent but also people who knew too much and could have seriously threatened his status. In addition, rather than growing, the group was actually losing members. The financial situation was certainly not desperate, as Pilet was quite a generous sponsor during the last few years of the order's existence. He gave, in fact, several million dollars between 1990 and 1994 and had made other donations before 1990. High-level members also paid monthly fees in cash to Di Mambro's secretary. It was becoming difficult to draw as much money as before, however, due to increasing reluctance on the part of some donors. Maintaining a number of full-time Di Mambro aides was certainly expensive, even more so because Di Mambro had developed a taste for luxurious living, which is evident from the heavy bills paid in high-class restaurants found among his personal papers. Finally, Di Mambro probably convinced himself that the movement was being subjected to police surveillance and that it was the object of a worldwide conspiracy. The Transit and the elimination of "traitors" probably seemed a workable solution to Di Mambro; this solution left behind the image of a mysterious Rosicrucian elite exiting a doomed world unworthy of it rather than one of a bankrupt order.

As far as the OTS's followers are concerned, we might conclude that religious behavior is not purely cognitive but should also be studied through the lenses of a "sociology of emotions." Randall Collins wrote (1990: 28) that sociological theories often "have a macro primacy" and need to be "micro-translated." When "we attempt a micro-translation of sociology – not necessarily an absolute micro-reduction, but a grounding of macro-concepts in real interactions across the macro-grid of time – we are led to see the importance of emotional processes." It seems increasingly clear that a number of middle-class men and women did, in fact, acquire within the OTS what they regarded as valuable emotions, a welcome supplement to their ordinary day-to-day lives. It was these emotions that sustained their allegiance to Di Mambro and Jouret and their ideas despite the realization by some members that a certain amount of deception had been involved. The feeling of being part of a secret community of initiates ready for the Apocalypse may, in turn, have seemed extremely valuable to men and women immersed on a daily basis in the routine of their business and professional lives. They regarded themselves as key actors at a turning point of human history and did not perceive Di Mambro's idea of a global conspiracy against the OTS as paranoid. Their main concern was to act in such a way that the "passage" to another reality could be successfully achieved.

The Transit appears as both a vindication and a vengeance. Leaders like Di Mambro expect unbounded loyalty from their followers. As Oakes puts it, "The followers usually fail to see that the charismatic leader demands trust in his person, not just in his vision or in the movement" (1997: 179). Consequently, even those dissenters who remained within the group and were still devoted to the cause but expressed growing distrust of Di Mambro personally had to be killed. Vengeance, of course, would not seem to be an appropriate behavior for a spiritual master. Di Mambro solved this problem by claiming that what would take place was the implementation of "Justice and Sentencing" – explained in an internal video of September 1994 as vengeance in an "impersonal" sense. Di Mambro claimed that he could forgive what traitors had done to him personally, but he could not forgive their sins against the Rosy-Cross. This was a mere rhetorical distinction because followers fully identified him with the Rosy-Cross as the recognized representative of the hidden Elder Brothers, the only one on Earth who had access to them. To convince disciples to follow him to another world after the passage through the "narrow gate" and to eliminate hated traitors probably was perceived by Di Mambro as a final reaffirmation of his crumbling authority rather than as an admission of defeat and escape.

Learning from the OTS Tragedy in a Comparative Perspective

Since the Jonestown tragedy in 1978, there have been a number of spectacular events related to small apocalyptic groups. Any attempt to interpret the roots of violent or self-destructive behavior should consider such cases in a comparative perspective in the interest of gaining useful knowledge that is applicable to possible future developments. Two cases are especially significant for a comparison with the OTS: the Peoples Temple and Heaven's Gate. The apocalyptic ideology of the three groups reflects the common feeling that members did not belong (or no longer belonged) to this world and that leaving it would mean reaching their real home on another planet. "I come from another planet," Jim Jones stated in a sermon in 1972. He further "suggested that many of his listeners had been with him on a more highly evolved planet," that they had come down, "and [that] Jones had come to release them from this world" (Chidester 1988: 82–83). "We go back to our home," proclaims the OTS in "Transit for the Future," while a suicide note left by one of the December 1995 victims proudly affirms: "I return freely and willingly to where I came from at the dawn of times." "I am about to return to my Father's Kingdom," declared Do (Marshall Applewhite) in a statement circulated in September 1995. Heaven's Gate in its March 1997 "Exit Press Release" explained: "We came from the Level Above Human in distant space and we have now exited the bodies that we were wearing for our earthly task, to return to the world from whence we came." Not only did members of all three groups feel ready to travel to a more hospitable planet, their judgment on this world was a very severe one. The world was considered to be corrupt, unjust, and doomed, and they felt rejected by it. Jim Jones saw the United States as an oppressive system, a prison. The Peoples Temple was facing a capitalist pharaoh eager to destroy the socialist ideals and challenges it represented. "We are rejected by everybody," commented Di Mambro in spring 1994 to his core group of followers. The OTS's "Transit for the Future" explained that human beings were simply trying to destroy the work of those who had spared no effort in bringing authentic freedom and well-being to the world. The tone was much less emotional within Heaven's Gate, although its members were well aware that very few people were ready to seize their offer of a "last chance to evacuate Earth before it is recycled."

The estrangement from this world had grown over the years. All three groups had considered relocating to another place on planet Earth, in the case of the Peoples Temple and the OTS in order to survive major disasters. But they had found that this was either not feasible or that other places gave no guarantee of safety. They expected only the worst from this world: the fate of the Branch Davidians at Waco or the Weavers at Ruby Ridge seemed ominous to both the OTS and Heaven's Gate. "Armageddon has begun" was the message posted by Heaven's Gate to newsgroups in September 1996. The message continued: "The servants of the Godly side have grown to despise this world and want to leave it, looking for someone or something to offer them a way out [. . .] still trusting that whatever is beyond must be better than what they have found here" (Perkins and Jackson 1997: 112).

All three groups also regarded themselves as being persecuted. In the cases of the Peoples Temple and the OTS, both leaders and members considered themselves the targets of a high-level conspiracy (Hall 1990: 283–284). Probably the most difficult thing to accept was that part of the actual or potential opposition came from former members, who had been trusted and knew a lot about what was going on inside the group. Interestingly, in the case of the Peoples Temple, "[c]ollective suicide was apparently first proposed as a strategy [. . .] in response to the defection of eight members in 1973 [. . .] as a way of preventing the church from being exposed to censorious attacks from the outside world" (Chidester 1988: 130). While the Peoples Temple and the OTS believed that a major threat was looming in the shape of apostates, ex-members were not a major stress factor in Heaven's Gate. However, Heaven's Gate did interpret ridicule and scorn by the media and the UFO Internet communities as persecution, thus confirming that the way opposition is perceived and interpreted within a movement may be more important that the actual amount of opposition itself.

These groups, believing that they no longer belonged to this world, considered themselves no longer bound by its laws. There was no place to which they could escape on this planet: "We seriously considered moving out of this country, but there seemed to be no place on the globe that would allow us as we would like," wrote Heaven's Gate's "Glnody" in his March 1997 "Earth Exit Statement." "There is no place for us to go but up," he concluded, and both Jones and Di Mambro would have warmly concurred with this statement. While these groups claimed that they did not belong to this world, they nonetheless wanted to make the headlines in it. As Jones said: "We've got to go down in history. We've got to be in the history books" (Chidester 1988: 116). The media-conscious OTS and Heaven's Gate carefully sent documents or press releases to newspapers and TV channels before annihilating themselves. Violence, where it occurs, may also be part of an effort to impress the world. Since they were writing at the same time a scenario for public consumption, it could be that such murderers came to see themselves as avenging angels, executing divine sentences in the final act of self-destruction. Staging a deliberately spectacular action becomes a supreme way of proving something to the world and of affirming in front of stunned spectators the value of a despised message. Deep estrangement from this world, perceived opposition (real or imaginary), and the feeling that there is no possible way to escape "but up" seem to constitute the ideal combination of factors leading to self-destructive and criminal behavior in small religious groups. The same probably applies to fringe secular political groups as well, although while they may see the option of punishing the traitors responsible for such situations as attractive, the goal of going collectively up is probably less comforting if there is no belief in another world. The role (and mental condition) of the leader of the group seems to be decisive in persuading followers either to choose the radical option or to adjust as well as possible to adverse circumstances.

It remains true that, in a case such as the OTS in particular, with the main actors gone, part of our interpretation continues to be conjectural. For instance, why should some members have perished with bullets in their heads, including a number of long-standing and trusted members of Di Mambro's inner circle, while others were "only" poisoned? There are elements in the logical unfolding and symbolism of the events that escape our understanding, and perhaps some key factors in the violent behavior of the group remain unnoticed simply because they defy the understanding of outsiders. Similarities provided by comparisons with other cases, however, lead us to believe that it is now possible to identify crucial factors with a reasonable degree of certainty.

References

Abgrall, Jean-Marie. *Les Sectes de l'Apocalypse: Gourous de l'an 2000*. Paris: Calmann-Lévy, 1999:

Anthony, Dick. "Brainwashing and Totalitarian Influence: An Exploration of Admissibility Criteria for Testimony in Brainwashing Trials." Ph.D. dissertation, Graduate Theological Union, Berkeley, CA, 1996.

Assemblée Nationale. "Rapport fait au nom de la Commission d'Enquête sur la situation financière, patrimoniale et fiscale des sectes, ainsi que sur leurs activités économiques et leurs relations avec les milieux économiques et financiers" (document n. 1687). Paris: Les Documents d'Information de l'Assemblée Nationale, 1999.

"Les sectes en France. Rapport fait au nom de la Commission d'Enquête sur les sectes" (document n. 2468). Paris: Les Documents d'Information de l'Assemblée Nationale, 1996.

Audit sur les dérives sectaires. "Rapport du groupe d'experts genevois au Département de la Justice et Police et des Transports du Canton de Genève." Genève: Editions Suzanne Hurter, 1997.

Bédat, Arnaud, Bouleau, Gilles, and Bernard Nicolas. 1996. *Les Chevaliers de la Mort*. Paris: TF1 Editions, 1996.

Caillet, Serge. *L'Ordre Rénové du Temple: Aux racines du Temple Solaire*. Paris: Dervy, 1997.

Campiche, Roland. "Quand les sectes affolent: Ordre du Temple Solaire, médias et fin du millénaire." *Entretiens avec Cyril Dépraz*. Geneva: Labor et Fides, 1995.

Chambre des Représentants de Belgique. "Enquête parlamentaire visant à élaborer une politique en vue de lutter contre les pratiques illégales des sectes et les dangers qu'elles représentent pour la société et pour les personnes, particulièrement les mineurs d'âge." *Rapport fait au nom de la Commission d'Enquête*. 2 vols. Bruxelles: Chambre des Représentants de Belgique, 1997.

Chidester, David. *Salvation and Suicide: An Interpretation of the Peoples Temple and Jonestown*. Bloomington: Indiana University Press, 1988.

Collins, Randall. "Stratification, Emotional Energy, and the Transient Emotions." In *Research Agendas in the Sociology of Emotions*, edited by Theodore D. Kemper. Albany: State University of New York Press, 1990: 27–57.

Delaforge, Gaetan. *The Templar Tradition in the Age of Aquarius*. Putney, VT: Threshold Books, 1987.

Hall, John R. "The Apocalypse at Jonestown." In *In Gods We Trust: New Patterns of Religious Pluralism in America*, 2nd ed., edited by Thomas Robbins and Dick Anthony. New Brunswick, NJ: Transaction Books, 1990: 269–293.

Hall, John R., and Philip Schuyler. "Apostasy, Apocalypse, and Religious Violence: An Exploratory Comparison of the Peoples Temple, the Branch Davidians, and the Solar Temple." In *The Politics of Religious Apostasy. The Role of Apostates in the Transformation of Religious Movements*, edited by David Bromley. Greenwich, CT: Praeger, 1998: 141–169.

"The Mystical Apocalypse of the Solar Temple." In *Millennium, Messiahs, and Mayhem: Contemporary Apocalyptic Movements*, edited by Thomas Robbins and Susan J. Palmer. New York: Routledge, 1997: 285–311.

Introvigne, Massimo. "Rapporti parlamentari e governativi sulle 'sette' in Europa Occidentale, 1996–1999." *Quaderni di diritto e politica ecclesiastica* August 2, 1999a: 385–408.

"The Magic of Death: The Suicide of the Solar Temple." In *Millennialism, Persecution and Violence: Historical Cases*, edited by Catherine Wessinger. Syracuse, NY: Syracuse University Press, 1999b: 287–321.

"Une Dérive vers le suicide et l'homicide. L'Ordre du Temple Solaire." In *Sectes et Démocratie*, edited by Françoise Champion and Martine Cohen. Paris: Seuil, 1999c: 300–313.

"Ordeal by Fire: The Tragedy of the Solar Temple." *Religion* 25 (1995a): 267–283.

Idee che uccidono. Jonestown, Waco, il Tempio Solare. Pessano (Milan): MIMEP-Docete, 1995b.

Lifton, Robert J. *Destroying the World to Save It. Aum Shinrikyô, Apocalyptic Violence, and the New Global Terrorism*. New York: Metropolitan Books, 1999.

Thought Reform and the Psychology of Totalism: A Study of Brainwashing in China, 2nd ed. Chapel Hill: University of North Carolina Press, 1989.

The Future of Immortality and Other Essays for a Nuclear Age. New York: Basic Books, 1987.

Marhic, Renaud. *L'Ordre du Temple Solaire: Enquête sur les Extrémistes de l'Occulte – II.* Bordeaux: L'Horizon Chimérique, 1996.

"Enquête sur les extrémistes de l'occulte." In *De la Loge P2 à l'Ordre du Temple Solaire*. Bordeaux: L'Horizon Chimérique, 1995:

Mayer, Jean François. "Les Chevaliers de l'Apocalypse. L'Ordre du Temple Solaire et ses adeptes." In *Sectes et Démocratie*, edited by Françoise Champion and Martine Cohen. Paris: Seuil, 1999a: 205–223.

"'Our Terrestrial Journey Is Coming to an End': The Last Voyage of the Solar Temple." *Nova Religio* 2 (1999b): 172–196.

Der Sonnentempel: Die Tragödie einer Sekte. Updated German edition. Freiberg: Paulusverlag, 1998.

"Des Templiers pour l'Ere du Verseau: les Clubs Archédia (1984–1991) et l'Ordre international chevaleresque Tradition Solaire." *Mouvements Religieux* 153 (1993): 2–10.

Oakes, Len. *Prophetic Charisma: The Psychology of Revolutionary Religious Personalities.* Syracuse, NY: Syracuse University Press, 1997.

Perkins, Rodney, and Forrest Jackson. *Cosmic Suicide: The Tragedy and Transcendence of Heaven's Gate.* Dallas: Pentaradial Press, 1997.

Richardson, James T., and Massimo Introvigne. "European Parliamentary and Administrative Reports and the Brainwashing Argument." Paper presented at the conference of the International Society for the Sociology of Religion (SISR), Louvain, July 1999.

Shupe, Anson, David Bromley, and Edward Breschel. "The Peoples Temple, the Apocalypse at Jonestown and the Anti-Cult Movement." In *New Religious Movements, Mass Suicide, and Peoples Temple: Scholarly Perspectives on a Tragedy*, edited by Rebecca Moore and Fielding McGehee. Lewiston, NY: Edwin Mellen, 1989: 153–178.

Wessinger, Catherine. *How the Millennium Comes Violently: From Jonestown to Heaven's Gate.* New York: Seven Bridges, 2000.

(ed.). *Millenialism, Persecution and Violence: Historical Cases.* Syracuse, NY: Syracuse University Press, 1999.

Wojcik, Daniel. *The End of the World as We Know It: Faith, Fatalism, and Apocalypse in America.* New York: New York University Press, 1997.

10

DRAMATIC CONFRONTATIONS:
AUM SHINRIKYÔ AGAINST THE WORLD

IAN READER

In August 1994, some months before the March 1995 nerve gas attack on the Tokyo subway that brought the Japanese new religion Aum Shinrikyô to world attention, Murai Hideo, then head of Aum's science and technology "ministry," informed a fellow devotee that "the time for confrontation" with the Japanese police was at hand (Takahashi 1997: 148). Acting on the orders of the movement's charismatic founder and leader, Asahara Shôkô, Murai supervised a number of Aum devotees in "secret work" manufacturing chemical weapons without the knowledge of the bulk of the movement's membership. This project was undertaken in preparation for the catastrophic endtime scenario that Asahara prophesied would occur by the close of the twentieth century in which the forces of evil would seek to destroy the movement. Aum had a sacred duty to stand up and fight for the truth and to defend itself against the "conspirators," who Asahara claimed were intent on destroying Aum, and to wreak vengeance on its enemies.

In other words, while from any normative standpoint Aum's manufacture and use of chemical weapons appear as acts of aggression, in the eyes of the movement's leaders they were defensive moves aimed at protecting its mission and fighting for the truth against hostile enemies. Aum Shinrikyô had encountered a great deal of antipathy, hostility, and conflict from various quarters, including hostile media treatment and concerted opposition campaigns by the families of devotees, disgruntled former members, and their lawyers. Aum also faced obstructive and sometimes aggressive and illegal hindrances created by neighbours and local authorities in the rural areas where it established its communes. Such hostilities had impacted badly on the movement and had, the movement believed, damaged its image in Japan and made it difficult to recruit devotees.

Aum had from the beginning been a world-rejecting movement that defined the everyday world as corrupt, evil, and in need of spiritual transformation, and it saw its own special mission as implementing this transformation. As such, it was unsurprising that Aum interpreted the opposition it faced as a manifestation of the corrupt world it was seeking to change and as a direct assault emanating from that evil world. These perceptions were intensified by the various setbacks Aum experienced in the brief period between its formation in 1984 and the subway attack of 1995, and they fed into what a prominent disciple, Noda Naruhito, was later to call the "persecution complex" that permeated the movement. (*Shūkan Asahi* 1995: 26). The result was an ever more fanciful set of conspiracy theories in which Aum saw itself as surrounded by conspirators ranging from the U.S. and Japanese governments to other groups that figure widely in conspiracy theories, such as the Central Intelligence Agency, (CIA), the Vatican, the Jews, and the Freemasons. All of these groups, Aum publications of the 1990s complained, were collaborating to destroy Aum and kill its leaders. (Reader 1996: 65–69; 2000: 156–158, 188–191)

These views were conditioned by Aum's polarized view of the world and by its apocalyptic visions that foresaw an imminent and final confrontation between good and evil. The actual opposition Aum faced readily fitted into this framework and provided it with "evidence" that the forces of evil were marshalling themselves against Aum. This gave rise to its further speculative construction of an all-encompassing opposition. Indeed, it is fair to say that Aum's construction of a series of enemies against whom it would have to wage sacred war, and consequently its espousal of a path of mass violence, were facilitated by the opposition it faced. The "persecution" that became a feature of Aum's rhetoric and the allegations of conspiracies against it in the 1990s was quite clearly an "imagined persecution" (Reader 1999), even if one that partly owed its origins to Aum's experiences of actual opposition from early in its history.

Although much of Aum's behaviour in the period in which it began to arm itself with biological and chemical weapons can be seen as a response to imagined or real opposition, this is a far cry from saying that Aum's violent confrontation with society occurred *because of* that opposition. Rather, the root causes of Aum's violence, which initially developed inside the movement and only later was directed at the world beyond Aum, developed from within the movement (Reader 2000: 229–249). Moreover, Aum's first acts of violence (beatings of disciples, the cover-up of an accidental death, and the murder of a disciple who threatened to expose Aum over this death) occurred before any serious opposition to Aum had developed (Reader 1999).

The causes of Aum's espousal of violence and confrontation were multiple: the personality of its founder and leader, Asahara Shôkô; the nature of Aum as a world-negating millennialist movement; and Aum's culture of extreme asceticism and its rejection of the everyday world as evil. There was also a series of internal problems that, coupled with Asahara's perceptions of external opposition, created a paranoid mind set that led to the emergence of a culture of coercion inside the movement and that escalated into full-scale violence. It was this combination of events and factors inside the movement that impelled Aum at critical points in its development toward ever more isolated and confrontational perspectives.

Even if the Aum affair should be viewed primarily as an example of the violence-producing dimensions of religion and of the ways in which internal factors can propel a movement toward violence, this does not mean that the external pressures on Aum were negligible or that one should discount them entirely as factors in leading it to violent confrontation. At critical junctures in its existence, the threats posed by groups opposed to Aum and the rebuffs it suffered in the public domain played a part in creating or intensifying the aggressive and paranoid attitudes within the movement. It is such issues with which this chapter engages. My intention here is not to analyze Aum Shinrikyô's path to violence and confrontation, but to look at the ways in which external pressures and, critically, Aum's perceptions of the pressures and opposition brought to bear on it contributed at vital stages to its internally engendered violence. In so doing, I shall comment on how the violence that originally arose inside Aum became externalized, on how Aum engaged in confrontations with the outside world as a result of its internal problems, and on how Aum's attitudes toward those it encountered played a cogent part in creating or provoking opposition to itself. I focus especially on the initial stages of Aum's engagement with violence and confrontation with Japanese society, for it was here that the stage and positions were set for Aum's later acts of violence, such as the 1995 subway attack. First, I shall briefly turn to the origins of Aum, to the experiences and nature of its founder, and to the type of movement Aum was.

Aum Shinrikyô: Origins, Founder, and Orientations

The dramatic dénouement envisioned by Murai and illustrated by the subway attack stood in sharp contrast to Aum's origins. Formed out of a yoga and meditation group established by Asahara Shôkô in 1984, it had initially been concerned with developing the spiritual consciousness of its disciples. Aum enabled them to acquire psychic powers through ascetic practice, and instructed them how to eradicate the spiritual impediments and negative karma that Asahara taught were the necessary concomitants of living in the spiritually devoid world of contemporary materialist society. Aum espoused a radical stance toward the world, rejecting mainstream society as materialistic and corrupt and encouraging members to devote themselves to ascetic and spiritual practices with Aum. This highly critical stance appears to have been conditioned by Asahara's own early experiences of rejection and discrimination at the hands of Japanese society.

Asahara was born Matsumoto Chizuo in 1955. Due to family poverty and blindness, Asahara spent much of his preadult life in a state-run boarding school for the blind. His feelings of abandonment by his family, discrimination because of his blindness, and later failure to enter a university left him with permanent feelings of rejection, frustration, and resentfment. Yet, he also had a very warm and friendly side and later, as a religious leader, he exhibited a personality that veered between the deeply kind, warm, compassionate, and charming and a tendency toward anger and aggression, especially in the face of opposition. In 1977 he left school, moved to Tokyo, and apparently broke off contact with his parents. He subsequently changed his name to Asahara Shôkô when he became the leader of a religious movement and later made it clear that he had rejected his past altogether (Kyôdô Tsûshinsha Shakaibu 1997: 23). He married in 1978, and his wife, Tomoko, came to hold a senior position in Aum.

After pursuing a career in acupuncture and healing and developing an interest in Buddhism, yoga, meditation, and asceticism, Asahara joined the new religion Agonshû, which incorporated these themes as well as promising adherents the possibility of attaining psychic powers (Reader 1988, 1991: 194–233). Agonshû taught that the world was facing a spiritual crisis and potential destruction from nuclear war or environmental disasters by the end of the twentieth century that could only be resolved through religious means. This aspect of its teaching attracted Asahara and many other young Japanese concerned about the future of society, and it subsequently became a predominant theme in Aum.

Dissatisfied with Agonshû because he felt it paid too little attention to ascetic practice, he quit in 1984 to establish his own religious group. The initial membership of this group was about fifteen, many of whom were still devotees at the time of the subway attack. Asahara appears to have been an inspirational teacher, attracting a growing number of disciples. Later media images notwithstanding, he was clearly a talented religious teacher, spiritual guide, and practitioner of yoga and meditation whose abilities played a critical part in drawing to Aum a number of ardent seekers and practitioners (Reader 2000: 54).

While Asahara and his followers strove to attain psychic powers and spiritual awakening through their practices, they also harbored an essentially pessimistic view of the world as corrupt and materialistic. In Asahara's view, all who dweltled in the materialism of ordinary society imbibed its negative karma, which inevitably caused them to fall into the hells at death and experience disadvantageous rebirths. It was only through rejecting the world and performing ascetic practices to purify the body and mind that one could attain salvation. This emphasis on asceticism was directly related to Aum's millennialism and to the sense of urgency and mission that derived from it. A series of visions and messages from various spiritual entities commencing in 1985 convinced Asahara that he had a special role in the imminent confrontation between good and evil and that he had been entrusted with a mission to purify the world by leading the forces of good in a final cosmic war. Such visions began to color his sermons and to assume a prominent focus in his teachings. Equally, these visions provided his followers with a sense of higher purpose: they were to be the "true victors," *shinri kassha*, forming the vanguard of his sacred army in its war against evil (Asahara n.d.: 154).

A Fragile Optimism and the Seeds of Failure

Despite its essentially negative view of the world, Aum's aspirations for the future were initially optimistic, holding out the hope that the "final war" would be fought on a symbolic, spiritual plane. In 1986 Asahara prophesied that nuclear war could occur before 1999 but stated that it would be avoided as long Aum could open two centers in each country of the world before that time (Asahara 1987: 87–88). Elsewhere he preached that if he could create a vanguard of 30,000 spiritually advanced beings by the end of the century, Aum would be able to purify the world of negative karma and bring about a peaceful transition to a new spiritual age (Mainichi Shinbun Shûkyô Shuzaihan 1993: 131; Reader 2000: 90–91).

In order to achieve such aspirations, Aum embarked on a number of ventures. In 1986 Asahara established a monastic-style order within the movement, the *sangha*, (this is the term used in Buddhism to denote the monastic community). Aum's *sangha* was to be an advanced "army" of spiritually enlightened beings who would rid the world of karmic evils and prevent the prophesied nuclear war. Aum also developed its "Shambhala plan" (*Shambhala* also being a Buddhist word used to signify an earthly paradise or a spiritual kingdom) aimed at building a this-worldly utopia through the acquisition of rural land on which to build "Lotus Village" communes where members of the *sangha* would live. Fired with missionary optimism, Aum opened its new communal center near Mount Fuji in August 1986 with "the bright hopes of establishing a 'holy land' as a model of heaven on earth" (Shimazono 1995: 397).

The apparent optimism of these prophecies and plans was, however, fraught with problems. Aum was effectively claiming sole responsibility for the task of world spiritual transformation while placing the onus on the world at large to receive its messages zealously. More problematically, world salvation was presaged on Aum's ability to grow at a striking and quantifiable rate through the unimpeded success of its *sangha* and communes. For a movement in its very early days with only a few hundred followers and a barely developed *sangha* system, the prospect of opening centers in every country of the world, of training 30,000 people to very high levels of spiritual attainment, and of developing adequate communes in which to nurture and train them would appear to be extraordinarily ambitious, if not simply unrealistic. In 1986 Aum only had a few centers in Japan and none elsewhere, had just begun to find the means of acquiring land for its communes, and had only three advanced practitioners who had renounced the world to devote themselves fully to their spiritual mission.

It did not take long to see that Aum's ambitious visions of its future were out of step with reality. Although its messages resonated with some Japanese, the steps that Aum emphasized as necessary to rectify the situation were too extreme to persuade the numbers of people it sought to renounce the world. The demand to break off all contacts with families, friends, and the past and to live an ascetic life appealed to a small number of devotees who enthusiastically dedicated themselves to Aum's highly structured monastic order and to its mission. It did not, however, attract sufficient people to meet the target of world salvation. By the mid-1990s Aum had persuaded about 1,200 followers to renounce the world and had gained perhaps 8,000 additional followers in Japan. This was a fair number for a movement with such extreme views and demands but far short of the numbers Asahara had claimed were necessary to achieve the mission of universal salvation. Moreover, Aum's attempts to open centers and develop beyond Japan had been almost entirely unsuccessful. Apart from a brief, turbulent expansion in Russia, Aum's overseas ventures in Germany, Sri Lanka, and the United States were resounding failures. Indeed, by the mid-1990s Aum had experienced massive failure in achieving the growth objectives needed to fulfill its mission of universal salvation.

Accidents and Murder: Internal Violence and the Damnation of the World

The sense of impending failure to attain its aspirations was a factor in Asahara's abandonment of Aum's previously stated mission of universal salvation and of its optimistic view that war and destruction could be avoided through spiritual means. This shift began in early 1988, when Asahara first appeared to suggest that Aum might not be able to achieve universal salvation (Asahara interview in *Twilight Zone*, January 26, 1988, cited in Numata 1996: 57). In early 1989, Asahara published a book entitled *Metsubô no hi* (a title meaning "day of destruction" and subtitled with the English word "Doomsday"). The book claimed that an end-of-century cataclysm was inevitable, that universal salvation was no longer possible, and that only those who followed the true way of Aum could henceforth be saved. Those who spurned this path of righteousness were effectively damned (Asahara 1989).

Underlying this change of view was Asahara's belief that the world had not heeded his call for spiritual action. The lack of tangible growth toward Aum's proclaimed goals meant that Aum appeared unlikely to achieve its previously affirmed mission. Consequently, I would suggest, Asahara transformed the nature of Aum's salvation activity and its goals while effectively placing the blame for the failure of its earlier mission on the world at large for not heeding his message. He shifted the emphasis from universal salvation through mass spiritual action to a more narrow salvation for the chosen few who believed in Aum. By accepting that mass destruction was inevitable, Asahara could continue with his self-created vision as a messiah while evading any blame for his inability to save the world. It was because of those who had ignored his teachings, rather than because of his failure to convert people to his mission, that world salvation could not be attained. Conversely, the world had rejected his message and hence deserved to be destroyed. Henceforth, as he declared in sermons from the latter part of 1988 on, all he could do was to save the Aum faithful. Everyone else was, rightly, doomed to a merited destruction (Asahara n.d.: 317; Reader 2000: 193–195).

Another, more immediate reason for the shift from the doctrine of universal salvation to one of selective salvation manifested itself in late 1988 and was related to Aum's first, unexpected and unplanned, criminal act. In the summer of 1988, it appears that Asahara began to pressure those close to him to perform austerities. His wife, Tomoko, for example, had proved a reluctant devotee and had refused to engage in these practices. Because of his belief that asceticism was a gateway to salvation, Asahara insisted on its performance by those around him; it is also likely that he saw Tomoko's refusal as a challenge to his charismatic authority. Whatever the reason he responded angrily, having Tomoko beaten until her resistance was broken and she agreed to follow Aum's spiritual path. This happened in September 1988, and she thereafter began to perform austerities, eventually becoming a highly adept practitioner who took on a senior role in the movement. Similar punishments were enjoined on others as well, and a culture of coercive asceticism took hold in the movement.

The argument behind such acts was that since the prospect of universal salvation was receding, it was incumbent on disciples to strive for their own salvation through ascetic practice. If they did not do so, they had to be made to conform for their own good. This, Asahara argued, was the behavior and the duty of a compassionate guru, who at times had to use cruelty in order to be kind and to lead his followers to salvation. Put another way, using violence would in normal terms be considered a bad deed that would have negative karmic repercussions on the doer. However, when used by an enlightened and compassionate teacher in order to save persons by making them perform austerities that would enable them to evade the hells at death and to attain salvation, then it was not an evil deed but one of the highest good (Asahara n.d.: 63–67, 111–112). This was an argument that came to be used increasingly both inside Aum and in Aum's conflicts with its opponents to legitimate the use of violence in the furtherance and defense of its mission. Equally, it is evident that another important theme underpinning Aum's uses of violence inside the movement, as with the beating of Tomoko, was the punishment of those who appeared to challenge Asahara's authority. This also was a pattern that later spread outside the movement. An underlying theme of virtually all of Aum's externalized acts of violence was the punishment of or retribution against those Aum felt had demeaned or opposed it.

The development of this culture of coercive ascetic violence and its concomitant legitimation of the use of violence for the sake of the guru and the mission had disastrous results for Aum. In the autumn of 1988 a devotee, Majima Terayuki, died during a bout of extreme asceticism ordered by

Asahara. Majima's death provoked a drastic crisis since the movement was about to apply for legal recognition under the Japanese Religious Corporations Law, a status that would enable it to get valuable tax breaks and other advantageous concessions. Applications were permissible after a movement had been in existence for three years, which in Aum's case would transpire in spring 1989. If news of this accidental death got out, it would have had catastrophic repercussions, destroying any chance of Aum's gaining this important benefit. Indeed, the news could well have jeopardized its very existence. It certainly would have undermined the position of a guru who claimed the ability to save his disciples and lead them to enlightenment yet caused their deaths through the practices he ordered. Sensing that Aum's very mission would be irrevocably destroyed by such revelations, Asahara and his closest disciples decided to cover up the death. They secretly burned Majima's body and disposed of the ashes. This was itself a criminal act in Japan but one that Aum's leaders clearly felt was preferable to the alternative. They had, in effect, determined that their mission was more important than the life of a follower or the law of the land.

The death of Majima was a disaster from which Aum never recovered. Indeed, it can be considered to be the critical juncture in the movement's history, the point at which Aum crossed into illegality and began its slide toward murder and mass violence. The death necessitated a change in doctrinal interpretation and orientation. Once Aum had, even accidentally, killed one of its own, it could no longer claim the ability to save all of humanity. In order to interpret the death of Majima to his close disciples without abandoning Aum's claims of spiritual prowess, Asahara had to emphasize a doctrine of selective salvation for only the most worthy. Since Majima had died, he clearly did not fall into this category; and his and other deaths that were to occur later could be interpreted not as a terrible accident, a reading that would place the blame for what happened on Asahara and his fellows, but as the result of his own unworthiness. Asahara thus absolved himself and his associates from responsibility for the death by creating a framework of interpretation that projected the blame onto the apparent victim rather than onto those whose actions had caused the deed. It was an explanation that was to be used with every subsequent criminal act that Aum committed.

The death of Majima and the ways in which it was dealt with bound the senior members of the movement together in a bond of criminality. It left them with a secret hidden within the movement that threatened its existence and had to be concealed at all costs, and it made them extremely defensive, if not paranoid, about anyone who tried to examine Aum's inner workings. Within a few months, this dark secret and the inner fears of Aum's leaders surrounding it manifested themselves in a crisis that led to Aum's first willful act of murder.

In February 1989, just two months before Aum's case for legal registration was to come before the courts in Tokyo, the scenario most feared by Asahara and the others who knew of Majima's death transpired. A disciple, Taguchi Shûji, who was party to the death and disposal of Majima's body, decided he could keep the secret no longer. His faith in Asahara had been shattered by the event, and he determined to leave Aum and inform the authorities of what had happened. Faced with a threat that would have proved fatal to his movement, Asahara ordered his disciples to kill Taguchi. Aum's mission, to say nothing of his own status, had to be preserved at all costs; in such terms, Taguchi was deemed disposable and murder in defense of the movement legitimate. The argument Asahara used to justify this action, as well as later Aum attacks and murders, was based on his interpretations of karma and the afterlife. If Taguchi were allowed to inform the authorities, he would not only destroy the truth but would incur terrible karma for wrecking Aum's mission of salvation. By killing him before he could do this, Asahara was effectively saving him from a far worse fate. This concept of killing in order to save someone henceforth became standard Aum doctrine; it was used to affirm the righteous nature of Aum's violent deeds and to legitimate the killing of those who might jeopardize Aum's well-being. It also removed any possible moral impediment to killing and, instead, encouraged the further use of violence by transforming such acts into sacred ones carried out to defend Aum and to "save" the unworthy "sinner" from falling into hell as a result of harming Aum's mission.

It is perhaps little wonder that *Metsubô no hi*, compiled in the aftermath of Majima's death and published at around the time of Taguchi's murder, expresses a far darker and more pessimistic picture than earlier Aum publications. In describing inevitable world cataclysm, the inability of Aum to save the world at large, the transformation of its mission into one centered on its own members and their survival, and the damnation of all who did not follow its path, Asahara had amended Aum's aspirations and visions in light of its recent experiences. He was also clearly worried that Aum might be on the point of fragmenting. In *Metsubô no hi* we have the first expressions of this fear. Asahara commented that Satan, who entered Aum's demonology at this juncture and who came to represent the evil world against which Aum had to fight, was seeking to infiltrate and corrupt the minds of his disciples. Even high-level practitioners, he claimed, could be tempted, and there had been defections caused by Satan's evil influence, while others had turned to spying against Aum and had had to be cast out of the movement (Asahara 1989: 46).

It was here that the first major indications of the paranoia and conspiracy theories that were to be the hallmark of Asahara's later sermons appeared. Within a few years of Aum's formation, and immediately after and in direct relation to the inner turmoil that had seized it, Aum had turned from a mission of world salvation to one of confrontation. Moreover, as Asahara's comments about Satan, defections, and spies illustrate, it was drawing increasingly sharp boundaries between itself and the world, becoming increasingly concerned about its internal integrity and fearful of its own collapse, and was developing a paranoid mind set in which it was beset by hostile forces both without and within.

Parental Conflict and the Development of Opposition

While Aum's turn to violence was conditioned by its problematic internal dynamics, it is clear from Asahara's comments about Satan and spies that he felt his movement was being undermined and damaged by hostile opposing forces. These fears were, in a sense, justified: Asahara's concern that the death of Majima could prove fatal to Aum's application for legal recognition was conditioned by his knowledge that a coherent opposition to Aum was materializing. It was, shortly after Taguchi's murder, to cause serious problems to Aum and to give rise to Asahara's first proclamation of overt confrontation with Japanese society.

The roots of this opposition are linked directly to Aum's activities and to the institutions it developed, notably its *sangha*, to implement its salvation plans. Aum enjoined those who entered the *sangha* to sever all ties with their former lives, including their families, and donate their possessions to the movement. This provoked angry responses from the families of those who joined.

The first member of the *sangha* was Ishii Hisako, a young female member of the original yoga group. Ishii, who renounced the world in 1986, had a formidable reputation in Aum as an ascetic practitioner and was one of its most influential members by virtue of controlling the movement's finances. She was implicated in Aum's later scandals and also became sexually involved with Asahara in the late 1980s (Egawa 1996: 158–161). Ishii's parents were angered when their daughter left her job and severed contact with them, and their anger was exacerbated when their inquiries about her brought abrupt responses from Aum (Arita 1995: 184–190). Fired by the zeal of withdrawing from a corrupt world and driven by a belief in the righteousness of its cause and the contrasting sinful state of those who objected to its activities, Aum treated such inquiries with contempt. This behavior illustrated a recurrent theme in its relationship with the world at large: The movement and its leaders rarely deigned to engage in an accommodating way with those who disagreed with it. Instead of mollifying the families of devout recruits or allowing them access to their alienated offspring, Aum appears to have repudiated them brusquely.

Such responses were based on Aum's sense of millennial certainty. The existing moral and social order in which the families of its devotees lived was going to be swept away and replaced by a different one inaugurated through Aum's actions. Since the world was immoral and evil, why should Aum respect its laws when they would soon be replaced by the new moral order Aum was constructing? Aum's millennial visions and its sense of righteousness, in other words, precluded it from seeking any real accommodation with those who might be upset by its actions.

The results were predictable. Aum's disdainful attitude merely heightened the anger of those who complained about its behavior. They became more vociferous and more convinced that Aum must be dangerous and have something to hide because of its aggressive refusal to allow access. This is precisely what happened with Ishii's parents, and it occurred repeatedly with other parents, relatives, and friends. The result was that an opposition distrustful of Aum's intentions and worried about the demands it appeared to place on devotees began to develop in the late 1980s.

The opposition had cultural and sometimes legal justifications on its side. Ishii was legally an adult able to make decisions about her future without recourse to her parents' views. However, the abrupt fissure of relations was highly problematic in Japanese culture, where individual motivations, especially of unmarried offspring, are widely considered to be subservient to parental and familial wishes. In some cases, the law was clearly infringed. Inoue Yoshihiro, who later became one of Aum's most militant members and played a major role in its crimes, joined it in 1987 at age seventeen, well under the age (twenty) at which he could legally have done so without parental consent. The fact that Aum allowed him to join its *sangha* when he was legally a minor, despite his parents' objections, placed Aum in direct conflict with, and demonstrated its underlying contempt for, the law of the land.

In spring 1989 Aum made its application for registration under the Japanese Religious Corporations Law. Normally such applications are straightforward, but Aum's met with vehement opposition from a number of people who complained about the way the movement had treated them. While these were largely the families of Aum devotees who had renounced the world, they included some dissatisfied former members who complained that they had given money to the movement but had receive little in return. The opposition, supported by local Tokyo politicians representing the interests of their constituents, was successful, and Aum's application was rejected in April 1989.

This decision was seen by Asahara as a direct assault by the authorities on Aum, and in an emotional sermon he complained of this attack on the truth. He asked his disciples what they wished to do: to abandon their struggle for truth and quit Aum or to fight for Aum. The response was unanimous: to fight for the truth and confront the authorities, a point Asahara reaffirmed by arguing that one *had* to fight those who degraded "the truth" (Asahara n.d.: 35–36). The fight was no longer merely on the spiritual plane. Aum went to court to get the decision overturned but also took its campaign to the streets, organizing vociferous protests against the decision, picketing the courts, and complaining of persecution.

In a remarkably short period, Aum had thus moved from a vision of sacred war on the spiritual level to one of confrontation with actual, identifiable enemies. Aum turned in the spring of 1989 from its benign and optimistic spiritual salvation mission to an overt declaration of confrontation with society. This confrontation was, as Asahara's sermon in the aftermath of the rejection of Aum's application stressed, essential for Aum's survival and the only course of action left (Asahara n.d. 4: 36). While the emergence of an organized opposition was not, it must be stressed, the most critical factor leading to this aggressive and confrontational stance, it was a highly contingent factor in the process, especially because of its emergence at such a critical time in Aum's history.

Confrontation, Murder, Humiliation, and the Manufacture of Weapons of Mass Destruction

In August 1989 Aum's campaign succeeded, and the April decision to deny it affiliated legal status was reversed. However, by this time Aum had attracted the attention of the mass media. In October 1989 the magazine *Sunday Mainichi* ran a seven-part series on Aum that accused it of breaking up families and exploiting its members and portrayed Asahara in a highly negative light. Aum reacted angrily to the articles, threatening lawsuits and condemning what it saw as media persecution, but the articles also galvanized the opposition and brought forth more than 200 new complainants against Aum. The result was the formation of the *Aum Higaisha no Kai* (Aum Victims' Society) and the engagement of a young campaigning lawyer, Sakamoto Tsutsumi, as its legal representative.

Sakamoto set about investigating Aum for what he believed might be illegal and fraudulent activities designed to acquire funds from disciples. In the process, he discovered that Aum had made false claims when promoting the spiritual benefits of its initiation practices. Asahara and his closest colleagues recognized that his investigations posed a serious danger to the movement, not only on this matter but also because further investigation might reveal the deaths of Majima and Taguchi. To forestall this possibility a group of disciples, acting on Asahara's orders, killed Sakamoto (along with his wife and son) in November 1989 and disposed of their bodies. It was not until September 1995 that the bodies were found after the perpetrators confessed to the deed. One of them, Hayakawa Kiyohide, told a court in January 1998 that Sakamoto posed a severe threat to Aum, that he had been killed to protect its mission, and that the murder was a manifestation of Aum's "salvation activity" (*kyûsai katsudô*) (http://www.asahi.com Jan 16 1998).

The murders were Aum's first aggressive acts committed outside the movement, and they can be connected directly both to the earlier deaths of Majima and Taguchi and to the growing tension between Aum and the world. Although no concrete evidence linking Aum to this incident emerged at the time, it was widely suspected of being behind the disappearance of the Sakamotos. This led to the growth of an even more concerted campaign against the movement. The campaign was spearheaded not only by the *Aum Higaisha no Kai* but also by friends and associates of Sakamoto, including the campaigning journalist Egawa Shôko (who wrote a number of highly critical books and articles about Aum) and the lawyer Takimoto Tarô.

In February 1990 Asahara made a misguided foray into the world of politics. Convinced that Aum needed to expand its base in order to attract new support, and that a high-profile election campaign could further this plan, he established a political party, the Shinritô or Party of Truth. Asahara, along with twenty-four Aum devotees, stood for election in the Japanese parliamentary elections. The results were disastrous for Aum and merely increased the pressure building up around the movement. The decision to engage in the world of politics caused unrest inside the movement, and several disciples quit as a result. Aum's election campaign was widely ridiculed in the media, which used the election to remind the public repeatedly about the possible links between Aum and the vanished Sakamoto family.

Every Aum candidate including Asahara lost heavily, and this humiliating rejection at the hands of the general public proved a bitter blow to the movement. Asahara attempted to externalize the blame for this catastrophic failure too by claiming that the authorities had conspired to defraud Aum of victory. The election debacle, in other words, added to the growing tide of conspiracy complaints that emanated from Aum and that illustrated how beleaguered the movement had become. Indeed, it was right after the election in March 1990 that Asahara began to talk openly in sermons about a "conspiracy" that had been formed against Aum. The conspirators included the Japanese and U.S. governments, Jews, Freemasons, and others. Aum's opposition was no longer just a group of disgruntled parents backed by lawyers and journalists; it had grown into a vast conspiracy to persecute and destroy the only source of goodness and truth left in the world. Henceforth, this conspiracy became a central plank in Asahara's teachings; it was used to demonstrate why Aum was unable to succeed in its mission and why it had to take up arms and fight.

This produced a further escalation in Aum's cycle of violence and malevolent intent. The Japanese public, which was presented with the chance of salvation, had chosen to humiliate Aum at the ballot box and therefore deserved to be punished. It was at this juncture that Asahara ordered a select group of disciples to engage in a secret plan to manufacture weapons of mass destruction that could be used to punish the unworthy in the inevitable war to come.

In the spring of 1990, Asahara's disciples constructed a secret laboratory where they manufactured biological weapons such as botulinum, the bacterium that causes botulism. In April of that year, an attempt was made to unleash botulinum in the center of Tokyo. Although a failure, it signified Asahara's intention to engage with his enemies on a grand scale. Aum had moved beyond its earlier attacks against individuals to the possibility of mass murder of the general public, who had become, by virtue of the 1990 elections, complicit in a conspiratorial campaign against Aum. Aum's polarization of the world was complete, and everyone who was not a member was an enemy who could justifiably be killed to protect Aum and its mission.

The Final Confrontation: Aum's Attack on the Tokyo Subway

Between the portentous spring of 1990 and the subway attack of 1995, Aum was consistently surrounded by controversy and conflicts. These were to a large extent a result of its own actions, compounded by the reputation it had gained after the disappearance of the Sakamotos and the election campaign. In May 1990, for example, Aum acquired land at Namino, in southern Japan, where it planned to build a commune. It concealed its identity during the purchase, an act that later led to the arrest of some Aum officials on criminal charges and to Asahara's complaint of persecution. When its true identity surfaced, the local villagers and civil authorities, who were fearful of having such a notorious movement in its vicinity, tried to block the commune's development. The result was that Aum became embroiled there and in a number of other locations in bitter disputes that ranged from physical confrontations between commune members and their neighbors to protracted court disputes with the civil authorities. The opposition Aum faced, especially at Namino, was not always legal. For example, the Namino authorities refused to accept the residence applications of Aum devotees living at the commune and also blocked their access to water, sewage, telephone, and other services. These actions were illegal, and the courts eventually ruled in Aum's favor in its disputes with its neighbours.

Aum's neighbors at Namino and elsewhere had reacted negatively to the movement because of its reputation, its underhanded dealings in acquiring land, and its disdainful attitude toward them. In viewing its neighbors as complicit participants in an evil world heading for disaster, Aum had made them into actual enemies and had managed to boost the hostile forces surrounding it.

Beginning in the spring of 1990, Aum secretly experimented with various weapons of mass destruction in preparation for the prophesied final war. The boundaries with the outside world became ever stronger, and it existed in a de facto state of conflict with the world at large and within itself. The activities of senior disciples such as Murai, who were engaged in attempts to make weapons, were one manifestation of this conflict. Others included the increasingly violent means leaders used to prevent followers from leaving the movement, the inquisitions and punishments meted out to any devotee suspected of being lax in faith, and attacks carried out on opponents who had campaigned against Aum and on other religious leaders suspected of opposing Aum (Reader 2000: 163–169, 203–219).

By the time Murai made his comment about Aum's imminent confrontation with Japanese society quoted at the beginning of this chapter, this confrontation had already occurred. Aum had accumulated a store of chemical weapons; carried out one attack on the general public using nerve gas in the town of Matsumoto in June 1994; and declared itself independent of Japan by forming its own "government" with Asahara at its head (Reader 2000: 208–211). The authorities also had become aware of Aum's activities, and preparations were afoot to move in on it.

In March 1995 events came to a head with Aum's attack on the Tokyo subway. This attack was intended primarily as a preemptive strike against the police. It was ordered by Asahara and coordinated by Murai when they learned that the police were about to conduct raids on the movement because of suspicions (subsequently confirmed) that it had committed earlier hostile acts and crimes. The sarin nerve gas attack, which killed twelve and injured thousands of rush-hour commuters, focused on the Kasumigaseki station in the heart of the government district. It failed to achieve its purpose. Two days later, massive military-style raids were carried out on Aum premises throughout Japan, resulting in the arrests of hundreds of Aum followers, the discovery of evidence linking Aum's leaders to crimes that included murder and the manufacture of weapons, and an ongoing series of trials that have seen several devotees sentenced to death for their roles in committing murders and many others sentenced to long periods of imprisonment. Many prominent Aum figures, including Asahara, remain on trial, and several face possible death sentences.

Despite failing to disrupt police investigations, Aum's attack sent out a number of dramatic messages. It illustrated Aum's hostility to mainstream society and its readiness to bring death and destruction on those who lived in it. The subway attack, directed at the nerve center of Japan, expressed in a concrete way the intention of Aum Shinrikyô to confront Japanese society and to strike out at what its leaders regarded as an evil world standing in antithesis to the sacred truths for which it was prepared to fight (Reader 2000: 26–28).

Conclusion

The enormity of Aum's actions in using chemical weapons to wreak mass destruction on the general populace, along with its extended history of violence against opponents and dissident followers, mark the Aum affair as one of the most dramatic incidents of religious violence in modern times. This chapter suggests that the origins of violence and confrontation, and of the doctrines that underpinned them, came from within the movement. Indeed, they were first expressed within the movement and only later were directed outside.

Yet, in analyzing how Aum's violence escalated so rapidly, attention must also be paid to the ways in which Aum's perception of external pressures on it fed into and exacerbated the impulses toward violence and confrontation within Aum. Some of these pressures were the result of real opposition, ranging from the unwelcome attentions of the mass media and the complaints of parents and the Aum Victims' Society to the hostile behavior of the villagers and authorities in areas where Aum built its communes. Such opposition and external pressures occurred at critical junctures in Aum's history when Aum's internal dynamics had rendered the movement precarious and liable to violence, and it thus played a part in heightening Aum's confrontational stance. The opposition to Aum that coalesced in spring 1989 to bring about the rejection of its application for legal recognition came at a sensitive time for the movement and was the catalyst that caused Asahara to call for his disciples to fight against Japanese society. Every subsequent manifestation of opposition, pressure, or protest against Aum added to this process.

At the same time, however, one should not lose sight of how important and useful such external opposition proved to be for Aum, enabling it to interpret its problems and strengthen its resolve. External pressures and opposition clearly helped Aum legitimate its critique of the corrupt and evil nature of society and hence for the need to fight against it in the service of truth. In a sense, Aum needed such external opposition and pressure so that it could emphasize its arguments about the evils of the world. The irony, of course, is that the opposition was initially provoked by Aum's zealotry and system of renunciation, which placed it in conflict with the parents of members and attracted a hostile press.

Real opposition, however, became transformed and magnified – as Aum's problems grew – into something far greater and more expansive. The critical event here was Aum's election defeat, which represented a loss of such proportions that it could only be explained by something as extraordinary as a world conspiracy, and could only be responded to by an act of dramatic retribution such as the failed botulinum attack on Tokyo. It was after Aum had become preoccupied with an imagined and all-embracing sense of persecution and opposition that it began to take steps to confront that opposition by manufacturing biological and chemical weapons that could wreak real havoc on the world. As Aum's paranoid construction of others' motives and imagined conspiracies grew, so did its belief in the inevitability of confrontation. As Murai's comment illustrates, Aum's disciples *expected* a confrontation to occur between the movement and the authorities. Aum had to confront the world because its polarized view of the world, in which the forces of good and evil were destined to engage in a final war, and its view that Aum was the only beacon of good and truth in the corrupt modern world, demanded nothing less. In less than a decade after proclaiming its mission to save the world, Aum had become embroiled in a rapidly escalating process of violence and opposition in which the one fed off the other until it reached the point at which Aum not only developed the capacity, through its chemical weapons program, to confront society and commit mass murder but actually did so.

References

Asahara, Shôkô. n.d. *Vajrayana kôsu. Kyôgaku shisutemu kyôhon.* Unpublished internal Aum text of fifty-seven sermons delivered by Asahara to disciples between 1988 and 1994, probably compiled around 1994.

　　Metsubô no hi. Tokyo: Oumu Shuppan, 1989.

　　Inishieeshon. Tokyo: Oumu Shuppan, 1987.

Egawa, Shôko. *Oumu Shinrikyô saiban bôchôki*, vol. 1. Tokyo: Bungei Shunjû, 1996. Http://www.asahi.com

Kyôdô Tsûshinsha Shakaibu (KDT) (ed.). *Sabakareru kyôso.* Tokyo: Kyôdô Tsûshinsha, 1997.

Mainichi Shinbun Shûkyô Shuzaihan (ed.). *Kiseimatsu no kamisama.* Tokyo: Tôhô Shuppan, 1993.

Numata, Kenya. "Oumu Shinrikyô no kenkyû- kagaku to shûkyô no kankei ni kanren shite." *Momoyama Gakuin Daigaku Sôgô Kenkyûjo Kiyô* 22 (1996): 93–128.

Reader, Ian. *Religious Violence in Contemporary Japan: The Case of Aum Shinrikyô.* Richmond, Surrey, England: Curzon Press and Honolulu: University of Hawaii Press, 2000.

　　"Imagined Persecution: Aum Shinrikyô, Millennialism and the Legitimation of Violence." In *Millennialism, Persecution and Violence: Historical Cases,* edited by Catherine Wessinger. Syracuse, NY: Syracuse University Press, 1999: 138–152.

　　A Poisonous Cocktail? Aum Shinrikyô's Path to Violence. Copenhagen: NIAS Books, 1996.

Religion in Contemporary Japan. Basingstoke, U.K.: Macmillan and Honolulu: University of Hawaii Press, 1991.

"The 'New' New Religions of Japan: An Analysis of the Rise of Agonshu." *Japanese Journal of Religious Studies* 15 (1988): 235–261.

Shimazono, Susumu. "In the Wake of Aum: The Formation and Transformation of a Universe of Belief." *Japanese Journal of Religious Studies* 22 (1995): 381–415.

Shûkan Asahi (weekly magazine), October 13, 1995: 26.

Takahashi, Hidetoshi. *Oumu kara no kikan*. Tokyo: Sôshisha, 1997.

MAKING SENSE OF THE HEAVEN'S GATE SUICIDES

ROBERT W. BALCH AND DAVID TAYLOR

In March 1997, all thirty-nine members of a UFO cult known as Heaven's Gate committed mass suicide in an exclusive suburb of San Diego, California. Their leader, Do, believed a spacecraft was about to take them to the Kingdom of Heaven, where they would be reunited with his partner, Ti, who had died in 1985. To make the transition, Do claimed that he and his followers had to shed their bodies since the body was only a decaying container for the soul.

The suicides had been carefully planned. Two notes found by the sheriff's deputies spelled out the details – a mixture of barbiturates and alcohol to induce unconsciousness, followed by suffocation caused by a plastic bag placed over the head and secured at the neck with rubber bands. The bodies were dressed in black uniforms displaying colorful shoulder patches with the words "Heaven's Gate Away Team," and each body had a travel bag next to it on the floor. The bodies were also neatly covered with purple shrouds. The evidence amassed by the sheriff's department and the medical examiner indicated that the suicides were undertaken voluntarily. No signs of struggle or violence were found, and the preparations included making two farewell videos in which the members appeared to be excited by the prospect of taking their lives.

The suicides were especially surprising because Ti and Do originally claimed that the only way to enter the Kingdom of Heaven was in a *living physical body*. They believed that death simply condemned one to another incarnation on Earth. How then did Do conclude that suicide was a viable alternative to physical departure, and why did his followers believe him? We will argue that the suicides resulted from a deliberate decision that was neither prompted by an external threat nor implemented through coercion. Members went to their deaths willingly, even enthusiastically, because suicide made sense to them in the context of a belief system that, with few modifications, dated back to Ti and Do's initial revelations.

To explain the suicides, we will show how each phase of the group's history set the stage for subsequent developments, until Do and his followers concluded that suicide was the only option they had left for leaving the planet. Our conclusions are based on twenty-five years of research on Heaven's Gate (Balch and Taylor 1976, 1977; Balch 1982, 1995), including twenty-two in-depth interviews with ex-members conducted after the suicides.

The Awakening: 1972–1975

We begin with the period Ti and Do called their "Awakening" because it formed the template for nearly every significant development that followed. Ti was born Bonnie Lu Nettles. She had been a registered nurse active in Houston's metaphysical circles, including the Theosophical Society and a spiritualist group that claimed to channel messages from departed spirits and space aliens. Do grew up as Marshall Herff Applewhite (Herff to his friends) in a strict Presbyterian family. After briefly studying for the ministry, he taught music at the University of Alabama and St. Thomas University in Houston. By the time he met Bonnie in 1972, he had started questioning orthodox Christianity and was developing an interest in alternative religious philosophies.

Bonnie and Herff felt an immediate connection, as if they had been together in a previous life, and soon they came to believe that their meeting had been preordained. Bonnie's marriage was disintegrating, and Herff had been fired from both of his university jobs, one following an embarrassing scandal involving a homosexual affair with a student. Herff struggled with his sexual identity for years and often spoke about his desire to overcome sexuality altogether. After losing his second teaching job, he began having dreams and visions that led him to question his sanity. In one vision, men dressed in white informed him that he was destined to fulfill a Christ-like role. For Bonnie this vision was prophetic. In her spiritualist meetings she claimed to have received information from an extraterrestrial that a mysterious stranger fitting Herff's description was about to enter her life.

Soon Bonnie and Herff were spending nearly all their free time together, and Herff's acquaintances marveled at Bonnie's influence over him. Bonnie had entered his life at a time when he longed for direction. She gave him a crash course in metaphysics, and he came to see her as a platonic soul mate. However, their relationship did not please Bonnie's husband, and he soon filed for divorce. Bonnie's obligations were weakened further when her two retarded daughters were institutionalized. Thus freed from social entanglements, she and Herff became increasingly reclusive, spending days alone together in a secluded house on the edge of town.

For Bonnie and Herff, the sudden coincidence of so many life-changing events could not have happened by chance. It was pure synchronicity, and it convinced them that they had a special calling. The disintegration of their previous lives had been God's way of weaning them from their human endeavors for a mission in which Herff would play the key role, with Bonnie acting as his guide. Shortly after leaving Houston on a road trip to discover their purpose, they wrote a manuscript describing their unfolding understandings. In a thinly veiled reference to Herff, they asked readers what they would do if Jesus chose to reincarnate as a man in Texas.

The answers they had been seeking came in 1973 after six months of traveling, during which they avoided social contacts, meditated, prayed, and supported themselves by doing odd jobs. In a powerful revelation, they realized that they were the Two Witnesses prophesied in Revelations 11. In that prophecy God gives power to two heavenly messengers who are restored to life after being martyred and ascend to Heaven in a cloud. Herff and Bonnie came to believe that the cloud was a spacecraft and that Heaven was a physical place that could be entered only in a living body aboard a spaceship. They called their resurrection the "Demonstration" because it would prove that they alone understood the secret of overcoming death.

Bonnie and Herff concluded that Earth was a garden that members of the Next Level had planted with the seeds of consciousness. Jesus had been sent to conduct the harvest, but it had to be postponed because the fruit needed more time to ripen. This time two individuals had been sent, with Herff in the role of Jesus and Bonnie acting as his guide. Immediately after the Demonstration, humans who chose to follow them would be picked up by spaceships and taken to the Kingdom of Heaven, where they would become immortal androgynous beings. To be eligible for membership in the Next Level, humans would have to shed every attachment to the planet. These included the same things Bonnie and Herff had given up: friends, families, jobs, possessions, and sex. Reflecting Do's personal struggle with sexuality, sex was expected to be one of the most difficult attachments to overcome.

Bonnie and Herff's favorite metaphor was that of the caterpillar becoming a butterfly. Just as they had done when leaving Houston, seekers had to withdraw from the world. This would begin a biochemical transformation of their bodies that would be completed following the Demonstration. Like butterflies, they would emerge from their chrysalis with new, more refined bodies, free from earthly limitations.

More pieces of the puzzle fell into place when Bonnie and Herff began to tell others about their mission. Convinced that time was short, they presented their message to anyone they thought might be receptive, insisting that humans drop everything and follow them immediately. However, they were dismayed to find that humans thought they were cranks, and the more they were rejected, the more their message took an apocalyptic turn. In a letter to a friend they noted that fires, floods, and other disasters seemed to follow them everywhere they went. Before long, it became clear that human civilization might have to be destroyed after the Demonstration.

Humans were not merely asleep but also under the influence of Satan, a former member of the Next Level who had chosen to turn against God. His unwitting helpers were a host of disincarnate spirits caught between human lifetimes. Because these souls could not indulge their human-level desires in disembodied form, they would attach themselves to humans and live through them by influencing their choice of activities. Most spirits were not evil (they influenced great composers and drug users alike), but they did Satan's work by clutching humans who threatened their vicarious pleasures by wanting to uproot themselves from the garden.

Satan's detemination to disrupt their mission was dramatized in 1974, when Herff spent six months in jail without trial for not returning a car he and Bonnie had rented with a borrowed credit card. This incident strengthened their belief that the Demonstration was near and led them to intensify their proselytizing. While in jail, Herff wrote a concise statement of their beliefs, and on his release he and Bonnie mailed it to dozens of spiritual teachers and New Age groups.

One of those fliers found its way to a group of seekers in Los Angeles who also happened to have been preparing for an ascension, though in spiritual rather than physical bodies. In another moment of synchronicity, Herff and Bonnie arrived at a time when the group was disintegrating and its members' personal lives were in flux, much as Bonnie's and Herff's had been. The messengers gave them two weeks to "walk out the door of their lives" and suddenly found themselves with twenty-four people who wanted to follow them. This was a clear signal that the harvest had begun.

The Chrysalis: 1975–1976

Now with a flock to tend, Herff and Bonnie changed their names to Bo and Peep. During the next several months, they recruited over 200 followers in a series of public meetings in the western United States. Some were over thirty and came from fairly conventional backgrounds, but most were young people from the counterculture. Despite their differences, they were seekers with weak ties to mainstream society who shared a desire for personal transformation. Bo and Peep saw this as evidence that they were ready for the message.

Bo and Peep relied on this readiness when recruiting followers. Believing that humans had to make a free choice to follow them, they did not try to pressure people into joining. In a succinct public lecture they would explain their message, answer questions from the audience, and then depart, leaving their followers to provide additional information. New members had to make their biggest sacrifices, such as saying goodbye to their relatives, even before joining.

For many, the most compelling aspect of the message was the promise of eternal life without having to die. Yet in a 1975 flier, Bo and Peep wrote that any member who was killed for his beliefs could still enter the Next Level:

> [He] would certainly resurrect in the simple, real sense, i.e., he would step aside . . . while his body heals itself, and then he would reenter it and take up his place in the membership of the next kingdom.

Thus the possibility that at least some members would die was acknowledged from the outset, but Bo and Peep rarely mentioned this in their lectures, and to members the likelihood of being murdered seemed so remote that it was virtually never discussed.

To help members enter the chrysalis state, Bo and Peep created a social cocoon that mirrored their own experiences. The group traveled constantly, stayed in isolated campgrounds, and survived by asking people for money, food, and gas. Members were discouraged from calling or writing to friends and relatives, and except in public meetings, they rarely identified themselves as a group. Within this encapsulated environment, they were expected to devote all their energy to overcoming their humanness. This entailed avoiding any activities that might draw them back into their human ways, such as reading, listening to music, using drugs, talking about the past, and engaging in sex.

Since the first step in the overcoming process was dropping out of society, it was only a matter of time before the media began reporting on people who had disappeared after attending Bo and Peep's lectures. Soon Heaven's Gate, then called Human Individual Metamorphosis (HIM), became a media sideshow. Reporters poked fun at Bo and Peep, experts claimed that the group was a cult that brainwashed its members, fearful parents drew parallels with the Manson Family, and one disgruntled defector publicly accused Bo and Peep of fraud. In a front-page wire service story, this person claimed to have started a "halfway house" for dropouts, which she called Hinder Evolutionary Ripoffs (HER). Bo and Peep saw these developments as further signs of Satan's opposition.

The negative publicity had two effects. First, it forced Bo and Peep into hiding because they feared assassination before all the "ripe fruit" in the garden could be harvested. Second, it heightened their sense of urgency. The end had to be near since Satan was pulling out all the stops. While living at a secret location in Oklahoma, Bo and Peep videotaped a "final statement" to be released after their departure, and in the meantime their followers stepped up efforts to get the message out.

Members fanned out across the country to hold more meetings, but without Bo and Peep their success was limited, disagreements arose, and discouragement set in when the Demonstration failed to happen. With the onset of winter, the regimen of camping and living on handouts wore thin, and soon defections soared. By the end of 1975, just eight months after the group began, over half of the members were gone, leaving only the most determined. Bo and Peep came to see this phase as a period of "pruning the vine."

The Classroom: 1976–1985

The next phase began in 1976, when Bo and Peep rejoined about 100 over-joyed followers and began making sweeping changes. The first significant change was to stop spreading the message. For months the pool of interested seekers had been dwindling, hecklers had been on the rise, and the media had been losing interest. Taking these developments as a sign that the harvest was over, Bo and Peep stopped holding public meetings. During this period they also changed their names again to Do and Ti, after the musical notes, with Ti's name always spoken first. The new order symbolized Ti's superior position in a "chain of mind" connecting members with the Next Level through Ti and Do.

The governing metaphor became the "Classroom." Assuming the role of teachers, Ti and Do began a rigorous program designed to prepare their students for graduation by teaching them to function as a finely tuned Next Level "crew." Comparing their students to astronauts in training, they instituted a kind of boot camp, first in Wyoming and later in other western states. At first, members continued to camp, but soon they moved into expensive suburban houses and began getting jobs such as waiting tables and repairing computers to support themselves.

Within each "craft," as the houses were called, everyday life was designed to simulate life aboard a spaceship. Strict procedures ordered the most mundane activities, such as using the toilet, buttering bread, and even sleeping, which was structured to prevent sexual arousal (e.g., hands above the waist and no sleeping on one's stomach). Private property was nonexistent, and members wore uniforms, for a time including hoods with mesh covering the eyes. Stringent routines permitted no time to dwell on the past or worry about what lay ahead. During one six-month stretch, students followed individualized schedules that specified activities down to the minute. For example, one member awoke from the first of four two-hour rest periods at 5:36 P.M, used the "bath chamber" between 5:57 and 6:12, took the first of thirty-two vitamins at 6:21, and then worked at "fuel preparation" (cooking) between 6:30 and 8:30. While performing "out-of-craft tasks" students distanced themselves from fellow employees by adopting a unisex appearance, identifying themselves as members of a monastery, and keeping records of their observations of humans.

One of the Class's first lessons was patience. In 1976 Ti and Do announced that the Demonstration had been canceled because the prophecy of Revelations 11 had been fulfilled by their "murder" at the hands of the press. Nothing was set in stone because their understandings were constantly evolving. The new information posed a severe test for some because it meant that much more time would be needed in the garden before leaving, and this further thinned the ranks.

Ti and Do constantly introduced new activities, but one that continued periodically for years was a routine called "Central," which was designed to teach students to focus on serving the Next Level. Every eleven minutes throughout the day, members were expected to check in at a central location, two or four at a time, and spend a minute silently asking what they could do to serve. Even figuring time excused from checking in, this could mean at least fifty visits to Central in a day. The practice appears mind-numbing since it was impossible to make one's checks while dwelling on the past or entertaining doubts, but students regarded Central as a positive exercise to be undertaken enthusiastically because it helped free them from human-level influences. As an ex-member explained, it was "an outward gesture of an inner commitment to always be available to serve others *joyously*." Students who did not share this enthusiasm usually dropped out, although they might be encouraged to leave. Ti and Do even bought bus or plane tickets for departing members and gave them money to help them get reestablished.

Late in 1976, Ti and Do did more than offer encouragement. Nineteen members who were thought to need more lessons at the human level were separated from the group and sent to Arizona, where they were instructed to get jobs and await further instructions. Ti and Do checked on them periodically but eventually cut off communication, leaving the Arizona contingent to drift back into the human world. By the end of 1978 the Class was down to forty-eight.

Other innovations strengthened the resolve of those who remained. For example, Ti and Do introduced a form of mutual criticism that involved pointing out ways in which members slipped back into human habits. Even seemingly innocuous human habits such as indulging an artistic spirit by doodling were discussed. These sessions were gentle compared to the encounter groups found in some communities, but the effect was similar, and so eager were students to change that they often called meetings for themselves.

Only by constantly asking for guidance from Ti and Do could students understand what the Next Level expected of them. Old methods of discerning truth, such as logic and intuition, were subject to human-level influences, and the possibility of individual revelation was ruled out by the belief that the Class was linked to the Next Level through the chain of mind. When Ti and Do were unavailable, students made decisions by asking themselves how their teachers would act in particular situations. The desire to emulate their teachers was illustrated by a banner in one craft that read: "I am in a classroom twenty-four hours a day. Everything I do is a test to tune in to my older members' mind."

Although canceling the Demonstration had reduced the sense of urgency, the Class never lost sight of the goal of being picked up by a spacecraft. Ti and Do instituted a nightly vigil of watching the skies for signs of Next Level activity, and once in Texas, Ti and Do even set a date for the lift-off. Anxiously the Class packed its belongings, drove into the desert, and spent the night in lawn chairs waiting for the ships. Though disappointed, members regarded the event as just another test.

Meanwhile, students' families were completely in the dark about these developments. Ti and Do did not allow members to call home until 1982, and three more years passed before students started visiting their families. Besides being extremely rare, these visits usually lasted only a day or two, and students revealed little about their lives except that they were living in a monastery and learning to work with computers. Since members appeared to be happy and free to leave if they wished, their families agreed not to interfere as long as they stayed in touch.

While reassuring, these contacts did not signal a weakening of the group's boundaries. In a significant turnabout prompted by a Class discussion of the soul, Ti and Do came to believe that their students had not been grown from human seeds after all. Rather, they were neophyte members of the Next Level who had been sent to Earth on a training mission in order to graduate to full membership in the Kingdom. From this perspective, parents were little more than instruments chosen to produce "containers" for incubating Next Level souls. The idea that the Class was an "Away Team" was beginning to take shape.

Crisis and Uncertainty: 1985–1988

Then in 1985, Ti unexpectedly died of liver cancer. Her death posed the biggest test the Class had faced because it contradicted the fundamental belief that the only way to enter the Next Level was in a living physical body. It must have been sobering to watch as Ti's ashes were scattered on a lake in a Dallas suburb. Not only had the students lost a beloved teacher, but there had been no resurrection, no spacecraft, no harvest, and not even a hint that the lift-off might be near. By then, however, the students were accustomed to being tested, and to our knowledge only one dropped out. Ti's death would prove to be the most important turning point since Ti and Do's awakening.

Do explained that Ti had been forced to leave her body because her "vehicle" could not withstand her energy. When it finally gave out, she had been recalled to the Next Level, leaving Do to complete their mission. In fact, Do was badly shaken by Ti's departure. He admitted that without Ti he often felt "underwater," and former members described him as "depressed," "weepy," and "lost." Do claimed that Ti stayed in contact with him but that her messages often were unclear. This led to indecisiveness and self-doubt. Do openly wondered if he was deluding himself, and once he offered $1,000 to anyone who wanted to leave the Class.

Although the students rallied behind him, Do felt it necessary to establish himself in his new role as the Next Level's sole representative. In a process he described as "grafting to the vine," students affirmed their loyalty to him. The most dramatic incident was a wedding ceremony in which he gave each student a gold wedding band in an emotional private meeting. Now, just as he was bound to Ti, his students were wedded to him. Students also began sending him "committal" letters in which they affirmed their devotion. Even ex-members who now believe they had been brainwashed claim that Do was completely sincere, never took unfair advantage of his followers, and expected no more from his students than he expected of himself. Members' bonds with Do became intensely personal in ways that once would have been considered thoroughly human. For example, when a student decided to leave in 1988, Do sat him on his lap and wept while holding him.

The Class's psychic distance from humans became even more extreme when Do introduced the idea of the Luciferians. Lucifer, as he called Satan, commanded an army of evil space aliens who were locked in cosmic battle with the Next Level. Previously the message had recognized the presence of tangible foes in the form of spirits, but the Luciferians were actual physical beings who, like members of the Next Level, traveled in spaceships. In a publication called "'88 Update: The UFO Two and Their Crew," Do devoted considerable space to "Lucy's" efforts to undermine the Class, citing things once attributed only to spirits.

It is not clear what prompted Do to expand on his ideas about Satan. Presumably Ti's death played a role since obstacles had always been attributed to lower forces. However, the "'88 Update" did not make such a connection. Nor did it cite any recent attacks on the Class. Most parents had given up on locating it; the Class was not being targeted by the anticult movement; ex-members were no longer denouncing it; and the Class kept such a low profile that hardly anyone even knew it existed. The only specific example of opposition cited in the "Update" is the "resentment" the group encountered during a short-lived effort to promote celibacy among humans. Rather than persecution, the Luceriferian theory appears to have reflected the spate of UFO abduction stories during the 1980s. Do could not believe that the Next Level would perform the medical experiments described by abductees. Only aliens who required genetic material for sexual reproduction needed to do that.

Despite the rhetoric about Lucifer, a former member of Do's inner circle claimed that the notion of cosmic warfare still was not dogma when he left the Class in 1994. Although the idea was used to dramatize the plight of humans, he claimed it was mainly speculation that was "fun to play with."

More important changes in the belief system came in the form of new understandings about the body and the soul. Since Ti obviously did not need a body to return to the Next Level, perhaps others would not have to physically board a spaceship to leave the planet. Her death had shown that the body did not have to be transformed after all. It was merely a "suit of clothes" that one put on to work in the garden. In this new view, the body became a decaying container for the soul – a "vehicle" to be traded in rather than transformed through a caterpillar-like metamorphosis. This at least was true of Ti and probably of Do as well. The fleeting nature of Do's own vehicle was driven home in 1988, when he almost died from tick fever. However, it would be years before Do considered the possibility that his students also might have to die. The goal still was to leave in a physical body, and as late as 1991 the Class undertook a water fast in preparation for the arrival of a spacecraft.

Reaching Out: 1988–1994

As stated in the "'88 Update," the group's dilemma was "WHAT TO DO WITH WHAT WE KNOW?" Do's solution was to begin spreading the message again. The first significant step was mailing the "Update" to UFO experts, book stores, and New Age centers around the country. This was followed in 1991 and 1992 by a video series entitled "Beyond Human – *The Last Call.*" However, only a few people wrote for information, and sincere inquiries were outnumbered by sarcastic replies. Later, the Class took the dramatic step of publicizing its message in newspapers and New Age magazines, including a $30,000 ad in *USA Today.* Perhaps reflecting the poor response to the group's previous efforts, these ads were far more apocalyptic than anything published before. For instance, the *USA Today* ad began with this warning:

> The Earth's present "civilization" is about to be recycled – "spaded under." Its inhabitants are refusing to evolve. The "weeds" have taken over the garden and disturbed is usefulness beyond repair.

Despite these efforts, the Class was shrinking. The most common reason for leaving was a feeling of personal stagnation, but to Do the defections suggested that time was short. Pointing out that ripe fruit falls off the vine if it is not picked, Do took the dropouts as a sign that the harvest was drawing to a close.

Toward the end of 1993, the Class was down to twenty-six students. Reflecting an urgency not felt since 1975, the group decided to blanket the country with public lectures in 1994. These meetings followed the same format as those in the 1970s, and as before, prospective members were expected to make an immediate decision. Although the Class doubled in size, some who joined were former members, and about half left within a few months. For Do, the poor response confirmed that the harvest was finally over. Other signs that the end was near included wars, earthquakes, volcanic eruptions, and the Waco standoff in 1993.

Except in 1994, when the Class was on the road, everyday life remained on course. Over the years, many of the more stringent routines had been relaxed or discarded. Students worked on a movie script based on their message, contacted New Age groups, attended UFO conferences, experimented with innovative diets, and attended movies for recreation, all the while trying to remain focused on their goal of returning to the Next Level. However, most still struggled with their human conditioning.

For men the biggest problem was "sensuality," the euphemism for sex. One ex-member reported having to look away when he saw attractive women on the street, and another fought to keep from becoming aroused by a particularly beautiful woman in the Class. The solution to these "mammalian" urges was castration. First discussed in 1987, it became a reality in the early 1990s, when two students flipped a coin to decide who would go first. Eventually eight men, including Do, had themselves castrated, and several others underwent chemical treatments to reduce their sex drive.

Searching for New Options: 1994–1997

Still without a clear sign from Ti, Do grew indecisive again. In 1995 the Class bought forty acres in the mountains southeast of Albuquerque, New Mexico, where it began constructing two large "earth ships" using tires packed with dirt as building blocks. Do envisioned an actual monastery but abandoned the project in midstream when the onset of winter made life uncomfortable for the older vehicles. By then Do was sixty-four, and several others were in their fifties and sixties.

Because of their remote location and thick, windowless walls, media stories later referred to these buildings as a "compound" and drew parallels with the Branch Davidians. The structures were designed more for insulation than fortification, but the location had been chosen to minimize contact with the outside world, including the government. The Waco incident frightened Do, who talked increasingly about New World Order conspiracies, and students often suspected that they were under surveillance.

As early as 1992, the Class began to explore the possibility of settling in a different country. Not only did Do hope to find a more accepting environment, but he believed that the Next Level was preparing to "till the garden" in North America. Eventually he and a few students visited countries all over the world, but after spending thousands of dollars on plane tickets and hotels, they concluded that every place was just as inhospitable as the United States. Their belief was buttressed by unpleasant experiences while flying to other countries, such as being interrogated for making last-minute ticket purchases with cash instead of making reservations with a credit card.

Although it seemed clear that the harvest was finished, the Class continued to advertise the message over the Internet. Its web site was sophisticated and used science fiction imagery to give a new slant to the message, but it generated few serious inquiries. Only two people, a young married couple, joined after contacting the group over the Internet, and one dropped out a month later.

During this phase, Do's health visibly declined. He looked tired, delegated more responsibilities to his students, and talked about assuming a "professor emeritus" role. Eventually he came to believe that he was dying of cancer, although later an autopsy proved that this was not true. For his students, the thought of going on without Do must have been unbearable.

"When Do came down to it," a former member explained, "he had explored all his options, and they all seemed like dead ends." The obvious conclusion was that it finally was time to leave the planet. Reflecting on the failure of the Internet campaign, an ex-member said, "We just were not able to interface with the public, and that was seen as more evidence . . . that it was time to leave." Another member claimed that the failure to find a suitable place to live only proved that there was no place left on the planet for the Class: "It is time for us to go home – to God's Kingdom, to the Next Level." The Class began using the name Heaven's Gate to symbolize the threshold on which it now stood.

While old options at the human level were being exhausted, the Class had been contemplating new ways of leaving the planet that did not require being picked up alive by a spacecraft. The door to this line of thinking had been opened by Ti's death. Since Ti had left her vehicle to return to the Next Level, it made sense to believe that the students could too. Ten years earlier, Ti and Do had said that death was a remote possibility, and now some students began to think about dying.

However, the idea of waiting for the vehicle to die naturally through disease or old age was out of the question. Not only had collective salvation always been integral to the message, but no one wanted to think what might happen if Do left first. The talk turned gradually to suicide. An option discussed after the Waco siege in 1993 was to provoke a fatal confrontation with government authorities. This possibility had its roots in Ti and Do's 1975 claim that members could enter the Kingdom even if they were murdered. On several occasions Do expressed his admiration for the willingness of the Branch Davidians to "go all the way." One suggestion was to use realistic water pistols to trigger a shootout, and later the Class even bought a few weapons, but the discussion was purely hypothetical and the guns were locked away because the students abhorred the idea of not being killed outright. A more direct method of taking their lives that was discussed was drowning, but this too was quickly dismissed.

The suicide talk escalated late in 1994 on the conclusion of the public lecture campaign. After describing a method for committing suicide that involved drinking a liquid and going to sleep, Do asked each member if he or she had reservations. Two ex-members who were present claimed that a few balked at the idea, but only one was so distressed that he left the Class. Now suicide was becoming a real possibility.

Early in 1996, seventeen students posted statements of their beliefs on the Internet. One all but admitted that the Class was planning suicide: "You see, death to us, has *nothing to do with the body* . . . I have made *my choice* to 'lay down my life *in this world*' and go with my Father, Do. . . . " A subsequent posting, which drew a parallel with the Jewish suicides at Massada, stated that the Class had thoroughly discussed the "willful exit of the body" and steeled itself to the prospect. The true meaning of suicide was deciding to remain on the planet.

Some of these statements made much of Lucifer's tightening grip on the human level. Luciferian influence could be seen in New Age counterfeits, government conspiracies, anticult groups, and human indifference to the Class's efforts to awaken humans. Although the group still had not received any active opposition, a new urgency was reflected in the title of the leading statement: "Last Chance to Evacuate Earth – Before It's Recycled."

Final Exit: March 23–25, 1997

Events started drawing to a close late in 1996. In November the Class held an estate sale to liquidate their possessions, and in January 1997 they purchased the

Away Team patches for their uniforms. Yet, a member who dropped out just six weeks before the suicides said that Do still believed they might be picked up in their human bodies, and other evidence suggests that members were prepared to continue waiting. For example, one student was given money to have his teeth cleaned in February 1997.

Despite Do's vacillation, several key events finally persuaded him that the moment of decision had arrived. The most important one was the advent of the Hale–Bopp comet, touted as the most spectacular comet of the twentieth century. It was due to make its closest approach to Earth on March 22, 1997, just one week before Easter, which Do saw as a meaningful coincidence. Ti and Do had dated their initial revelation from the arrival of the Kohoutek comet in 1973, and Do's interest in Hale–Bopp was fueled by a rumor, popularized by talk show host Art Bell, that a spaceship had been sighted behind it. Do speculated that Ti might be returning for him and the Class. Even after failing to locate the spacecraft with a telescope purchased for that purpose, Do became convinced that the comet was a sign that the end of the Class was at hand.

Ti and Do had always believed in synchronicity, and now everything seemed to be falling into place: Do's failing health, the conclusion of the harvest, the arrival of the comet, and the approach of Easter. As the comet drew closer, the students visited amusement parks and gambled in Las Vegas, but these excursions only strengthened their resolve to leave. "Everything of this world has been offered us," one student wrote on the Internet, "and I can honestly say, 'Thanks, but no thanks.'"

While the suicide plan took shape, the Class added the flashing words "RED ALERT!" to its web site. In three final "Earth Exit Statements" students cited human ignorance, corruption, violence, drug trafficking, and persecution as reasons for leaving. All options at the human level had been tried and discarded. "We are returning to Life," Do said in his farewell video, "and we do in all honesty *hate* this world." In their own videotaped statements the students laughed, wept, scolded humans for their blindness, and poured out their thanks to Ti and Do for providing them with an opportunity to enter the Next Level:

> I don't know what I did to deserve to be here, and I'm embarrassed that I can't express, without getting emotional, how good I feel about what I'm doing now and how good I feel about being here. And being given this opportunity to go to the Next Level – just the opportunity, the *gift*, is overwhelming. . . . I'm the happiest person in the world.

To the laughter of her classmates, a student gave the Star Trek salute and said, "One last thing we'd like to say is, thirty-nine to *beam up!*"

Then the suicides began. Do referred to them as their "final exit" because he and his followers already had exited from society, and now they were leaving the human level altogether. The suicides were conducted according to a deliberate, well-thought-out plan. They occurred over a three-day period, with one group designated to die each day and certain others appointed to straighten up after those who had left their vehicles. At the conclusion, three students assisted Do and then took their own lives. The purple shrouds may have symbolized the resurrection, but it may also be significant that purple was Ti's favorite color.

A Sociological Perspective on the Suicides

In the context of the group's history, suicide was a rational response to circumstances as they were perceived by Do and his students. Events in each phase of the group's evolution set the stage for subsequent developments, until suicide appeared to be the only option for leaving the planet. The factors leading to the suicides can be divided into three categories: (1) conditions that predisposed the group to radical action, (2) situational factors influencing the assessment of options, and (3) precipitating events that transformed suicide from an option to a reality.

The Predisposition to Radical Action

Long before the suicides, Heaven's Gate had demonstrated a propensity for extreme behavior. Not only did members submit willingly to extraordinary disciplines such as Central, but many of the men voluntarily had themselves castrated, Do being foremost among them. The factors predisposing the group to radical action include its belief system, method of selecting members, social organization, leadership, and external environment.

Belief system. The group's belief system is especially important because it provided the cognitive framework that members used to interpret their personal experiences and the world around them.

Heaven's Gate was based on the goal of going to heaven in a spacecraft. Although the means of boarding the ship changed in the end, the goal itself remained constant and shaped virtually everything members did throughout the group's history. The goal generated a sense of urgency, and even after years in the Classroom it could rekindle enthusiasm. It also set the Class up for failure because it was a tangible physical event that students believed would not happen if they became complacent.

This goal reflected a dualistic cosmology that divided the universe into sacred and profane realms. The Kingdom of Heaven promised purity, freedom, and eternal life, whereas the human level offered only an empty existence and ultimately a meaningless death. Lucifer controlled the Earth, and so powerful was his grip that the garden would have to be plowed under after the harvest. Admission to the Next Level not only required breaking social and economic ties with the past, but overcoming every aspect of one's humanness. In the beginning, Ti and Do believed that the transition required a literal physical metamorphosis, but even after this idea was discarded, Do never abandoned his conviction that the body itself was profane.

This dualism became more extreme over time. Belief in Satan and spirits evolved into an elaborate Luciferian conspiracy, and the group's rhetoric became more apocalyptic. More importantly, changes in the belief system completely separated the true self from the human body. Members came to see themselves as nonhuman souls who were merely occupying temporary life-support systems while on a mission to an alien world.

The theme of death was present in Heaven's Gate from the beginning. Originally, Ti and Do believed the prophecy of Revelations 11 required their death and resurrection, and though they did not emphasize it, they stated as far back as 1975 that members could enter the Next Level even if they died before the spacecraft arrived. Belief in the Demonstration was dropped, but the specter of death reappeared when Ti died, and the fact that she had left without her body shaped future discussions about how the others might leave.

Membership selection. The members who ultimately took their lives were the product of a long attrition process that left only the most committed. Life on the road in 1975 quickly weeded out the halfhearted, and even most who stayed eventually dropped out. Still others were asked to leave. Just as members had not been pressured to join, they were not pressured to stay, so leaving was relatively easy for such a high-demand group. The attrition process left only those most willing to submit to the rigors of the Classroom.

Social organization. The Class entailed an intense resocialization program within a monastic environment that demanded extraordinary self-sacrifice. The chrysalis metaphor is apt because the Classroom constituted a liminal phase between the human world and the Kingdom of Heaven (Turner 1969). Like a tribal rite of passage, it was characterized by separation from society, sexual abstinence, the minimization of sexual differences, the absence of personal property, humility, unselfishness, total obedience, sacred instruction, and the suspension of family obligations. All these characteristics have been shown to be associated with a high level of commitment (e.g., Kanter 1972).

Leadership. Within the Classroom, Ti and Do were the sole purveyors of knowledge, and they were free to modify their beliefs in response to changing circumstances. New information typically was revealed through signs embedded in seemingly ordinary events, and these signs were especially compelling when they occurred as synchronicity. Because of the chain of mind, only Ti and Do had the ability to interpret these events correctly. Ti played a role even after her death because students believed she continued to provide direction for Do.

Do was both an emissary from the Kingdom of Heaven and an exemplar of how to think and act like a member of the Next Level. His sincerity as well as his affectionate fatherly style generated intense devotion and a compelling desire to emulate his thoughts and actions. In Freudian terms, the individual member's superego ceased to perform its critical function because Do had become the ego ideal for the entire Class (Downton 1973).

External environment. Ti and Do's concern about outside opposition had its roots in actual experiences, such as being fired, imprisoned, and rejected for their beliefs. These experiences inspired their dualistic outlook and laid the foundation for the Luciferian theory. However, opposition ended in 1976 when the group went into seclusion, and nothing the Class did afterward generated anything approaching persecution. After Ti died, Do's concern about external threats became increasingly independent of actual events, and minor ridicule and general indifference were treated as evidence of a vast conspiracy of lower forces. In the end, Do's *perception* of external events was all that mattered.

It is important to note that, except for the death imagery and disparagement of the body, most of the factors identified previously characterize hundreds of totalistic religious groups, but only a minuscule number end in suicide. Heaven's Gate certainly had a proven capacity for radical action, but it took several unanticipated developments to transform the group into a "suicide cult."

By the early 1990s, the Class had pursued a wide range of avenues for achieving its goal. Students had left their worldly lives, endured tests on the road, trained in the Classroom, publicized their message, and searched the globe for a better place to live. Yet the Class was still here. In effect, it had endured almost twenty years of failed prophecy. As Do and others aged, the option of further waiting appeared less and less realistic. None of these developments reflected active outside opposition

Ti's death changed the matrix of options by suggesting a new alternative. Members already had come to believe that the body was just a suit of clothes, and Ti's departure provided confirmation. The Waco incident also affected the group's thinking by suggesting that students might be murdered after all. It also provided a dramatic model of commitment. We can imagine two converging trend lines: the closing of old options at the human level and the simultaneous emergence of new options involving death. At the point where the lines intersected, the hypothetical talk about dying was transformed into a clear intention.

Precipitating Factors

The preceding developments created a heightened state of readiness. In addition to their proven capacity for radical action, members believed they had exhausted their options at the human level, and they had been discussing suicide for at least four years. All that remained was the right combination of circumstances to convince Do that the time had come. In the end, the suicides were not triggered by an external threat, like the government's actions in Waco or Leo Ryan's investigation of the Peoples Temple, but by Do's perception of a synchronistic conjunction of events as compelling as the coincidences that had led to his Awakening. Not only did the members share Do's belief in synchronicity, but his interpretation made sense in the context of long-held beliefs. From the students' perspective, everything in the group's history had led the Class to this final, inevitable step.

That history can be summarized as a process of progressive, *deliberate disconnection* from society.[1] Initially the process was mainly social and economic, but the fundamental objective of Heaven's Gate was to disconnect *mentally* from everything human, including the body. Suicide was merely the logical conclusion. Once the decision had been made, the suicides were carried out with the same methodical precision that had characterized the Class for over two decades. Death signified graduation – the moment when the students would toss their hats in the air. Suicide marked the end of the Classroom and the beginning of new lives as full-fledged members of the Next Kingdom.

References

Downton, James V. *Rebel Leadership: Commitment and Charisma in the Revolutionary Process*. New York: Free Press, 1973.

Kanter, Rosabeth Moss. *Commitment and Community: Communes and Utopias in Sociological Perspective*. Cambridge, MA: Harvard University Press, 1972.

Turner, Victor T. *The Ritual Process: Structure and Anti-Structure*. Ithaca, NY: Cornell University Press, 1969.

---

[1] For earlier accounts of Heaven's Gate, see the following:

Balch, Robert W. "Waiting for the Ships: Disillusionment and the Revitalization of Faith in Bo and Peep's UFO Cult." In *The Gods Have Landed: New Religions from Other Worlds*, edited by James Lewis. Albany: State University of New York Press, 1995: 137–166.

Bo and Peep: A Case Study of the Origins of Messianic Leadership. In *Millennialism and Charisma*, edited by Roy Wallis. Belfast, Northern Ireland: Queen's University, 1982: 13–720.

Balch, Robert W., and David Taylor. "Seekers and Saucers: The Role of the Cultic Milieu in Joining a UFO Cult." *American Behavioral Scientist* 20 (1977): 839–860.

"Salvation in a UFO." *Psychology Today* 10 (1976): 58–66, 106.

LESSONS FROM THE PAST, PERSPECTIVE FOR THE FUTURE

J. GORDON MELTON AND DAVID G. BROMLEY

Dramatic Denouements involving new religious movements have become the focus of a surge of scholarly attention over the last decade. For a time after the occurrence of the Peoples Temple episode, there was a tendency to treat scattered violent incidents idiosyncratically, as few historical counterparts had been studied by social scientists. The occurrence of several high-profile episodes over the last decade created the impetus and opportunity to develop a more general understanding of these Dramatic Denouements. In order to achieve greater theoretical specification, we have deliberately limited the focus in this volume to a small set of events that have key elements in common rather than theorize broadly about the complex, multifaceted relationship between religion and violence. The dynamics of conflict between control agencies and governmentally sponsored guerrilla groups, for example, might well differ in some important ways from the events analyzed here. In this concluding chapter we consider three important issues: the likelihood of future violent incidents, the sociopolitical context within which such incidents are likely to occur, and the perspective gained from analyzing recent cases that might be brought to bear on any future episodes.

Future Episodes

There are a number of reasons to anticipate future incidents that resemble in some measure the episodes analyzed in this volume. At the most fundamental level, this expectation is based on the observation that the histories of the major religious traditions are replete with the creation of both unity and division, harmony and conflict. However this observation might be expanded and contextualized, it is abundantly clear that religion and violence are no strangers. Recent U.S. history has been a remarkably pacific period in religious history, and there has been an unfortunate tendency to assume that this quiescence is the usual state of affairs. But even a cursory examination of contemporary and historical global events provides massive evidence to the contrary. Religion constitutes a distinctive form of social authorization, one that holds the potential to challenge as well as legitimate the existing social order. From this perspective, the simple demographic facts are that new movements continue to form across the globe, and some of those movements will stand in radical resistance to the social orders in which they emerge. While it may be true that only a tiny proportion of new movements are likely to become involved in violent episodes of any kind, the growing pool of movements creates that statistical probability.

To this eventuality must be added the fact that awareness of religious movements is increasing even more rapidly than their number. Indeed, every national and international compilation of religious movements adds numerous groups, mostly those of recent vintage but also many with lengthy histories that are just now being discovered. It is therefore likely that in the years immediately ahead, there will be an exponential increase in the number of extant movements identified and recorded by scholars who are now beginning to expand their fields of study to include movements outside the boundaries of Euro-American nations. These soon-to-be-discovered movements will then become part of the calculus of the possible dangers posed by new religions. Developing an appropriately sophisticated interpretive framework will require taking into account the increased number of movements, the historical contexts of movement–societal relationships, and the extreme volatility of sociopolitical conditions in many nations.

One further caution is in order. If the recent past serves as a meaningful guide, future episodes may well involve small and unacclaimed movements. As Melton and Bromley point out, the well-known controversial groups at the heart of the cult controversy have not been particularly prone to violence. Chapter 8 on the Branch Davidians and Chapter 11 on Heaven's Gate are particularly instructive in this regard. Both movements existed for extended periods of time in relative obscurity, in relatively low conflict with outsiders, and without any visible clues to the climactic events in which they were to become involved. In fact, none of the four movements examined in this book – or others such as the Church Universal and Triumphant, the Peoples Temple, and the Rajneesh – were particularly large, powerful, or aggressive throughout most of their histories. If this pattern holds, incidents will be difficult to anticipate. Responding to episodes that do occur is likely to be a consummate challenge, as comprehension and containment will likely beoccurring simultaneously.

The Changing Sociopolitical Context

Whatever the actual occurrence of Dramatic Denouements, changes in the organization of movements, countermovements, the media, and control agencies have profoundly altered the sociopolitical context in which they will occur. New religious movements are much more likely to conceive of themselves transnationally and organize themselves globally. For example, the surge in the transplantation of nonwestern religious movements to Europe and North America since the 1960s, as well as the transplantation of new movements from western nations to other nations around the globe, is now well documented. Many of these movements are organizing transnationally, regarding themselves as independent of the political jurisdictions in which they are located. Transplantation means that violent episodes occurring in one nation may have direct implications for a number of nations, and transnationalism creates a different kind of challenge to governmental officials than the historical pattern of movements attempting to form a "state within a state." The same can be said for governmental control agencies. Only a short time ago, national political leaders and citizenries alike were likely to calculate vulnerability to radical religious groups in terms of events occurring in their immediate geopolitical environs. This calculus has now shifted to a global level. Control agencies are increasingly attuned to international events that are regarded as having domestic implications. As a result, the degree of threat perceived by control agencies may be based on events occurring virtually anywhere. An important parallel development has been the emergence of a global network of information collection and dissemination, fueled by the development of the mass media, the Internet, and other communication technologies. Events that even a few years ago would have largely escaped public notice now receive immediate and sometimes substantial media coverage. This is not simply a matter of the rapidity and extensiveness of news coverage; it also involves a lag in developing frameworks for interpreting the meaning of violent episodes. The facile and readily available "dangerous cult" template still tends to be invoked in response to confrontations between movements and the social order. The effect of such media coverage is to reinforce the kind of cult stereotype that is being vigorously rejected by most scholars studying new religious movements. Finally, the strength and influence of oppositional movements have fluctuated over the last several decades. In the United States, the anticult movement has declined in its political influence, although its "cult" and "brainwashing" characterizations continue to retain considerable cultural legitimacy. At the same time, oppositional movements have gained influence in Europe. Where once oppositional movement influence flowed from the United States to Europe, the reverse might occur in the future. In any event, the ebb and flow of countermovement influence is now international in nature, producing more complex and unpredictable consequences in any future episodes.

The volatile political situations in western Europe, Japan, Russia, and China merit special commentary. The European situation currently is complex, with countries adopting divergent responses to episodes of violence. With a few minor exceptions, Europe was relatively free of violence involving new religions until the Solar Temple murder/suicides in 1994. French-speaking nations responded particularly vehemently, producing a coalition between elements of the French government and the *Association pour la Défense de la Famille et de l'Individual* (ADFI), the country's primary cult-awareness organization. A parliamentary committee and ADFI produced a report in 1996 that identified 172 "sectes" (the equivalent of the term "cult" in the United States) operating in France that had become a source of concern, based on allegations of what was termed "mental manipulation" (the equivalent of what has been labeled brainwashing or mind control in the United States). Initially, an observatory was established to study sectes and propose ways to oppose them; in 1998 a new office, the *Mission Interministérielle de lutte les sectes* (the Interministerial Commission to Make War on the Sects) replaced the observatory. Specific sanctions were sought for selected groups, but all 172 groups were compelled to fill out extensive reports on their financial dealings. Subsequently, the commission proposed legislation to criminalize mental manipulation.

In Germany a well-established cult-monitoring network has been anchored by the pastors appointed by the Evangelical (Lutheran) Church for that purpose. In the wake of the Solar Temple episode, anticult agitation intensified. In this case the controversy centered on the Church of Scientology, which the government refused to recognize as a religious organization. In 1996, the Bundestag established an Inquiry Committee to examine the "so-called sects and psychogroups." Contrary to prevailing expectations, however, the committee's 1998 report concluded that the great majority of new religions do not pose a serious problem and called on the government to cease using derogatory labels such as "cult" and "sect." Even in the case of the Church of Scientology, official observation was discontinued after two years. A Belgian governmental commission identified 189 sects and established a sect observatory in 1997; Austria followed a similar course, establishing a sect observatory in 1998. By contrast, Switzerland (despite a French-style report from the Canton of Geneva) and Sweden rejected governmental intervention, with the Swedish report directly criticizing the French initiative. The United States actively entered the European debate through the Commission on Security and Cooperation in Europe (the Helsinki Commission) as an agency to encourage compliance with human rights agreements concluded under the auspices of the Organization for Security and Cooperation in Europe (OSCE), which was established in 1975.

The Aum Shinrikyô's gassing of the Tokyo subway station traumatized a nation accustomed to the safety of its urban environments. Soon after Aum was identified as the possible source of the attack, a variety of measures, some quite harsh, were proposed. A coalition of lawyers formed, some of whom were already involved in cases against the Unification Church taking the lead. Legislation ultimately was passed, but it was far milder than the bills originally proposed and was specifically drafted to target Aum. In addition, however, governmental agencies have undertaken a series of high-profile prosecutions of groups promoting alternative healing methods that have resulted in member deaths. The Aum episode also had a profound impact on the Russian Federation, which had recently abandoned its long antireligious tradition and enacted religious freedom provisions in 1990. However, with the discovery that the majority of Aum members actually were Russian converts, support for anticult legislation mounted. In 1997, a new Law on Religion was passed that created a distinction between traditional religions. A variety of restrictions were placed on foreign religions based on the contention that traditional Russian religions needed protection from the activities of new foreign religious missionaries. The Russian Ministry of Health had already established an office to aid victims of "totalitarian sects" ("totalitarian" carries a particularly offensive connotation in Russia). In the wake of the national law, many of the states in Russia began employing local laws to suppress the activities of religious groups they regarded as problematic. Under the new law, the government can revoke or deny registration to otherwise law-abiding religious communities, and it distinguishes religious "groups" from religious "organizations." The latter status requires the entity to have existed in Russia for fifteen years.

The political jockeying over whether and how much social control should be exercised over new religions may continue for some time. Whatever the final disposition in various nations, greater surveillance and control will exist in some countries. Such measures may escalate or prevent conflicts that may occur in the future. Further, the political solutions in some countries are influencing the choices made in others, as the responses of Sweden and Switzerland to the French legislation exemplify. It is difficult to draw any firm conclusions about shifting movement–societal relations at this juncture, but it is clear that future episodes will occur in a much more complex, global sociopolitical context.

The Movement for the Restoration of the Ten Commandments

Even as work on this volume was well underway, there was another episode of violence that underscored a number of the observations made in this book and documented in particular our expectations about the probability of future events and their sociopolitical context. Here we briefly review the March 2000 episode involving the Movement for the Restoration of the Ten Commandments (MRTC) in Uganda because it is suggestive of likely future scenarios.

The MRTC traced its origin to visions of the Virgin Mary given to Credonia Mwerinde (1952–2000) as early as 1981.[1] Mwerinde was told to renounce the sin in her life, change her ways, and prepare for a future mission.[2] Over the next several years she received additional messages from Mary, although she did not immediately reveal these publicly, expressing God's grief over the abandonment of the Ten Commandments even by (Roman Catholic) church members. The Virgin called on the faithful to reject envy, jealousy, selfishness, argumentation, pride, fraud, hypocrisy, anger, rudeness, ruffianism, hatred, and enmity and to replace these with faith, hope, charity, repentance, forgiveness, gentleness, truthfulness, justice, and happiness. She also called for more prayer and Bible reading, full participation in the church's sacraments, and observance of the Ten Commandments.

---

[1] It appears that Mwerinde's father, Paulo Kashaku (d. 1991), was also a visionary and as early as 1957 had seen his daughter in a vision. He had a vision of Saint Joseph, the Blessed Virgin Mary, and Jesus in 1988, shortly before his death.

[2] *A Timely Message from Heaven* (1991: 1). This book, published by the movement, contains the major documents that shaped its beliefs. The perspective on the movement presented here has been put together from this book, a large collection of news reports (which have to be read with extreme care), and correspondence/conversations with a number of colleagues who have researched various aspects of the group. We are particularly indebted to Jean-François Mayer, Massimo Introvigne, and Jean Rosenfeld.

The visions renewed the attack upon malevolent magic that had been spread in Rhodesia in the 1950s by the Mchape (witchcraft eradication) movement, and the rapidly mounting death toll from war and AIDS were pronounced as signs of divine punishment of sinners.[3]

Angelina Migisha (1947–2000) had received messages from the Virgin from childhood since the 1950s, but in 1984 she had a vision of the Virgin and Jesus during which she was informed that it was time to reveal the messages she received publicly. She subsequently announced that twelve new apostles, six men and six women, were to be selected with the assistance of the Virgin and Jesus.[4] At about this same time a third woman, Ursula Komuhangi (1968–2000), Credonia's niece, identified with the emerging MRTC.[5] In 1989, the three women recruited Joseph Kibwetere (1932–2000), who had independently had a vision of the Virgin, to their cause. The Movement for the Restoration of the Ten Commandments could really be said to have been launched by these four. Kibwetere, a Roman Catholic layman, was the oldest of those who would be chosen apostles and functioned as bishop for MRTC. Over the next few months, the remaining eight apostles were chosen.[6] Each eventually reported visions and received messages from the Virgin and Her Son. Among their number were several priests and nuns who had been introduced to the world of Marian visions prior to their contact with Migisha.

Collectively, the visions shared by this group pictured various disasters, many reminiscent of those visited on Egypt in the days of Moses, that would descend on the people in the months and years ahead. They also contained specific complaints about changes instituted by the Roman Catholic Church since Vatican II, particularly changes in the administration of several sacraments. Beginning in 1989, the group began to speak openly about their messages from heaven to their neighbors, and in 1991 they published the messages in *A Timely Message from Heaven: The End to the Present Times*. This book formally announced the intention of the still small group to initiate a Movement for the Restoration of the Ten Commandments. The twelve explicitly declared that they were not a new religion, but a movement calling all believers (including Protestants and Muslims) back

---

[3] It has also been suggested that the MRTC should be related to a larger community of Marian apparitions that included the better-known apparitions from around the world and some received locally in Uganda.

[4] *A Timely Message* (1991: 119–120).

[5] Ibid. (34).

[6] Ibid. (44–46).

to observance of the Ten Commandments. At this juncture, MRTC was operating as a reformist revitalization movement within the Roman Catholic Church and was very loosely connected with the larger global network of groups that were oriented to the multitude of messages received from the Virgin Mary during the nineteenth and twentieth centuries. These groups also overlapped the network of conservative Catholic groups that rejected many of the changes within the church instituted during Vatican II.[7]

From its beginning, an apocalyptic element was an integral part of the MRTC's teachings, as it had been for many of the Marian movements. Because of its sinfulness, the present generation would be brought to an end in the near future. The Earth was compared to a tree that at the end of its season was made bare of (human) fruit. Possibly setting the stage for the final event, one vision predicted three days of darkness that would come upon the Earth. When this occurred, all the faithful were to go into a building prepared for this purpose, shut the doors, and remain secluded. All activities for the next three days were to take place within the confines of that sanctuary. At the end of that time, three-quarters of the world's population would be dead. The remainder would inherit a new redeemed Earth. The MRTC's apocalyptic teaching became more clearly defined throughout the 1990s.

Kibweteere reportedly predicted cataclysmic changes at the end of 1999 that would result in the deliverance of the group. These appear to have been false reports. All of the predicted changes were for the end of 2000 (the actual end of the Millennium). Indeed, as late as January 2000, MRTC forwarded a letter to the government office in charge of registering religious groups announcing that its mission was concluding and that there would be no year 2001.

The movement gained a physical headquarters when Mwerinde donated farmland she owned in Kanungu, a trading center in the remote Rukungiri district of Uganda. A variety of buildings, including a school building and a chapel, were constructed throughout the late 1990s at the headquarters complex. The movement's school at one point boarded as many as 300 pupils but was closed in 1998 by authorities because it failed to meet government standards and because there was some objection to the curriculum. Eventually, Kanungu was designated as "Ishayuriro rya Maria" (Rescue Place for the Virgin Mary).

MRTC's focus on a lifestyle based on the Ten Commandments led to adoption of a highly ordered life that included celibacy. As with many African

---

[7] Ibid. (44).

new religions, the members adopted a simple, uniform dress of green, black, and white. The movement also developed a form of sign language that replaced speech as much as possible (except during worship services), and contact with nonmembers was minimized. MRTC apparently prospered throughout the 1990s and experienced steady growth, mostly attracting former Roman Catholics. The primary source of conflict for the movement was strained relationships with relatives who did not join the movement.

Whatever the complex set of events that led to the climactic episode of March 17, 2000, may have been, MRTC leaders evidently made a decision no later than early March to end the movement's existence by systematically orchestrating the deaths of its membership. A critical factor in the decision-making process may have been that many members began demanding the return of their donations to the movement. These demands probably threatened the group's financial viability. The deaths that followed occurred in two phases. During the first phase, there were deaths in various movement centers around the country. Cursory examinations of the bodies suggested death by poison, strangulation, and stabbing. Apparently some 400 members, the majority of them dissidents, were killed and buried in mass graves at six different locations. The second phase involved the many members residing in Kanungu. Word circulated that the Virgin was about to appear and that members should prepare for their deliverance at her hands. They slaughtered cattle, purchased a large supply of Coca-Cola, and indulged themselves with food. They also began to stock up on gasoline, ostensibly for fueling a recently purchased generator. Some members sold property and destroyed personal items. On the evening of March 15, they gathered for a party at which the food and drink were consumed. Two days later they gathered at their meeting place, where the windows were already boarded up, as prescribed in their early revelation. After a brief period of singing and chanting, there was a violent explosion and consuming fire. No one escaped the barricaded building.

The mass death on March 17 ultimately led to the discovery of the bodies of those who had been killed earlier at the other MRTC sites. Initial reports of the event the following day referred to a "doomsday cult" that had conducted a "ritual mass suicide."[8] Only when hundreds of additional victims were discovered did media interpretations move in the direction

---

[8] It should be noted that the idea of suicide was imposed on the incident in the very first tentative news reports on March 19 before any investigation had been conducted by authorities. In the several months during which the story was unraveling, two further

of homicide.[9] Given the remote site and meager resources, a limited number of autopsies were performed. After considerable fluctuation, the final count of victims offered in mid-July was 780. It appears that MRTC leaders perished in the fire with their followers, but their bodies were never identified and formal warrants for their arrest have been issued. While the leaders and possibly some followers died at their own hands, most members probably were murdered.[10] In the wake of the episode, Ugandan officials issued a call for a thorough investigation of the deaths. They were joined by officials from Rwanda, Kenya, and Togo in proposing investigations of current minority religions and possible legal actions to combat the growing religious pluralism facing Africa. While the political outcome remains undetermined at this writing, there is every reason to expect that several African nations will pursue a course similar to that of European nations impacted by violent episodes.

In its broad outlines, the MRTC episode is consistent with the theories and case studies presented in this volume. Its chief distinguishing trait is the apparent murder of a large proportion of the membership. Given the group's remote location, its cataclysmic demise, the limited official investigation, and the fragmentary information available about key dimensions of the movement (history, theology, membership, leadership, current and former members), a comprehensive analysis of the incident will be most difficult, and many questions will probably never be answered.[11] And

---

accounts of mass suicide, both false, were also reported in the international news and were tied to the events in Uganda.

[9] Among the data that first suggested homicide rather than suicide was the means of death, by explosion and fire, rather than poison, the preferred means of suicide.

[10] This incident, like those discussed elsewhere in this volume, is extremely complicated. It is obvious that some people, those who planned and executed the explosion and fire on March 17, committed suicide. It is also obvious that many were killed and tossed into mass graves prior to March 17. In addition, the authors conclude that death by homicide of the great majority of those who died on March 17 is most consistent with all the evidence we have as to what occurred. Further, we believe that the leaders of the movement died in that conflagration.

[11] Just before this chapter was readied for the press, the study of the movement that had been undertaken by members of the Religious Studies Department at Makerere University appeared as *The Kanugu Cult-Saga: Suicide, Murder or Salvation?* (Kabazzi-Kisirinya, Nkurunziza, Deusdedit, and Gerard 2000). Their report remains preliminary and concentrates on questions of background and context more than on the movement itself. Further study, including at least one doctoral dissertation, is underway and will possibly shed additional light on the incident. The authors are particularly grateful for the informal communications of the findings by Jean-François Mayer, who conducted preliminary resaearch in Uganda in August 2000 and continued to pursue research in Uganda through 2001.

comparisons with other episodes are constrained by both the dramatically different cultural context in which MRTC formed and its predominantly peasant membership base. The episode is useful, however, in confirming at least some of our expectations concerning possible future events. The movement was one of thousands of new religious movements in Africa; it had existed for a number of years but was quite small and obscure even in its immediate environs. At the same time, it was connected to the worldwide Marian tradition in Catholicism that often includes indigenous ideological and organizational elements. In this regard, its apocalyptic theology and tight-knit organization were not radically different from those of other such movements. The movement does not appear to have aroused public alarm. There was some conflict with the families of converts and a dispute with governmental officials over the adequacy of its schools, but apparently there were few visible indications to the local populace or public officials that the movement was headed toward a catastrophic end. Further, the threat that the MRTC leadership experienced and their radical plan to bring the movement's history to a close were concealed from most members and virtually all outsiders. Indeed, MRTC first achieved public attention at the moment of its cataclysmic end. Even given the magnitude of the violence, a decade ago these events might have attracted little public attention in the West. The intense if short-lived media coverage the episode received is substantially attributable to an increased sensitivity to violence by religious movements and the globalization of news reporting. The reflexive response of the media was that of yet another "cult" committing "mass suicide." It is likely that MRTC will join the list of episodes invoked to legitimate applying the dangerous cult template to future events. In brief, then, the elements that now sound familiar – a small, obscure group that has existed for some time, is theologically and organizationally distinctive in some respects but traditional in others, remains relatively invisible publicly but evolves in the direction of more radical ideology and organization, encounters an internal crisis about which many members and most outsiders remain unaware, ends its history in a climactic moment, thereby precipitates official investigations of other new religious groups, and becomes part of a media-constructed image of dangerous cults – are all found in this episode.

Lessons Learned – Perspective Gained

The preceding sections of this chapter strongly suggest that there will be future episodes of violence of the kind examined in this volume and that they will occur in a much more complex and politicized environment. It is therefore useful to identify some of the insights gained concerning the social conditions under which Dramatic Denouements of the kind analyzed here occur.

- In understanding the occurrence of violent episodes, it is imperative to move beyond broad, encompassing movement and control agency characteristics. For example, among the attributes most commonly linked to movement extremism and volatility have been millennialism, totalism, and charismatic leadership. Melton and Bromley point out, however, that these attributes lack discriminative power. A great many movements possess these characteristics but show no signs of proclivity toward internal or external violence, while movements that do not exhibit this constellation of characteristics have been quite violent. Thomas Robbins proposes a distinction between a general millennial orientation and what he terms "catastrophic millennialism," with the latter constituting a particularly volatile movement orientation. In a similar vein, Lorne Dawson rejects a deterministic linkage between charismatic authority and violence, arguing instead that the sources of instability are located in the mismanagement of recurrent problems of charismatic leadership that find their roots in the problematic process of maintaining charismatic legitimacy. Eileen Barker is careful to draw a distinction between various kinds of cult-watching groups, arguing that they possess very dissimilar characteristics and objectives that translate into different patterns of interaction with the movements they monitor. It is important to affirm that none of these three formulations should be construed as moving toward a sharper "profile" of a dangerous group. All of the contributors caution that the dynamics of violent episodes are quite complex and cannot be reduced to lists of movement or control agency characteristics. From this perspective, the finer distinctions offered in these chapters serve better as *sensitizing concepts* than as *predictors*.
- An enduring paradox for interpreters of social behavior is its concurrent manifestation of continuity and discontinuity, a quality exhibited by movements and control agencies alike. Several of the analyses of specific episodes of violence call attention to extended periods of continuity followed by radical discontinuity. For example, Balch and Taylor note that Heaven's Gate exhibited a longstanding belief that movement to the Next Level would involve physical transportation of corporeal humans; deciding instead that physical death was necessary for advancing to the

Next Level established the basis for the group's decision to take their own lives. Ian Reader observes a parallel pattern in Aum Shinrikyô. Its condemnation of conventional society and its sense of persecution existed for some time; it was the group's legitimation of violence to control dissidents that led to the ultimate confrontation with authorities. While several analyses identify the specific moments in the histories of these movements when radical organizational and behavioral changes occurred and the dynamics operating at those moments, a more thorough understanding of any continuities across movements awaits further specification.

- One of the lessons that clearly emerges from both the theoretical formulations and episode case studies is that violent episodes are fundamentally *interactive* in nature. That said, it is equally true that the *primary impetus* toward violence may emanate from either movement or control agents. This point is supported by the contrasting analyses in the Heaven's Gate and Branch Davidian cases. Robert Balch and David Taylor acknowledge the influence of external influences on the trajectory of Heaven's Gate, but they are quite emphatic that it was largely developments within the movement that account for its final climactic departure. By contrast, John Hall emphasizes the role of external agents – oppositional groups, the media, and regulatory agencies in the Branch Davidian conflagration. Since most cases involve interactive exchanges, it probably is more useful to think in terms of dangerous *situations* rather than dangerous *organizations*.

- If most Dramatic Denouements involve interactive exchanges between movements and societal institutions, then it is important to understand the internal dynamics on both sides in equal depth and detail. To date at least, social scientists studying religious violence have directed less attention to the study of control agencies than to movements. Comparable analyses of the destabilizing attributes of these agencies is equally integral to future analyses of violent episodes. For example, there is evidence that police officers are most likely to resort to force in arrest situations when their authority and legitimacy are challenged; that public protest situations have sometimes degenerated into simultaneous riots by both protestors and police; and that police are likely to rationalize the excessive use of force where there are strong police subcultures in which all outsiders are viewed with mistrust. Some of the basic findings on control agents could be fashioned into a more sophisticated understanding of control agency behavior. Some beginnings have been made in this volume. Stuart Wright in essence argues that destabilization of government control agency behavior is most likely when those agencies become isolated from other moderating relationships, an observation that resonates with findings on religious movements. Eileen Barker identifies certain kinds of cult-watching groups as having organizational forms and objectives that lead them to be provocative and as thereby moving situations toward greater polarization.

- One of the more interesting and complicating patterns to emerge from both the theoretical and case study chapters is that violent episodes do not necessarily involve entire movements or control agencies. Rather, relatively small subgroups may orchestrate these episodes. Robbins suggests this possibility by including among the characteristics of destabilizing totalism increasing control by charismatic leaders and lack of critical feedback. This is also implicit in Lorne Dawson's discussion of charisma management problems when he identifies leader isolation and overidentification with the leader by followers as sources of destabilization. The case study chapters are even more pointed. It is particularly clear from Reader's analysis that only a tiny minority of Aum Shinrikyô members were aware of the group's amassing and use of chemical weapons, and Introvigne and Mayer make it clear that a small inner circle of Solar Temple members planned and carried out the murder/suicides. An analogous observation can be made about the operation of police agencies in the Branch Davidian episode. The initial raid took place after the Bureau of Alcohol, Tobacco, and Firearms (BATF) had essentially polarized the situation by manipulating the assistance of some agencies and excluding others in such a way as to maximize its own control. Given the BATF's radical stance toward the situation, the potentially moderating influence of other law enforcement agencies was precluded. As the subsequent standoff unfolded, there was tension between tactical and negotiation units the resolution of which may have contributed significantly to the final outcome. The virtual invisibility of inner circle politics and early tendencies toward violence are troubling, of course, particularly when combined with the fact that most rhetorically bellicose groups never cross the line into violent confrontation. Suspicions by movements or control agencies that violence is planned or imminent are extremely destabilizing in situations in which tensions are already escalating. Since the inner circles of both movements and control agencies often are inaccessible to social scientists, it is important not to base expectations of movement or control agency actions on rank-and-file behavior.

- One of the major lessons derived from the incidents examined here is that they can have profound, far-reaching implications beyond the immediate turmoil and loss of life. Violent incidents have also had a significant impact on other movements not involved in the episode, political coalitions, and law enforcement agencies. The confrontation between federal agents and the Branch Davidians clearly stands out with respect to the impact on other movements. The Oklahoma City bombing has been directly linked to the Davidian episode, and a number of Christian militia groups took the confrontation at Waco as evidence of the federal government's hostile intentions toward them. Balch and Taylor note the apprehensiveness experienced by Heaven's Gate members following the federal raid on the Davidians. The Church Universal and Triumphant was influenced by that episode to open negotiations with federal officials and ultimately to reorganize in a way that diminished the risk of provoking the authorities. There have also been major political ramifications. More than any single event, the murder/suicides by members of the Solar Temple empowered the current reaction to religious movements in several European nations. The Aum Shinrikyô sarin gas attacks produced unprecedented legislation that authorized governmental officials to monitor and regulate the activities of the reconstituted movement (Adelphi) and regulatory actions against a range of movements in Russia. Finally, law enforcement agencies have come under intense scrutiny in the wake of these episodes. For example, Japanese police were criticized for failing to detect the threat posed by Aum Shinrikyô earlier. In the United States, the confrontation with the Branch Davidians triggered a series of official investigations. Official reports clearing federal officials of wrongdoing notwithstanding, the legitimacy of both the BATF and the Federal Bureau of Investigation (FBI) was badly tarnished by the episode and resulted in agency reorganization.
- Finally, the most consistent observation uniting the chapters in this volume is that *polarization* is a key factor in Dramatic Denouements. Contributors make it clear that polarization may occur as a result of either movement or control agency dynamics. Dramatic Denouements therefore are not inherently attributable to either movement extremism or control agency provocation and usually involve some measure of interactive influence. Factors promoting polarization include the

qualities of movements and control agencies, on the one hand, and interaction dynamics, on the other hand. In the former category fall such characteristics as secrecy, ideological and organizational radicalization, crises created by charismatic instability, rejection of established normative constraints, and destabilization produced by internal dissent and apostasy. The latter category includes qualities such as elimination of third parties, formation of oppositional coalitions that create unified adversarial relations, mutual definitions and stances that orient to the other as subversive, and mass media amplification and stereotyping. An important caveat that also is explicit in several chapters is that virtually all of these characteristics possess subjective as well as objective dimensions. That is, it is extraordinarily important how the members of parties involved in the situation *perceive* events and actions. For example, several contributors refer to "perceived persecution" or a "sense of threat"; they observe that the apparent perception or sense of danger experienced by participants was not shared by other parties and that it was difficult to apprehend in analytic retrospect. It is difficult to overemphasize the importance of explanations that include the perceptions of all parties involved in Dramatic Denouements both in theory building and in conflict resolution processes. If, as is often the case, a small leadership group on either side is orchestrating events, it is particularly critical to gain access to their perception of the nature, meaning, and significance of unfolding events.

This brief synopsis of insights gained from the theoretical and case study analyses presented in this volume leaves no doubt that it represents only an interpretive inauguration. Each of the theoretical issues and each of the cases is slowly evolving into an analytic project of its own. On both counts the challenge is formidable. It involves gleaning information and perspective from cases in which much of the vital information and key potential informants are now lost. Nonetheless, the gravity of the issues serves as its own mandate for the task ahead.

References

A Timely Message from Heaven: The End of the Present Times. Rukungiri, Uganda: The Movement for the Restoration of the Ten Commandments of God, 1991.

Kabazzi-Kisirinya, S., R. Nkurunziza, K. Deusdedit, and B. Gerard (eds.). *The Kanugu Cult-Saga: Suicide, Murder or Salvation?* Kampala, Uganda: Department of Religious Studies, Makerere University, 2000.

INDEX